THE LONESOME TRAVELLER

Jerry Gray

THE LIFE AND TIMES OF CANADA'S SINGING LEGENDS

THE TRAVELLERS

BookLocker
Trenton, Georgia

Print ISBN: 978-1-64719-738-4
Ebook ISBN: 978-1-64719-739-1

Published by BookLocker.com, Inc., Trenton, Georgia, U.S.A.

Printed on acid-free paper.

BookLocker.com, Inc.
2021

First Edition

Library of Congress Cataloguing in Publication Data
Gray, Jerry
The Lonesome Traveller by Jerry Gray
Library of Congress Control Number: 2021918029

Ontario Place Forum opening concert, 1971

The Folksinger's Credo

You don't go into folk music to make a lot of money. You go because you have a commitment to the music of the people and their struggles in life. That's why it's also so relevant. It's the music that satisfies your heart, and that's why you do it. It's in your heart and in your blood, and that's why you do it. The music is always relevant, because it sounds like it was written yesterday.

The songs are ethical, and we have to share them with others.

And even if we come from different places on the globe there is a commonality of conditions that we sing out for.

~ Source Unknown
   Adapted by Jerry Gray

TO ETTY & YEHUDA

THANK YOU FOR BEING
LIFE-LONG FRIENDS
AND FANS

TABLE OF CONTENTS

INTRODUCTION

In 2000, Rob Bowman of York University wrote the liner notes for a new Sony CD which included songs from each of the seven LPs (six in Canada, one in the U.S.) and four singles that The Travellers had recorded for Columbia Records during the 1950s and '60s. It was released in 1999. He wrote:

> "Before there was a Canadian music industry, The Travellers were blazing a pathway. Before Canada had its own national anthem, The Travellers were waving the flag, writing and singing a Canadianized version of 'This Land Is Your Land'. Before multiculturalism became a buzz word that defined the reality of what it meant to be Canadian, The Travellers were singing Ukrainian, Native Indian, French, Israeli, African and Italian songs as well as material from at least fifteen other countries. Before the 1960s served to imbue much of contemporary youth with a political consciousness, The Travellers' repertoire was rife with songs of social significance. Simply put, when The Travellers formed in late summer of 1953, they were significantly ahead of their time."

My name is Jerry Gray. After speaking to a group, a number of years ago, someone in the audience asked me when I would write my life story and what I had done while I was a member of The Travellers.

Since their beginnings in 1953, the group had many firsts in Canadian culture. We were selected by political, governmental, and social organizations to lead and represent Canadians on many issues. The Travellers and I helped guide Canadians as we sang songs from all the regions of Canada. The Travellers' cultural ideas helped Canada to grow in maturity. In 1967, when The Travellers were hired by the federal government to appear in concert in every province and territory, we did a record 186 performances. Since many Canadians are not aware of all the accomplishments of The Travellers. I will be detailing many of the significant performances and stories in this book, and will also tell the story of my life. It will also tell the story of how the Canadian version of This Land Is Your Land was written.

Shortly after Theodore Bikel's death in 2015, I began to reflect that, when it came time for my passing, even though not remotely under consideration by anyone, including me, there would be no one around to tell my convoluted story accurately. That is one of the reasons I am writing this text—so people will know who I was, or had been.

About forty years ago, I had done a lot of TV work and, when I went to a restaurant or a movie, people would buzz and point me out. About twenty years ago, a gentleman approached me, looked me up and down, and then poked me with one finger. He said, "You used to be somebody." I loved his line, and I had to answer that, "I still am!"— the only retort I could come up with on the spur of the moment. But I always liked that comment, so hopefully I still am. But I often wonder, who will be there when I pass away, to include me when they ask, "Where have all the mavens gone?"

I write this memoir of my life now, so that my children and grandchildren and friends, and fans, can hear the stories of where I was and what I was doing during those many times I had to be away while they were growing up. Despite my busy schedule, I always hoped I found the time to spend as much time as possible with them, and to provide as much life guidance as I could.

For everyone else, I want to share the story of someone who always cared for his fellow man, and did his best to tell their stories and sing their songs.

The Travellers never had a fan club or people who stepped up to tell their stories, although there were many newspaper articles over the

years. As I tell this story, you will come to appreciate how often we lived up to our name.

So now, sit back, relax and join me and The Travellers on our unique and oh-so-Canadian musical adventure. I hope you'll find reading these stories as interesting and as much fun as it was for me to live them.

CHAPTER 1:
I AM A WEARY AND A LONESOME TRAVELLER

College and Spadina

My parents were born in Lithuania—my mother in Vilna, and my father, in 1902 in the shtetl of Mariampole. My father, Hershl Grizhbutsky, was the youngest of a family with two older sisters. He never spoke much about his growing up. I have a picture of him at about age twenty-one. He was wearing a military uniform, but I doubt if he'd enlisted; he was probably drafted for a year into the Russian Army. His two older sisters married when they were young. I have a family photo of them with their husbands—my father at about age twenty-three, and their mother in front of a small rural farmhouse. My dad later moved to the Lithuanian capital of Vilnius, or Vilna. The next photo I have is of him in what appears to be a political office in Vilna. Sadly, we never discussed these pictures. I also knew he had some religious upbringing, but after he arrived in Canada, he led the life of a non-religious man.

In Vilna, he met my mother, Merke Shapiro. They must have carried on some type of relationship there because they met up again, by design, after they both had arrived in Canada. My mother was the youngest of five children. The eldest, by twenty years, was Goldie, who went to the U.S., married in Detroit, and raised a family of four children. The next brother and sister both married and remained in Vilna. The next brother, Zalman, was red-haired and musical, and even though the family was not religious, he served as a cantor in a synagogue in Vilna. Because of his red hair, he was known as "Zalman der Roiter" (the redhead). The youngest was my mother who was pretty and very popular, as well as musical and athletic. I have photos of her at the beach and at the gym participating in gymnastics, and always with a smile on her face.

My mother arrived in Halifax early in 1928 before heading to Winnipeg in search of a distant cousin. She was then advised to meet Hershl, her intended, in Toronto, as he was also arriving by ship in Halifax 6 months later. I found a sworn application made out by a rabbi in Vilna, declaring that Hershl was actually her cousin, and that's how my father got into Canada.

When Mirke first arrived in Canada, the immigration officer changed her name to Mary Shapiro. When Hershl arrived in Canada, he became Harry Gray, because neither he nor the immigration officer knew how to spell Grizhbutski – or even Hershl for that matter. So, they mutually agreed that he would be called Harry Gray. I have always thanked that Halifax immigration officer who performed this official name change, simplifying things for all of us.

In September of 1928, my parents went to a rabbi and were married. Home was a second- floor room on Nassau Street, one block from Kensington Market, which was heavily Jewish at that time. My father began a career as a photographic assistant developing pictures for a photographer. My mother found work in the nearby needle trade on Spadina Avenue. My sister Helen (Chaika), was born on September 7, 1931, as the nation sank into the Depression. Two years later, I arrived on October 3, 1933. I believe that the number three has always been my lucky number. My mother reported that I was an unhappy baby because of some chronic minor sicknesses that prevented me from sleeping.

We were now a family of four and more space was needed. We moved to a third-floor apartment at 464 Spadina Avenue, just four doors south of the center of the Toronto Jewish world, near the corner of College Street and Spadina Avenue. Music lovers in Toronto will recognize the address as that of the later El Mocombo night club. At the time, the owner of 464 Spadina was Mr. Jubas. The Jubas family had two sons, one a little older than my sister and one slightly younger than me. Mr. Jubas had a barber shop on the ground floor, and the front was shared with Mrs. Hinton, who ran a grocery store. That word in Yiddish, "der hintn", is the same as one's "rear end", which led to much laughter whenever we spoke about the name of the storeowner below us.

There was no play area at College and Spadina, but there was an empty lot half a block south at the corner of Nassau Street where some derelict milk wagons were parked. That was my playground. In my early years, like my parents, I spoke nothing but Yiddish as there were very few children on my block, and television was still twenty years away. So, I listened to radio shows like *The Shadow* and *Jack Benny* to help me learn English.

Both College and Spadina streets had electric streetcar lines and, at the corner where the power lines above intersected, sometimes the power poles on the street cars would disconnect from the upper electric wires and sparks would start shooting out while the streetcars were reconnecting. I was fascinated by the electrical spark display that lit up the sky.

Spadina Avenue had several Yiddish theatres nearby, a number of small synagogues, and many Jewish-owned drugstores and bookshops on the edge of Kensington Market. My block boasted a bowling alley, a pool room, and the famous Crescent Grill which served eggs and bagels all day to the many cab drivers and bookmakers in the area. When I was a boy, it was exciting to know that these bookmakers were gambling and placing bets on races. Across the street was Balshin's Gas Station where you could get tires during the war without having special coupons. The street hummed with political intrigue and the presence of unionists from many of the nearby needle trade industries. When the official meetings at the nearby Labour Lyceum ended, the arguments moved out onto the street. This was my first political exposure during the "Hungry Thirties", but I was too young then to understand the issues people were arguing about.

In October 1938, when I was about to turn five, I began kindergarten at Lord Lansdowne Public School on Spadina Avenue, just north of College Street. Walking to and from school each day, my friends and I had to pass the original Benjamin's Jewish Funeral Home near my home. We always walked quickly and quietly so as not to disturb the dead in there.

But in November, my school year suddenly came to an end when I developed "mastoiditis", an infection in the mastoid bone behind my left ear. Penicillin had not yet been invented, so every day my mother

wrapped my head in a scarf and we walked or took a streetcar to the Sick Children's Hospital at College and Elizabeth Streets to have the affected area scraped and drained. After Christmas, I was well enough to return to kindergarten, but only once a week. But I had missed so much of the year, including basic "cutting and pasting" techniques, that for the rest of my school life I never mastered those skills, right to the present day.

By that time, my father had become a house painter, and bought a car to carry his supplies to his jobs. My parents, although schooled in basic religious practices from their upbringing in Europe, never joined a synagogue. For that reason, and with no family in Toronto, I never even entered a synagogue until age sixteen when I went to a relative's bar mitzvah in Detroit. This meant, of course, that I never had my own bar mitzvah at age thirteen, a religious ceremony that leads to a Jewish boy officially becoming a "man".

The Jewish Labour League

My parents had joined the Jewish Labour League Mutual Benefit Society, a left-wing labour-oriented organization with an office located three blocks away at College and Brunswick Avenues. The Labour League ran after-school Yiddish classes where children learned Yiddish language, history, and music. On Sundays, the men and women would gather in groups, or "branches", to discuss current events according to left-leaning protocols, and hear eminent speakers like J. B. Salsberg, who was a member of the provincial legislature. Sunday was also the day that families could get a low-interest loan to buy a house by borrowing from a credit union called an AKTSIA, run by the Labour League.

On Sunday afternoons, the large meeting hall was used for rehearsals by The Toronto Jewish Folk Choir, conducted by Emil Gartner, a noted Viennese conductor. This wonderful man somehow blended the working men and women, housewives, seamstresses and other needle trade workers into a choir which rivaled the professional Mendelssohn Choir – the one conducted by Sir Ernest MacMillan. My mother sang soprano in the choir, so, when she could not get a

babysitter, on Sunday afternoons my sister Helen and I would sit in the rehearsal hall with instructions to "blayb shtil", or "be quiet!"

We were actually privileged to be at those wonderful rehearsals; to hear guest artists like Paul Robeson and Jan Peerce rehearse with the choir before performances at Massey Hall. My sister had an excellent voice. Both she and I appeared in junior concerts held at outside theatres like the Strand Theatre, later called the Victory Theatre, where we made our first concert appearances at a very early age. The first time I sang a song on stage, I was only five years old. It was choreographed by my Yiddish teacher, Nechama Yanofsky, the mother of Zal Yanofsky, who later became a charter member of the group, The Lovin' Spoonful.

My mother had a fine voice, and back in Vilna she had sung in a choir. She had also been part of a gymnastics troupe. It seemed that my mother's gene pool affected me in both sports and music, the only areas where I excelled. Because of my early ear operations, my mother was adamant that I should not play an instrument like a horn or clarinet, one that required "blowing". In Yiddish, this was known as a "bloozing" instrument, not akin to a "blues" instrument. What about a stringed instrument? Well, in my early athletic experiences, anyone who carried a violin case was considered a "sissy." The boys I hung around with were athletes and not "sissy musicians". As a result, you would never find me with an instrument case of any kind.

My father was more of an intellectual who spoke up at political meetings and was well-read in Jewish classics and general politics. He did not have many outside interests and did not talk about my interests or my mother's singing.

The Birth of Camp Naivelt

Since 1925, the Jewish Women's Labour League (the women's auxiliary of the Jewish Labour League) had been leasing some property on the Credit River near Brampton, Ontario. Here they had established a children's camp, which they called Kinderland. The location was serviced by the Canadian National Railway that ran from

Union Station in Toronto. The CNR had acquired the land from Eldorado Mills, built a picnic ground on the Credit River, and a small amusement park on the property, and re-named it Eldorado Park.

The Labour League soon began attempts to purchase about 103 acres of the land, but the CNR was openly resistant to selling to a Jewish organization—a reaction typical of the anti-Semitism in Canada in the 1930s. However, in 1936 when the CNR discontinued rail service and abandoned the tracks, the Labour League managed to acquire the property through an individual who was not directly linked to the League. This person then transferred it to the Labour League, who then sold 8,000 shares to members for $5.00 each.

The picnic grounds had an indoor recreation area, two bridges spanning the Credit River, a covered picnic area with tables and a snack bar, and an amusement area with a merry-go-round badly in need of repair. This merry-go-round had a spot with a brass ring that, if you managed to grab it as you went around, you could win a prize. That old merry-go-round proved to be too costly to renovate and was ultimately torn down, but it had a great interest to me and even inspired me. A few years later, a carnival near my home in Toronto also had a merry-go-round with a brass ring, a later inspiration of life choices for me

The Labour League, composed entirely of left-wing, Jewish immigrants wanted to create a new political world in Canada, so they called their new acquisition, "Camp Naivelt", meaning literally, "Camp New World". The picnic ground was left as it was, and people would come by bus or car to spend a day of their weekend in the country. My father's newly acquired car gave him the opportunity to take his family to Camp Naivelt. We could now drive to the camp in less than an hour rather than take a bus to Brampton and then a cab for three miles, or take the train to Churchville and then walk about half a mile. The other alternative was to meet at 7 Brunswick Avenue, on Sunday morning, pay a few dollars for the round trip, and travel on the back of an open truck outfitted with benches.

Camp Naivelt had two sections: One was the original Camp Kinderland – the children's sleepover camp, with room for 250 kids and counselors all escaping from the city's summer heat. Most

campers were subsidized by a sliding scale of fees that were tailored to the family's income. At first, they all slept in tents until a building program made it possible for everyone to sleep in cottages. The kids took part in Yiddish plays and sang songs that mirrored the "new world" credo of the camp's name. Many Jewish children came to Camp Kinderland from the heat and grime of downtown Toronto, and left with happy memories and a tremendous spirit of hope.

The rest of the campground was reserved for adults and families, who could lease a plot on one of the three hills of the camp. These people first built a wooden tent platform, and then pitched a tent on it for sleeping. Later, they would build a kitchen opposite the tent flaps, and thus had a place where they could sit and be out of the weather. In time, families built either a complete cottage or, as in our case, my father and I built a two-bedroom cottage with a living room and attached it to the wooden kitchen which, by the early 1940s, eliminated the need of a tent entirely. Our cottage still stands today on Hill # Two, as Cottage #24.

The sides of the sloping hills led to the top where the cottages were located were dotted with weekend cabins used only for sleeping that people would rent for weekends, and sometimes even for a full week. By now, there was a large dining hall. The children ate meals first and were replaced in a second seating by visitors and cabin holders who ate after the children had left.

The camp also had a concert hall called "the dance hall", where cultural events took place. This became the focus for singers and actors who were able to perform in song, drama, readings, and concerts. At first, all the swimming took place in the Credit River, but in the late 1940s the camp built a large swimming pool which is still in use today.

Camp Naivelt was where I first learned about folk music and presentation, and where The Travellers and other musical artists and performers actually began their careers. This is the summer community we grew up in, and it continues to the present day. Camp Naivelt has been recently recognized by the Ontario Historical Society for providing places for musicians and performers like The Travellers to begin and flourish in the arts. We all worked collectively in trying to create a new political and cultural world for Canadians to be aware of, and for us, to be able to take a part in. You'll hear more about Camp Naivelt throughout this book, and see how its ideas helped in the formation of a true Canadian and Yiddish culture.

Growing up at Manning and Bloor

The year I was six years old, our family moved from College and Spadina to our new home at the corner of Manning Avenue and Bloor Street. The new address, 646 Manning Avenue, was sort of the reverse of our old address at 464 Spadina. This new house had a garage filled with paint cans and ladders and it was accessed through a laneway in the back. Living in our own home was a new experience for the whole family, as opposed to living in a rental flat.

Our house was heated in winter by a coal-burning furnace, and the ashes had to be emptied several times a week. We used the ashes on the icy sidewalks to prevent slipping and sliding in the winter. Some strong young men delivered the coal through a basement window directly into a bin in the furnace room. These young men always arrived covered with coal sweat on their faces and bodies from carrying the coal sacks to the window and emptying them down the chute.

The water tank in our home was heated by a "jacket heater", a small furnace that also burned coal. As I grew older, my father began to rely on me to empty the ashes from the furnace as well as from the jacket heater, and take them out to the roadside where city trucks would come and carry them away. After a night without the water heater on, someone had to load coal into the water heater early in the morning in order to heat enough water for washing dishes, clothes, and ourselves. As I grew older, that job again became my responsibility.

My father was not a tall man—five foot three inches—but he worked hard as a house painter. As I got older, I helped him from time to time by carrying ladders and paint, and supporting the ladders against three-story houses. I was also conscripted to paint parts of homes, like a fence, that required no painting finesse. For these tasks I received only a bare allowance.

During the 1940s, there were no supermarkets. Food was available at individually owned grocery stores, and drug items could be bought at local drugstores. I attached a carrier to my bike to work for a grocery store. I delivered groceries for them on weekends and after school and received a very minimum wage, and an occasional gratuity.

Two blocks east of our home was Palmerston Boulevard, a street with large houses owned mainly by physicians and dentists who generally had their offices on the ground floor. These doctors all required magazines for their waiting rooms, so I wormed my way in to getting contracts for delivering the magazines of the day, like *Liberty, Maclean's, Life* and *The Saturday Evening Post*. The magazines were delivered by boys like me, and every Friday was collection day. As I made the rounds, the money I collected meant I could go to the movies on the weekend.

There were four movie theatres along Bloor Street within four blocks: the Metro, the Bloor, the Midtown, and the Alhambra. During the winter, I would solicit jobs cleaning snow from porches and sidewalks for a weekly amount. I was now getting into sports at school, and these local jobs enabled me to earn a small amount of money which I used to buy sports equipment like baseball spikes, gloves, and athletic shoes, and a bicycle.

One block south of my house was the playground and sports field for Harbord Collegiate. I spent my summer days there running races, playing softball and quoits—a game similar to horseshoes but with rubber quoits (a small rubber ring). I won many races, and this allowed me to start competing in the City of Toronto Police Games held annually at the Canadian National Exhibition stadium. For seven consecutive years, from age nine to fifteen, I won at least one medal every year in the 100 or 220-yard dash, or broad jump.

Harbord Playground did not have an under-age-thirteen or fourteen softball team, so I played softball for the legendary Toronto Elizabeth Playground team, known throughout the city as "The Lizzies". I also played softball for the Toronto YMHA softball teams, as well as other teams around Toronto. Actually, the first softball team I played for was called the Toronto Newsboys, a team coached by Louie Goldstein, a local polio survivor from an earlier epidemic in Toronto. Long-time friends, Len Ura and Benny Haber, were on that team. We played many sports with or against each other throughout high school, and later in golf and tennis. I am glad to report that both men are still alive and active, still spinning yarns about which team was the best that we ever played for or against.

NEWSBOYS BOW IN MII ET SOFTBALL FINALS

Toronto Newsboys softball team went to the deciding game of the T.A.S.A. midget finals before bowing to Kenwoods, 18-11, at Fred Hamilton playground last night. The Newsboys are shown in the above picture. Back row, left to right: Ken Bookie, Lou Goldstein, Norm Christie, Len Ura, Julius Gelman, Norm l..., Sid Pinkus. Front row, left to right: John Nushownis, Jim Mu..., ...aro, J. ..., B...ny Haber, John Heta and Sheldon Langer.

Jerry Gray, 1st row, 3rd from right

In 1953, the year I turned twenty, I won the city championship with a fastball team that played on a Mount Pleasant Road softball diamond. I also played hardball with the Columbus Boys Club in an Italian community. I was the only Jewish guy in that league. Throughout those years, I never got cut from any team I tried out for, and always played the entire game.

Both my sister Helen and I went to Clinton Street Public School, located between Harbord and College streets. In grade five, all the kids took some kind of academic test for which they never gave out the results. But my teachers kept alluding to my academic standing by saying from time to time that I was perhaps slipping a bit academically. I attended that school for eight years. I had a hunch these were IQ tests that became part of my permanent school record.

Performing at Massey Hall

In 1945, when I was in grade six and Helen was in grade eight, a music specialist from the Toronto Board of Education Music Department visited every city school and listened to every senior class student as he or she was singing. I can still remember the names of those music experts: Miss Derry and Mr. Eldon Brethour. They were looking for 125 students to appear in a massed choir at the annual May Spring Concert held at Massey Hall in Toronto.

Helen and I were the only two from Clinton's 1,200 students to be selected. For us, that meant we had two rehearsal-day holidays away from school, plus the date of the concert. It was very exciting! The following year, Helen went on to high school, but for the next two years when I was in grades seven and eight, I was again the only student from Clinton selected for that honour.

In June of 2018, Massey Hall closed its doors for two years of renovation, and performers like Gordon Lightfoot played a part in the closing ceremonies. As you read in the introduction, The Travellers played Massey Hall probably long before any other folkie, but for me it began first with the massed public-school choirs in 1945–47. I also went to Massey Hall in the early 1940s to hear Paul Robeson and Jan Peerce sing with The Jewish Folk Choir, as my mother sang in the choir. After The Travellers started in 1953, we performed in four concerts at Massey Hall with Pete Seeger in the 1950s, and then with Judy Collins in 1961.

In one of Pete Seeger's concerts, he showed up on stage for the final rehearsal with a log and an axe. He began chopping the log while he sang a work song and covered the stage with wood chips. The stage manager, whom we called "Hester, the mike tester", told Pete he could not do that without a protective tarp, which she then produced. The show went on as planned, and that same summer Pete did the same thing on the Camp Naivelt stage.

My dad was only 5'3" and I maxed out at 5'6" but, despite my size, I easily took part in school athletics, trying to prove myself more than adequate in sports skills. In grade eight, my final year at Clinton, I was the captain of the volleyball team and we won the City School Championship. One month later, I was named captain of the softball team and while we went to the city championship, we lost in the final. The day before that last game, our pitcher, Alan Lackstone, rode his bike down the hill in High Park too quickly, crashed into a tree and broke three ribs. Our substitute pitcher walked in ten runs, and that's why we lost. I was named the star of the game because I hit an "inside the park" home run at the fenced-in, Sunnyside Stadium. You'll hear more about Alan and me a little later in this story.

Through my sports activities I had a lot of friends, and we would often ride our bikes from Clinton School all the way to the mouth of the Humber River in west Toronto. There we would use our bikes as collateral, and for fifty cents each, six of us would rent two rowboats and row out into Lake Ontario. One August day, we came upon a middle-aged couple rowing beyond the breakwater, where the waves were much higher than closer to the shore. When their boat overturned, the six of us went into action. We managed to rescue the woman, but no matter what we did, we could not find the man.

Reporters from the *Toronto Telegram* came to our school and took photographs. The next day, there was a major story in the local paper, *The Evening Telegram*, with pictures of all of us. The story lauded us for saving the woman's life before the city lifeguards were able to show up. Sadly, it was several hours before they were able to locate his body. That was the first time anyone had written a newspaper story about any of us. I still have the newspaper picture story of that event as it was the last thing I did while at Clinton Public School.

Jerry Gray, left

I finished grade eight with an over 80 per cent academic record. My scores would have been much higher, except for the fact that I almost failed two subjects: penmanship and art! Remember, when I was in kindergarten and missed most of the year from illness? This resulted in my missing out entirely on several basic subjects, like cutting and pasting. Eight years later, that loss of time resulted in my almost failing grade eight. Can you believe that? Maybe not!

Harbord Collegiate and Football

When I entered high school at Harbord Collegiate, known as HCI, as an undersized thirteen- year- old, I quickly discovered there were no inter school teams such as basketball or football that a boy my age might try out for. The school offered only inter-class teams, so I played for my class team in touch football, volleyball, and basketball. We won the championships, and I still have those crests that were given out at the end of the year.

I joined the YMHA at 15 Brunswick Avenue near College Street. There, I began swimming, and playing basketball. A series of clubs began there among members the same age, and the Y gave them a club leader who led them through their early years. I met some new friends from my old Kensington Market area and we all formed "Club Reagan". We all played on the same YMHA softball team, and won the local city championship.

In the fall I entered grade ten at HCI, but because of my October birth date, I was a year ahead of most of my friends. We all decided we would try out for a new bantam football team for "under age fifteens", the first bantam football league in the city schools.

About fifty boys showed up for the first practice, and that day my close friend and Club Reagan team mate, Marv Tameanko, broke his leg! At the second practice, after the Jewish mothers' telephone network was activated, only twenty-five boys showed up. Parental signature was necessary for anyone to play football. For my part, I signed the permission forms myself.

Even though I had reached what would be my maximum height of 5'6", I was the only one with any football experience, so I was named quarterback and captain of this first bantam team.

We fielded a magnificent team that first year, with a backfield that consisted of our last year's record-breaking 4 x 100-yard relay track team. This was an era when, in Canadian football, the forward pass was just beginning to be used, and touchdowns were awarded five points rather than the six they are now.

Harbord football teams rarely won more games than they lost, but this team was different. Football newspaper results showed that in the first game, Jerry Gray scored two touchdowns, as HCI won 12-0. The season went the same way, and after five games we were undefeated, untied and un-scored upon. We went to the city finals against Malvern Collegiate and lost 12–5. Five wins in one season was well above the standard for Harbord football teams, but HCI won the City Cheerleading Team trophy using Canadian, and later British actress, pretty Toby Robbins, who also won the Miss Cheerleader trophy.

I'll finish this section by mentioning my full Harbord career in football. In the 1949–50 season, I played as a reserve quarterback. We defeated Central Tech 12–0, St. Mikes Collegiate 16–1, and Bloor CI, 22–0. Next game we tied with Parkdale 5–5, then we defeated Oakwood 11–0. This was a beginning for me because when the #1 quarterback was injured, I played the whole game throwing two touchdown passes, one to Zel Goldstein, and one to Marvin Tile. In the semi-final, we lost to eventual champion, Riverdale 18–5.

Zel Goldstein scored nine touchdowns during the season and in the spring won the city 100-yard track championship. Zel went on to become co-owner of the Hy and Zel grocery chain. Marvin Tile became an orthopedic surgeon and was given The Order of Canada for his work in developing hip-replacement surgery. Marvin appears again later in a humorous event during my music career.

Grade twelve began when I was elected captain and appointed as starting quarterback. We won only one game, tied two and lost three, and missed the playoffs. I scored one touchdown in the season and also made the second all-star team for the city league. Not bad for a guy who did not grow past his five-foot six height, not a great height for a quarterback, but I was very quick.

On the last day of that season, I played the entire junior game, offense and defense. Then when the junior game was over, the coach told me I'd be playing quarterback in the second game, because the regular senior quarterback was injured. That night, I was definitely tired! I was only able to do this because it was the last game of the season, and we were not in the playoffs.

The grade thirteen football season was my last at HCI. We won three and lost four, not too bad for an HCI Senior Team. Harbord students usually spent only one year in grade 13 and went on to university; few played for two years whereas most other schools' grade 13 students played for two years. In the last football game of my career, I celebrated by scoring two touchdowns! My record at Harbord included scoring two touchdowns in my first bantam league game and two again in my last game for HCI, plus two touchdowns in the first game of my life, as a thirteen-year-old in another league, which I'll tell you about soon. I was the only quarterback in Harbord history to have won more games than he lost. I won an award at the later commencement exercises for my record-setting, four-year career in football at HCI.

Harbord Collegiate and Basketball

It was clear early on that I had leadership ability in sports. That leadership ability manifested in other areas throughout my life. Perhaps it's part of the reason I'm still around at age eighty-five, and still able to perform on stage and teach in lecture halls. My athletic career at HCI was enhanced by my three-year stint with the Harbord basketball teams. My first year on the HCI junior team, I was a second-stringer, but I played in all the games. We won nine games and lost two, the last one in a semi-final game against Malvern.

The next season, 1950–51, I was again appointed as team captain. Our leading scorer was club-mate Marvin Tameanko, now over six feet tall and well recovered from his broken leg. Throughout the season, he was the top, "go to" scorer except for two games when I scored 25 points, and was second in scoring. In the pre-season, we played ten games against teams not in our conference, winning nine of them, and then we won all six season games without a loss. In the quarter final, we defeated Danforth Tech 50–29, and I was the top scorer. The semi-final game against Bloor Collegiate was a record-breaker in a two-game total point semi-final.

In the first game, Marvin Tameanko set a Toronto record of 41 points as we won 73–55. In the second game, we lost 70–66 but won the total point series. Hank Galka of Bloor set a new city scoring record of 48 points! We won the total-point semi-final easily.

The final championship game against Riverdale Collegiate was tied after regulation time. As the game ended, we were down one point, and my best friend, Marvin Kopel, had two foul shots. He made one and missed the second to tie the game, but we lost in overtime 48–43, as Tameanko left the overtime early with five fouls.

The player I played against in this game was Ron Stewart who, like me. was only five foot six inches tall. We each scored eight points against each other. Ron later became a record-breaking football player at Queen's University, and for many years played as an all-star in the

CFL for the Ottawa Roughriders. He later became a lawyer and worked for Elections Canada. My close friend, Marvin Kopel, and I made the Toronto all-star team, to be repeated several years later at the University of Toronto!

My final basketball year at Harbord was grade thirteen. It was 1952, and there were only a few players left from last year's team. Marv Tameanko was back, along with Marvin Kopel. We won six games, lost four and missed the playoffs. Tameanko did not have as successful a year as last year, allowing me to be top scorer in three of our games.

In my final game at Harbord, I had to leave with a dislocated finger in the fourth quarter. This was the end of my major sports career at Harbord, an enviable record of performance. I was captain of both the Harbord swim and track teams, and won several individual and swim relay medals. I also played several games for the Harbord Hockey team, not my best sport, but I am the first and only Harbordite who played on five interscholastic teams. It is still a record at the school as no one has played on more than three teams since my record-breaking year in 1952.

Well, I'm tired from even thinking about all these games and events, but they are a big part of my life. My years at Harbord allowed me to grow up as a person by being captain of just about every team I played on. I also gained a good reputation at Harbord, an achievement which helped me begin my second and third careers after leaving Harbord. Two more careers? Wait and see.

Harbord Collegiate and Musicians

Before beginning grade nine at Harbord in 1946, I was still one of the shortest kids in the class. But I had already learned that I had strong abilities in two areas—music and sports. Harbord had a long history of musical accomplishment with both its orchestras and musical operettas.

Many composers graduated from HCI who went on to Canadian and international fame. Victor Feldbrill was many years older than I but I knew his family, and he went on to become the conductor of the

Toronto Symphony Orchestra as well as of many other orchestras around the world. Past ninety at the time of this writing, he was recently given a Lifetime Award by the Toronto Musicians Association. I was the only one at this event who showed up who remembered what he had done musically, and the only one who had actually known him. Composer Srul Irving Glick was also a classmate of mine at Harbord. He had a winning charm and great success as a composer, until he died too early in 2002.

That summer of 1946, there was a travelling carnival visiting Christie Pits Park, two blocks from my home, at Bloor and Christie Streets. I went to the carnival and won a lamp at a baseball throwing stand, and then I went for a ride on the merry-go-round. Just like the merry-go-round at Camp Naivelt, it had a spot, as you went around, where you could try and grasp a brass ring and win a prize. That summer, I managed to grasp the legendary "brass ring", and won another free ride. This experience influenced many of my decisions going forward into a career which I had not yet chosen. Like the brass ring at the carnival, all my efforts in life were attempts to "win the brass ring."

Playing Sports in Toronto and being Jewish

As I mentioned earlier, when I arrived at Harbord for grade nine, there were only inter-class teams available for kids my age. But I wanted more, so after asking around, I learned about a football league for thirteen-year-olds in Trinity Park at Gorevale and Queen Streets. It was led by Carmen Bush, a renowned coach at nearby Columbus Boys Club, a mainly Italian sports club. They steered me towards the Toronto Kiwanis football team (Trinity K Club).

Only two Jewish guys showed up for the first practice; me and my Clinton P.S. friend Alan Lackstone. Alan and I had been stalwarts on the Clinton softball and volleyball teams, winning championships in our final year. Because the Harbord C.I. school area had about eighty per cent Jewish students and very little success in football, the incident of two Jewish students trying out for a predominantly Christian football league was considered comic—both to the other players as well as to the coaches.

In the first game, the K Club played against Columbus Boys Club. Alan Lackstone made the first touchdown of the game. In the second half of the game, I scored two touchdowns. My coach, Frank Cornacchio, congratulated me after the game and then said, "You looked like a rabbi running from the bakery with a bread in your hand!" I took it as a sort of "compliment" that mirrored the racist situation in the downtown west end of Toronto at that time. Cornacchio later changed his name to Cornack, perhaps to hide his own Italian roots. We played in two more games, with Alan scoring one more touchdown, and me scoring one more as well, then leading the league with three.

Throughout my athletic career, I often played these games where the prejudice by the other team came through loud and clear. For example, one year at Harbord, we played a football game at Christie Pits against St Michael's Collegiate and, before the game, their team lined up against us and sang, "We're gonna kill you f—g Jews." It was indeed a bloody game, but we defeated them, much to their dismay.

Here is another example: When I played softball for the YMHA and we were playing against McGregor Playground at their home field in Parkdale, a non-Jewish area of Toronto, I played centre field. In the last inning, I parked my bicycle nearby and, after the last out, I hopped on my bike and rode up a hill to get out of the area quickly in order to avoid any confrontation that might take place after the game.

In all my sports ventures, I ended up playing for mainly Jewish teams, and we were often the subject of derisive catcalls before, during and after the games. This verbal abuse extended to my mid-life when I played squash for the YMHA in a city squash league. I think that, because of my height, I made it a kind of crusade (really?) in all my endeavours throughout my life to show people that we Jews were a strong people.

When I began participating in athletics at age thirteen, I never told my mother that I was playing football, and usually signed the participation forms myself. Luckily, I incurred no injuries. My family's revelation about my all-encompassing sports activities came later as part of my graduation from Harbord.

At Harbord, I was also in a music appreciation class. But I was never in an instrumental music program due to restrictions my mother imposed, or those I imposed upon myself. The summer was filled with playing on softball and baseball teams in the area, and basketball at the YMHA on Brunswick Avenue. I even joined the West End YMCA to play basketball on the weekends because the YMHA was always closed on Friday and Saturday. In this way, I played seven days a week.

In grade ten I was not yet old enough to play on the school's basketball team, so I played in a city league for the YMHA. I also swam for Harbord, but with only five swimmers in my age group, we were all relegated to the relay teams. When spring arrived, fresh from being football finalists, our track team once again won the city 4 x 100 relay championship. The three boys who left to go to other schools— Walter Bulchak, Fred Wine, and Herb Handler—became all-stars at their new schools. We remained lifetime friends and, just like me, they all became dentists. They also all predeceased me. The end of that year, 1952, was the end of an era for me at HCI.

The summer was filled with baseball on Mondays and Wednesdays, and softball on Tuesdays and Thursdays. My softball team won the York Township championship. I also won more medals at the Toronto Police Games, a part of the City Playground track and field championships. That summer, I also began spending more time with my mother in our Camp Naivelt cottage where I began my music career.

Harbord Collegiate, and the Politics of McCarthyism

In September 1948, I entered grade eleven at HCI. The head of athletics was Mr. Stapleton Caldecott, a retired Sergeant Major who had served in World War II. He took me aside when I returned from summer vacation, and said, "Jerry, are you still a member of that Jewish Communist Group?"

"What are you talking about?" I asked. "Why are you asking me this? It has nothing do with my activities here at school." Well, he hemmed and hawed, and then told me I was "under observation." And then he left.

I was the youngest player on the junior boys' football and basketball teams. That year, I made those teams as a first team player and, although two years younger than anyone else, I was made quarterback for the football team. I was also on the swim and track teams, and vice president of the Boys' Athletic Association. In my fourth year at HCI, I would be president. But at the end of the school year when I got my report card, I was stunned to see a "C", a bare pass in physical education. I was upset and angry, but I decided not to complain because, in my heart, I knew it was Mr. Caldecott who had given me that mark.

After the spring 1952 results came out, I spoke to Mr. Caldecott about my mark. He told me the reason I got only a C was because I could not do a proper somersault. Now, everyone on the school staff knew I could not do a summersault because I had had mastoiditis in kindergarten. The balance in my inner ear had been altered by the infection, which prevented me from doing certain things. I could easily dive off a platform tower, but I could not do a somersault. This was another result of my childhood mastoiditis: no somersaults—along with the aforementioned failure to master cutting and pasting.

It's true that I was a member of the United Jewish People's Order Youth Group, a subgroup of the organization my parents were members of, as well as being an assistant athletic advisor in the UJPO junior athletics programs. But I had no political involvement in any of the politics at the UJPO at this age. Even so, Mr. Caldecott made it clear that he considered me to be a Communist agent in the school.

In grade twelve, I reached the height of my athletic career. I was made captain of the Junior Football team for the next year, and I was the only person in the last twenty years to be on five intercollegiate sports in one year. Yet here I was being privately ridiculed by the athletic department head for allegedly detrimental political conduct.

This was not the end of Mr. Caldecott's self-appointed suspicion of Jerry Gray, in this era of McCarthyism.

Harbord 1951–53 – Final Years

In 1951, my athletic career at HCI had been exemplary, and even record-setting. I had played on all the interscholastic teams, captaining many of them. That summer, I worked as a lifeguard at Camp Naivelt. The job involved teaching group swimming to the many overnight campers in both morning and afternoon classes. Between classes, the pool was used by camp residents and their guests, and I was on duty as lifeguard.

On duty as lifeguard at Naivelt Pool, 1952

Part of my job involved maintaining the proper pool water PH balances as prescribed by provincial laws, and entering the mechanical room under the pool to "backwash" the pool filters every evening. The older people that used the pool rarely swam; instead, they did the "machaye" stroke, a Yiddish name for standing in the pool at waist level and occasionally moving your arms. Some of the younger adults would come to the pool after work and challenge me to a race of one or two lengths.

It was during this summer when my "on stage" musical career began. The accompanist for the Jewish Folk Choir was Fagel Gartner, wife of the conductor, Emil Gartner. Every Saturday night, there was a concert with visiting singers who were guests in the camp during the week. Following the concert, there was a "youth" campfire, held outside the young people's centre near the concert hall. The younger people, along with the children's camp staff, would gather for an hour or two and sing the folk songs we had grown up with. We sang songs in both Yiddish and English; we sang labour songs, and songs of peace and social protest.

I was familiar with all these songs, for I'd inherited my mother's musical ability which included good timing, a confident voice, and a natural ability to create harmony easily, something not too many others could do.

Early in the camp season, Fagel Gartner approached me at the pool and asked me to sing a solo on stage. She taught me a song called "Papir Iz Doch Vays", The Paper is White, a Yiddish courting song from Poland. After I performed this song that night, the applause was lengthy and loud, so I had to repeat it. I loved the experience and was quickly hooked into performing. I also loved the song and still sing it when I do a Yiddish program.

On other occasions, my long-time friend Jerry Goodis and I would sing some Yiddish duets together, and we were both Stan Kenton and Woody Herman fans, Jerry was three years older than I, and we discovered we sang very well together. We started a small choir of ten to twelve young people, and called it the UJPO Youth Singers. This group sang at several nearby summer camps and union meetings. By the fall, we were a bona fide group of singers.

When that pivotal summer ended, I returned to HCI for grade thirteen to prepare for provincial exams leading to university. Every year, the T. Eaton Company and the Robert Simpson Company would select two incoming grade thirteen students, one male and one female, to represent the school as its representative on each of the companies' student boards. The school reps were chosen over the summer, and were usually selected from those who were student council reps or athletic leaders, or persons of note in the school. Since I was the top athlete at the school, and was also incoming president of the Boy's Athletic Association, I, as well as others, assumed that I would be selected by the school to be one of the student reps. But that did not happen. One of the male reps rightfully selected was the president of the Student Council, and for the first time in its history, the other male selected was a boy entering grade twelve! Later, in the day, when I asked the previously-mentioned head of Phys Ed, Mr. Caldecott, why I had not been selected, he simply stated that he did not have to give any reason for his decision. When I went to the principal and asked, he told me that Mr. Caldecott had not nominated me, and had given no reason publicly for his choices.

The year was 1951, and it seemed to me that McCarthyism had crossed the border and blacklisting had begun in Canada. I was devastated, as I was one of the most active and well-known students in the school. I decided that questioning this decision further would be futile, as no one was prepared to take a stand and there was no way to appeal. It was certainly an unhappy welcome to my final year at Harbord Collegiate.

I played my usual sports as captain of both the football and basketball teams, and also took part as a member of the swim team. Mr. Caldecott did not coach any of those teams during that year. That spring, the teachers' union went on a work-to-rule strike against doing extra-curricular work. I ended up coaching the track team so that the students would be able to participate in the spring track meet at Varsity Stadium at the University of Toronto. When the team trials began and the strike ended, I told Mr. Caldecott that, for the first time in my HCI career, I would not be participating on the track team. Several others on the senior track team also chose not to participate. They understood why I was taking this position, and they were standing in solidarity with me. This was the first setback that I'd had politically in my life, but it was not the last.

A Question of Religion – and Justice Delayed.

In the grade thirteen examinations, I ended up with about 81 per cent, standing in the top twenty in a class of about one hundred students. By that time, I had made my career choice, and applied to the Faculty of Dentistry at the University of Toronto.

About twelve of the top twenty in my class went into medicine at U. of T., and about five went into dentistry. In 1952, the application to the School of Dentistry contained a line that asked for the religion of the applicant. When I was turned down, I was upset. But I also knew that prior to this, many Jewish applicants to Medicine and Dentistry had been turned down, even if their scholastic record was higher than that of other applicants.

At that time, Harbord Collegiate had the highest percentage of Jewish students in the province, and also the highest number of applicants to the professional faculties. In previous years, many applicants who had been refused by the University of Toronto applied to other universities, where they had their applications easily approved.

There were very few dental schools in Canada in 1952, so I had few options. I went to Roy Ellis, the dean of the Faculty of Dentistry in Toronto. Roy was an ex-Australian who had heard from a high school faculty committee about previous students who were not accepted. His excuse was that sometimes the committee did not accept too many students from one school, and that might have been the reason for my being turned down.

The next day, I returned with a print-out of Harbord's grade thirteen students and their final results. I pointed out the two Harbord applicants who had been accepted into the U. of T. Dental School, with marks at least ten per cent less than mine. Those two students were not Jewish.

The reason for my being refused was clear. It was now too late to be given a place in the 1952 freshman class, so Dean Ellis suggested that, if I went into Arts for one year and did well, or, if I returned to Harbord and rewrote several Grade 13 papers and did well, I would be accepted the following year. Justice delayed, perhaps.

Choosing my first option, I registered in liberal arts at the U. of T. The semester began, but I did not enjoy the arts courses. Then fate intervened. In late September, I received a call from my music mentor, Fagel Gartner. She had formed a choir of eight singers who would represent the UJPO in a cross-Canada tour, and she asked me to join. Travelling across the country by train, we would perform concerts in many of the large and small western Canadian cities on the way back. The women in the group, called the UJPO Folk Singers, came from the Jewish Folk Choir, and my sister was asked to participate as well. I would be the youngest person in the small choir, and the only male! I took the offer and joined the group.

Fagel Gartner and the UJPO Folk Singers

The choir began by rehearsing its repertoire for several weeks in Toronto. Then, in early October, we drove east to perform our first concert for the UJPO in Montreal. Our performance went very well, and many people found it amazing that a successful musical tour could be mounted with non-professional singers. However, while we were not professional, we were good.

When we returned to Toronto, we left on a CPR train from Union Station for the three-and-a-half-day train trip to Vancouver. Every day, we found time to rehearse, even though we were without a piano. We ate three meals a day on the train, and slept in bunks in the sleeping cars. We made short stops in Winnipeg and Calgary where the UJPO had branches; their members brought bagels and other goodies to the train station for us. We promised to return on our way back, as we would be singing our way east across the country. When we finally arrived in Vancouver, our bodies were vibrating from three consecutive days on the train. From there, we took a ferry to Vancouver Island.

We saw salmon jumping up the river while we travelled and we did concerts in Port Alberni, Nanaimo, and Victoria. After a quick stop at Victoria's Butchart Gardens, where we sang one concert, we took a ferry back to the mainland. Three concerts in Vancouver followed, where we met many local UJPO members.

From Vancouver, we took the train back through the Rockies to Alberta. We made stops in Lethbridge, Medicine Hat, and several rural communities, and finally ended up in Calgary for a couple of days. After fitting in a side trip to Banff and Lake Louise, we then did a couple of concerts back in Calgary.

Concerts followed in Edmonton, and then on to Saskatchewan for concerts in Saskatoon, Moose Jaw, and Regina. From there, we headed to Manitoba for three days of concerts in Winnipeg. In each city, we were billeted in people's homes to allay expenses, and received a daily stipend of expense money. Winnipeg, with a large Jewish population, came out for the three concerts at the College Theatre. In the cities of Vancouver, Calgary, and Winnipeg, we managed to get off the train and spend a couple of afternoons touring the area.

After we left Winnipeg, we did a concert at Fort William (later called Thunder Bay) where we sang at the Finnish Community Hall, and spent some time at a Finnish sauna. By the time we were approaching Sault Ste. Marie, we were starting to feel a little homesick. After one show, we continued to Sudbury where we were hosted by the Mine, Mill and Smelter Workers' Union. We did two concerts there where we sang a bunch of union songs. The next morning, we finally caught the train back to Toronto. It had been an amazing experience, but we were all glad to be home.

Jerry Gray with Claire Klein, Vancouver, 1952

The following May, I returned to Harbord to execute my second plan. I rewrote three former class two (over 75%) grade thirteen marks, and managed to turn them into three first-class (over 85%) honours. When I filled out my new application to the Faculty of Dentistry, I noticed that the question about religion had been deleted from the application form. (Apparently, Mr. Borovoy and the Jewish Alpha Omega dental society. and others had lobbied in Ontario.) After I submitted my application, I was accepted into the School of Dentistry with ease.

When I could not enter Dentistry immediately, I felt I had lost a year of my life. However, my experience touring with the group gave me my first learning experience about the music business. The tour had been a path-finding and educational experience for me as I learned about the country, for it was the first time any folk group had toured across the country in this way. In spite of that experience, the politics and discrimination of the early 1950s were hard to forget.

Gary Cristall, who we worked with in 1967 in Ottawa during Canada's centennial year, later wrote a book, *A History of Folk Music in English Canada*, about Canadian folk music tours, and used my diary of this trip as the basis for one chapter. He thought it was amazing that we were able to do such a successful tour across the country at that time.

The tour was repeated the following year, without my sister, Helen, who had married, but with the addition of my friend Jerry Goodis. Of course, I couldn't tour again with the group because I was now in my first year at the Faculty of Dentistry at the U. of T.

The Canadian tour record was later broken in 1960 by a "new" group of folk singers called The Travellers, and later, broken again by The Travellers who, in 1967, performed 186 concerts across Canada as part of the 1967 Centennial celebrations.

This 1952 trip across Canada helped develop in me the interest in performing Canadian songs for Canadians, something never done before by any folk group.

McCarthyism Returns

My high school graduation ceremony took place when I was away on my one-year musical tour across the country with the UJPO Folk Singers. But in absentia, I was awarded three athletic and citizenship awards. My parents were there on my behalf and accepted each award to a standing ovation for each presentation. They were likely amazed, because, remember— I'd never told them about my sports activities, and that I had signed all my own permission forms. Of course, they knew that I participated in sports, but they didn't know to what extent that was.

When I returned to my high school just before entering U. of T., I encountered Mr. Caldecott in the hall. Stopping me, he asked again if I was still part of that "Communist" organization. I ignored his question, and him, and I walked away. Clearly, McCarthyism[1] was still at the school.

---

[1] **McCarthyism**, refers to a period of time during the 1950s that saw American Senator Joseph McCarthy produce a series of investigations and hearings in an effort to expose supposed communist infiltration of various areas of the U.S. government. The term has since become a byname for defamation of character or reputation via

As I write this book, it seems to have reappeared, by a different name in America. In 1953, when all of Stalin's atrocities, such as the "Night of the Murdered Poet, came to light, I made the decision to leave the UJPO.

The University Years

Soon after I entered first year pre-Dental, I discovered we were facing a forty-hour work week, including three hours on Saturday mornings. In my first year, I played on a junior (under-age-21) city league basketball team that won the Toronto championship. However, in the provincial final, we lost to Niagara Falls whose star player was one of the Triano family in the Falls. Two players on my team were from the Riverdale Junior basketball team that had defeated Harbord, in overtime, two years earlier in the city championship. One was Ron Stewart, whom I've previously mentioned.

I met Ron some twenty years later as we boarded a plane from Moncton to Charlottetown. We sat together, and I noticed that his palms were sweating profusely with what he explained was a "fear of flying". Here was one of the greatest Canadian footballers, standing five feet six, same as me, being afraid of a flight from Moncton to Charlottetown, with no hills en route! We had a drink upon landing and talked about the city final when we had played against each other, and how we each had scored an equal number of points that day.

During my travels across the country and around the world with The Travellers, I often met people I'd known in my younger years. Back at the Harbord playground, I had occasionally played baseball with Morley Safer of "60 Minutes". Once in the London airport, I met him just before he joined the television news show, *60 Minutes*. We talked about growing up on the same street near Harbord, and about his work at the CBC before he joined CBS News.

---

widely publicized indiscriminate allegations, based generally on unsubstantiated charges. https://www.britannica.com/topic/McCarthyism

1953 The Birth of The Travellers

The summer before I settled into my Pre-Dental years, five members of our small choir of fifteen UJPO Folk Singers decided to break away and form a new group. One of these was Sid Dolgay, the oldest person in the group and the only person we knew who played an instrument. Sid played a mandolin type of instrument called a mando-cello, but he played it like a guitar. He played in a mandolin orchestra in Toronto and had some radio experience. The second person in the group was Jerry Goodis, the president of the Youth Division of the UJPO, and he soon became one of Canada's most well-known ad-men. His partner in the ad agency, Goodis-Goldberg, was Sam Goldberg, an ex-musician whose sister, Tanya Gould, was the accompanist for Viennese folk singer, Martha Schlamme, in New York City. Sam Goldberg became our first manager. Two other people in the group were Oscar Ross, Jerry Goodis' lifetime friend, who also joined the ad firm as artistic director, and my sister Helen, who had been a soloist with the larger Jewish Folk Choir. Last but not least was myself, who was still a teenager and a college freshman, but now a seasoned veteran of cross-country stages as well as the Naivelt Hootenanny singalong scene.

The Travellers: Jerry Gray, Jerry Goodis,
Simone Cook, Oscar Ross, 1955

We began by rehearsing three songs: "The Strangest Dream" by Wade Hemsworth, "The Lonesome Traveller" by Lee Hays of The Weavers, and "Solidarity Forever", a union song from the Joe Hill era. written in 1916.

We decided to call ourselves "The Travellers", using Lee Hays' song, and "The Lonesome Traveller" would be our signature song. At one point, we considered a name similar to The Weavers. We were a Canadian group after all, so why not call ourselves "The Beavers"? Maybe going on stage with false buck teeth? But saner heads prevailed and we gave that up, and called ourselves The Travellers.

We initially thought we would tour Canada, perhaps even the world, and the music would come from around the world also. That's why we called ourselves The Travellers. As we started learning other songs, we were approached by the UJPO to sing for them at their annual convention in Toronto. We said we'd be glad to do it, but we only had three songs prepared. They said, "That's fine." So, we did the three songs, the audience asked for encores, and we repeated the same three songs to loud and long applause. Nine years later in 1962, when we appeared in Moscow, we sang a Russian song, and the audience insisted by prolonged rhythmic clapping that we do it a second time.

In August 1953, Camp Naivelt had invited veteran folk singer, Pete Seeger, to appear in concert. Pete was part of The Weavers, the group which had formed in late 1949 by appearing in a Greenwich Village night club, and were held over for seven months during which they were "discovered" by Decca Records. They released two 78's of the songs "Goodnight Irene", "On Top of Old Smoky", "Wimoweh", and "Tzena Tzena". All four songs topped the American music charts for many months. Because of their popularity, the group toured nationally.

In 1952, The Weavers, composed of Fred Hellerman, Lee Hays, and Ronnie Gilbert along with Pete Seeger, were named by a right-wing magazine, *Red Channels*, as being Communists. Before the year was over, the group had broken up. All their public appearances and record contracts had been cancelled and they were blacklisted on American radio and television networks, and in concert halls.

Pete's 1953 appearance in Canada at Camp Naivelt, was one of his first chances to appear on stage again. Pete was the guest artist at the camp's Saturday Night concert series. Our fledgling Canadian folk quintet, The Travellers, attended that concert. Afterwards, Pete was invited to one of the Camp's family cottages, and the impromptu evening lasted into the wee hours of the morning. The Travellers were there, and Pete taught us a song that Woody Guthrie had written in 1940 called "This Land Is Your Land", along with a song called "We Will Overcome". Pete had learned the "Overcome" song on a visit to the Georgia Sea Islands' Black communities, and had filed it away for future use. Woody had written "This Land" as he travelled across the U.S. by thumb, rail and his wits, in 1940. When he reached New York City, he met Pete Seeger. Woody put the song in his pocket and never started singing it until 1949, just when his voice began to fail him. He had a condition called Huntington's Chorea, much like Lou Gherig's disease, which caused him to lose his ability to sing, and he would die at age 55 after 15 years in a sanitarium.

This Land is Your Land – The True Story

Pete Seeger had begun to sing the song in concert, and was just about to record it with The Weavers when the group was blacklisted and the record company refused to release it. In a short time, Pete Seeger, Woody Guthrie, The Weavers, <u>and</u> the song were blacklisted from airplay. Pete figured that maybe a Canadian group would not have to fight the American blacklist. Accordingly, he asked if we would take charge of the song and write some new, additional, perhaps "Canadianized" words to keep Woody's song around until (as he phrased it) "the political clouds rolled by".

Making "This Land" Canadian became our prime project, at the same time as we were learning new songs to add to our repertoire. We came up with many new versions as we tried out new words. The American line "from the redwood forests to our mighty mountains*"* was changed to "from the Arctic Circle to the Great Lake waters". We also altered the second verse, which contained the line, "to the sparkling sands of our mighty deserts" when someone said to me, "We don't got no mighty deserts in Canada." He was right of course, so we changed that second line to "from the fir-clad forests, of our mighty mountains"—something we have in abundance in Canada!

In Sudbury, Ontario, we tried a new version during a twenty-song program for the Mine, Mill and Smelter Workers' Union at their convention in 1954. As it happened, someone at that concert owned a tape recorder and recorded it. By now, we had arrived at almost the final version of the song except for the words in the second line of the chorus: "from Nova Scotia, to the Vancouver Island".

At the time, I was doing some research on songs from Newfoundland and came across a song that said, "there's lots of fish in Bonavist' Harbour". When I returned to Toronto the next day, I found a map of Newfoundland and discovered that the easternmost village in Canada was Bonavista. What a lovely name I thought, and the perfect one to book end "Vancouver Island". That's when the last word was changed, and we arrived at the final version of the song that everyone knows. At their next rehearsal, The Travellers started singing the line "from Bonavista", and it fit both musically and geographically. In the meantime, I have what I think to be the only recording of that Sudbury concert, containing the phrase, "from Nova Scotia".

Not long afterwards, a U.S. folksinger and banjo player from California named Guy Carawan appeared with The Travellers in Toronto, and we sang the new lyrics with him. He was very excited about our version, and left town not only praising our new lyrics, but also saying that he'd really enjoyed the enthusiasm we sang them with. So, the Canadian version of the song was born, and then approved by an eminent American singer. This life-altering event effectively changed our theme song from "The Lonesome Traveller" to "This Land".

Now our challenge was to find an audience for the new Travellers and for our new song, "This Land". When Guy Carawan returned to the U.S., he toured around the country and ended up at a music camp in 1959, run by a Tennessee Labour Union group. Their music director had just died in a car accident and they needed someone to take over her job. This was the time when Dr. Martin Luther King Jr. was beginning his work, and the U.S. civil rights songs were being sung. Pete Seeger then joined Guy at the camp as they rewrote the civil rights anthem into "We Shall Overcome". Guy served for the next thirty years as music director at that camp, which became the jumping-off point for many civil rights protest workers as they wrote their songs.

While I was in my first year of Pre-Dental, I thought that The Travellers needed another musical instrument, so I decided to learn how to play the five-string banjo, an instrument championed by Pete Seeger. I soon discovered that Toronto music stores did not carry such an instrument, so I scoured the pawn shops and managed to find an old banjo without a case for fifty bucks. I used a shopping bag to carry it around.

Now I had to find a teacher. There were no banjo players or teachers in Toronto, but Pete came to the rescue when he arrived in town with a copy of a book called *How to Play the Five String Banjo*, authored by him and mimeographed by his wife, Toshi. I had a great many recordings of Pete playing banjo and singing on Folkways recordings. I even had a small 78 RPM record of Pete and the Yiddish singing duo, The Barry Sisters. They had recorded a Yiddish song at a Los Angeles studio owned by an army buddy who had served with Pete in the entertainment section during World War II in the South Pacific. It turned out that his wife was one of the Barry Sisters! Together they recorded a song called, "Hey Djhankoye", about a Jewish collective farm area in the Ukraine, with the Barry Sisters singing the original Yiddish words and Pete doing the English translation.

Every evening, I would plunk out the banjo exercises in Pete's book. Then, while lying on my back in my bedroom, I began to play and sing along with Pete's recordings. I announced that I would be ready to play with the group within three months.

In 1953, the CBC television network was established. After watching some of the early TV programs, we decided to audition for a spot on the new network's summer replacement shows. We got an invitation to do a TV show, and I was able to perform with my banjo within the three months, just as I had announced. At that point, I joined the Musicians Union, and today I am an Emeritus Lifetime member.

So, in this short period of time, you have the beginning of The Travellers, the writing of the Canadianized version of "This Land", and learning how to play the banjo—all while having forty hours per week of dentistry classes. That year was a time of beginnings, with a bright future ahead. But it was not easy in Canada to get appearances, and there was no one in Canada before us that could lead the way. So, we developed different ways ourselves, by knocking on CBC producers' doors and cold-calling them. It seemed to work, as you'll soon see. There was no playbook on how to start a folk group, so we invented one.

During The Travellers' early years, while I was still a dental student, we made an impact on the television critics of the 1950s. Before the group had made its first recording in the mid- 1950s, we received very positive reviews that are worth sharing here because they inspired us to continue what we had started:

"Happily, free of pretentious oddities. They have versatility and exuberance".

~Clyde Gilmour, *The Globe and Mail*

"The Travellers stand a better chance of succeeding, reason: Showmanship."

~ Alex Barris, *The Globe and Mail*

"They are infinitely better than their brassy brothers… wove a spell of folk songs brimming with exuberance and happiness in a style that is entirely their own."

~ Robin Green, *The Globe and Mail*

"A young, fresh, and exuberant group of Canadian Folk Singers staged an exciting and winning program at Hart House Theatre last night. All their numbers have vigour and sincerity, plenty of showmanship and professional polish. They are undoubtedly bound for greater success."

~Stan Rantin, *The Toronto Star*

Reviews like these inspired us to continue striving towards our dreams. One of our first dreams was to appear on TV and perform music that would be accepted by both audiences and critics alike. We set new goals to make recordings and to appear on concert stages. You'll have to read on to see if we succeed.

1953-1958

In September 1953, when I entered my first year of Dentistry at the University of Toronto, I had to pay over $2000 to register, and that was all money I'd saved from my summer jobs at various places. I worked the month of June at Camp Naivelt, painting the new swimming pool before we put the water in. I also painted the large dining hall that seated 250 people, and then I assumed my job as head lifeguard, with two other friends, Morry Patt and Marty Kane, acting as my assistants for that summer. The camp season ended in late

August, so I worked as a lifeguard on the Toronto waterfront, as well as at Sunnyside Pool, the largest public pool in Canada, until classes started after Labour Day. I'm still in touch with Morry Patt and Marty Kane, and earlier this year we attended Marty's eightieth birthday celebration. Morry is two years younger than me, our mothers were both born in Vilna in Lithuania, and we both celebrate our birthdays on the same day.

Because university expenses were now a reality, I found I could no longer afford to keep playing the same amount of sports as I had during the previous eight years. I had to work to remain in school, so I became a referee of interfaculty basketball and football games at both the U. of T., and for the Toronto Secondary School interscholastic games I'd played in for the previous five years. So, during the week I refereed games at Hart House at noon, and then at various high school gyms after 4:00 P.M. Two evenings a week, for several years I also coached for the Toronto Indoor Playgrounds at Bloor Street Collegiate, and coached some teams there as well. Because I didn't have a car, it was a tight schedule, balancing all these jobs around my class schedule, but at least it gave me some income.

The next job I had to fit into my schedule was rehearsing and performing with The Travellers. We sang for trade unions at rallies and on picket lines, and I had also started giving seminars on the music of the labour unions for the United Auto Workers at the CAW (Canadian Auto Workers) education center on Lake Huron. We also sang on campus at fraternities, at several campus events, and began a five-year period of singing for the Campus Hillel Foundation[2] at their opening evening of the year. This venue gave us a chance to sing not only songs about Canada and the labour movement, but also the backlog of Yiddish songs we knew from our growing up years.

It was easy for us to sing for these events at Hillel, because in the early years the student president at Hillel, was law student Alan

---

[2] **Hillel: The Foundation for Jewish Campus Life** (known as **Hillel International**) is the largest Jewish campus organization in the world, working with thousands of college students. Named for Hillel the Elder, a Jewish sage known for his formulation of the Golden Rule, Hillel is represented at more than 550 colleges and communities around the world. https://www.hillel.org/

Borovoy, who was later followed by Steven Lewis. Alan had been two years ahead of me at Harbord Collegiate, and like me he worked with The Jewish Labour Committee while an undergrad. Later he became the first president of the Canadian Civil Rights Union, a position he held for some forty years.

Steven Lewis was the son of David Lewis, the head of the Federal CCF[3] Party which later became the NDP. With sponsors like that heading Hillel, it was easy to sing all our pro-labour and protest songs about social housing ills with impunity. In the summer, Alan Borovoy was the director of Camp Ogama in Muskoka, Ontario, and hired The Travellers to appear. As the camp divided into sections for an international Olympiad, we sang a series of international songs, followed by a series of fireside concert hootenannies at the lake. It was kind of amazing to see all these Forest Hill kids, who'd been entrusted to Alan Borovoy for the summer, returning home singing songs like "The Talkin' Union Blues", and "Solidarity Forever". These kids were part of the upcoming 1960s' folk song generation, later joining the civil rights protests

Pete Seeger was in a similar situation. Because of the McCarthy backlists, Pete could only sing at schools and summer camps, where both he and The Travellers imbued the spirit of protest in leading to their later political involvement during the early 60's.

Auditioning for the CBC

In the fall of 1953, the CBC (Canadian Broadcasting Corporation), the government-owned radio network, began their first season of television. After watching the early programming of *Uncle Chichimus* and the early music shows, we decided this was a medium we could

---

[3] The **Co-operative Commonwealth Federation (CCF)** was a social-democratic political party founded in 1932 in Alberta by a number of socialist, agrarian and labour groups. In 1944, the CCF was elected in Saskatchewan and formed the first social-democratic government in North America. In 1961, the CCF became the New Democratic Party, or NDP. https://en.wikipedia.org/wiki/Co-operative_Commonwealth_Federation

easily be a part of. So, we contacted Peter McFarland, a CBC TV producer. After several calls, our manager, Sam Goldberg, got us an appointment to audition for *The Haunted Studio*, a summer replacement series about a TV studio haunted by former musicians. We prepared three songs.

At the audition, we sang three songs, and Peter McFarland lit a pipe. After a few minutes of musing, he asked if we had any more songs. So, we did three more songs. The pipe remained lit, and more musing followed along with another request for more songs. When we finished, he asked about other songs, so we did three more—now having sung a total of about twelve different songs. More musing followed.

Sam asked if he liked our presentation. "Yes!" he said, "I liked what I heard starting right from the first song. But I was so enthralled with the music, this was really like a private concert!" A comment which caused us all to grin--a bit.

Peter McFarlane then hired us to perform a couple of songs on one of the shows in the middle of that summer. This was the early days of live TV. We got a two-hour rehearsal call where we ran through the song, and they "blocked "it out—meaning they placed us in certain positions on the studio floor to get the camera angles correct.

At the next rehearsal we went to those positions and sang the songs so they could situate the sound booms and camera angles. Next came the final rehearsal followed by a break, and then the show was done live. Videotape had not yet been invented, but they had what was known as a Kinescope copy, which they could refer to later. This meant the show could be seen by audiences everywhere, but it was another decade before the performers could actually see what they had done. Well into the 1980s, I continued to call the CBC, asking if their archives department had begun transferring all the early TV shows onto videotape. I was hoping the quality could be saved if they were salvaged onto videotape, and later on to DVDs. I think I spurred them on to review their procedures regarding "old shows", and eventually I received a lot of copies of some those early shows that featured The Travellers, but not all of them.

The Travellers live in CBC TV studio, 1955

Over the next ten years, we went through this procedure for each TV show we did, and always had to rely on others to tell us how it went. Most people we knew did not yet have a TV, so they would go and visit a friend who had a TV, and watch the show. Soon they had <u>all</u> become experts at telling us that "you blinked when the camera was on you," or "there was a shadow at the back of the set while you were singing," or some other technical flaw that we had no part of. But we were in demand, so we called other producers at the CBC to see if we could get on a different show. It was an exciting time! TV was still so new, and people who did not know anyone with a TV set would stand at the windows of TV stores to watch the shows.

When we were doing that first show, Sid Dolgay, was the only instrument-playing member of the group, and therefore the only "musician" in the group. As such, he was included in the musicians' union contract, while the rest of us were on "work permits" from ACTRA (the Association of Canadian Radio and Television Artists), one show at a time. The musicians got a better rate of pay than the non-musicians, but that situation lasted only until the second show because by then I had taught myself to play banjo. When I went to the rehearsal, there were other musicians around who had played with the symphony, and with other radio shows and concerts for many years. People like legends Bert Niosi and his brothers took us under their wing and promised to show us how to ensure we were not taken advantage of. His brother, Joe Niosi, (a bass player who stood bigger than his bass fiddle) gave me a card just as the rehearsal was ending. When I read the card, it said, "Don't give up your day job!" That was the stock card they gave to all newbie musicians.

By the next rehearsal, we'd been given a friendly introduction to the musicians' union. The other musicians on the shows we did, actually liked it when The Travellers appeared because we arrived with a song that was prepared, and required no extra accompaniment by the members of the "house band". So, when we went to block out and rehearse on camera, the band would take an extended break and go out for a smoke, or other refreshment.

My *Dentantics* Entr'acte

In my first year of university, I was asked to take part in the dental school ritual of being in a show at Hart House Theatre. It was their annual show called *Dentantics,* and would require several months of rehearsal followed by three days of performances in March. Because of my busy schedule, I had to tell the producer I simply did not have the time to do this. They said I could have a solo part that required no rehearsal time, but which was important to the show. It was called an "entr'acte," and would occur when all the actors had to leave the stage so they could close the curtain and make set changes. Once the curtain had closed, I would go out in front and do a three–four-minute entr'acte, hopefully followed by a long applause. When I finished, the curtain would re-open and the show would continue.

Hart House Theatre at University of Toronto, 1955

I came up with an act based on a class we had taken that year about medicines used in dentistry, some of which came from the Belladona family of drugs. When it was time for my entr'acte, I came out dressed as a Caribbean sailor called "Jerry Belladona," (an obvious take off on a famous calypso entertainer with a similar name) and I sang the song

"Jamaica Farewell". I did not do it in "blackface". The arts writer for *The Varsity,* the university newspaper, wrote a review of our show predicting that "the *Dentantics* show will be much better than the medical show, *The U.C. Follies,* or the engineers show, *Skule Nite,* over the next three years, because of a young performer, Jerry Gray, who will steal the show any night he's "on". For the next three years, I fulfilled my job by being a permanent entr'acte. The reviewer was Moishe Reiter who, still a law student at U. of T., gave me the same type of review every year. We became long-time friends, and he became a very good lawyer, obviously, with an excellent eye for talent!

Meanwhile, I continued practising my banjo prowess, and Sid Dolgay and I, were being reviewed in the Toronto newspapers. The overall consensus was that, with the banjo now playing the rhythmic tone of the music, it freed up Sid Dolgay to play some solo lines on the mando-cello, substantially enriching the group's overall arrangements and increasing their musicality both in concert and on TV. In his historical liner notes for the 2001 Sony LP, THIS LAND, Rob Bowman wrote: "As unorthodox as this combination was, it worked perfectly."

After that first TV show called, *The Haunted Studio,* changes began taking place in The Travellers. My sister Helen got married in 1955, and several months later she was pregnant. She managed to stay long enough to sing with us for the various dates we had booked. After she left, Simone Cook, a member of the Jewish Folk Choir, stepped into her spot. Simone had a different type of voice than my sister, and while Helen had a wonderful voice, and even though she was my sister, I think the group sounded better with Simone's voice, as she fit in very well with the rest of us.

After the *Haunted Studio,* a new TV show appeared called *The Cross-Canadian Hit Parade Show,* with Winnipeg transplant Wally Koster, as the singing host. In our guest spot, we were dressed as miners coming out of a coal pit, and I sang the lead in "Sixteen Tons", the # 2 hit in Canada at that time. By this time, some people in my 3rd year class had begun asking questions about "someone they'd seen on TV last night that looked a lot like me." During this year, I had started seeing patients in the Dental School's clinic, and some of them asked if I had been on TV lately! I always answered that it was probably my brother, not me. They, of course, did not know that I had no brother.

Our spot on the *Cross-Canadian Hit Parade Show* turned out to be Oscar Ross's last appearance with us. Just before our second TV show in 1955, he decided to leave the group to become a mime—like the famous Marcel Marceau. Right after Oscar left, we did a concert at Camp Naivelt, and Oscar was on the same bill in his new role as a mime.

A friend named Martin Meslin sang with the Youth Singers, which were sort of junior singers like the triple A minor league baseball players waiting their turn to go up to the majors. Marty stood about six-foot-two and towered over me, but had a pretty good voice and was an attractive-looking singer with a bright smile. He did one TV show with us, a few other gigs in some summer camps, and an on-air pilot for a new TV show in Wingham Ontario, near Owen Sound.

I think Marty's heart was not really into being "on the road" with a singing group, so he decided he needed some time to think about it, and traveled to Europe with his wife. We had a couple of important TV dates coming up and he could not commit and asked to be excused, but we thought we really needed to do this next gig. We were right, because the new TV show was important for us. Losing a person in the group was always a problem. Each group of people creates a unique sound together, and if one leaves, the dynamics of the sound and the appearance of the group both change. You always hope it will work out in time.

When Marty left, we did not replace him, but even so he marched for me at my wedding two years later in 1957. We had now experienced some major changes from the original group that had formed in 1953.

Right after the *The Canadian Hit Parade Show* we were asked to do a spot on *The Jackie Rae Show,* a TV show that included a lot of Toronto's jazz musicians including reed player Moe Koffman. Moe had just recorded "The Swingin' Shepherd Blues", which became one of the first hits ever recorded in Canada. In 2001, Moe Koffman and

The Travellers were the first two artists presented with the new Lifetime Achievement Award by the Toronto Musicians Association.

On November 30, 1955, The Travellers were asked to be a part of a CBC Radio Network Show, called *Songs of My People*, a multicultural show of songs from around the world. We had many international songs in our repertoire, and ultimately received a lot of positive write-in comments about our performance.

Word was now getting around about the new group in town who were singing songs about Canada, including a new song called "This Land Is Your Land". In late November 1955, The Travellers made a second appearance on *The Jackie Rae TV Show*, and Moishe Reiter wrote a column about me in *The Varsity*, the U. of T. daily newspaper.

On February 1, 1956, we were asked to take part in the second season of a TV talent show called *Pick the Stars*, where performers would appear on TV and viewers could vote on the acts by what is now called "snail mail". The winners would then continue for another month. This show was a ground breaker for me personally because I was playing the new banjo that Pete Seeger had generously taken the time to order for me from Boston's Vega Company.

On our first appearance on *Pick the Stars*, we were given about four minutes for our performance. We chose a song from a particular area of Canada, and then for the last minute we did several verses and choruses from "This Land Is Your Land". Letters of support rolled in and included many comments about our singing "This Land". Those positive comments allowed us to continue to further episodes, and each time we would do a song from a different part of Canada and then finish up again with the chorus of "This Land".

On the February 1 show, we inaugurated Martin Meslin into the group and a month later we were invited to perform on a show at the Wingham TV station. It was a pilot for a country music series starring Earl Heywood, a local country musician hailing from that area of Ontario's "corn belt". When we arrived in Wingham, we had an amusing time trying to find the TV studio. First of all, we had driven up from Toronto on a dark and snowy Sunday evening, and arrived around 7:00 pm. The whole town was dark, so we rolled up the main street looking for a motel. We could not see one, and the only light on was at a funeral parlour, and the door was unlocked.

We parked and went in, but no one was around. So, in keeping with the weather and the situation, Jerry Goodis climbed into a coffin that was displayed on a table, and stretched himself out. Suddenly, the owner came in and asked (naturally) what we were doing there? At that time, Wingham was still a very small town with apparently no motel. The funeral director had a big laugh, and then he guided us through the snow to a motel on the edge of town near the TV tower. The next morning, we showed up at the TV station on time to tape the pilot. They gave us a country themed set to sing on, and western duds to wear. We sang, as close as we could get to, country songs, and left for home the next day.

This was Marty Meslin's last show as part of the group, as he departed after two TV shows. We won our second attempt to advance on the *Pick the Stars Show*. In a column for the *Toronto Star*, TV critic Alex Barris commented that The Travellers were on their way to stardom. 1956 was indeed a successful year for The Travellers, and for me too.

The previous summer, we'd travelled to the Laurentians to sing at Camp Beaver, a UJPO sister camp to our Toronto camps Kinderland and Naivelt. It was there that I met a girl named Greta, the first girl I could call a "girlfriend". We were from the same background, Jewish and left of centre, and she was now working as a teacher in Montreal. Like me, Greta had also been an accomplished athlete in her Montreal high school, Baron Byng, which, just like Harbord CI, and was about ninety per cent Jewish. Later that same year, she came to a Toronto UJPO convention, where we renewed our relationship. The following year, in 1956, she accepted a job teaching in Clarkson, Ontario, about halfway to Hamilton. And then she moved from Montreal to Toronto. Later, in order to save money, she moved into my parents' home with me but, because of my obviously busy schedule, we did not see much of each other except on weekends.

Here comes more of the busy schedule as I advanced through Dental school with the end now in sight. When the Travellers sang at Camp Beaver, it was the first time I'd ever heard of Wade Hemsworth who wrote songs about his adventures in Northern Ontario. As a budding engineer with Ontario Hydro, he'd been dropped into that black-fly ridden area, and wrote his iconic song called simply, "Blackfly". Of course, his other very famous song is the "Log Driver's Waltz". Once I heard "Blackfly", it stayed with me as a signature song for my whole career, and we recorded it on our first album which is now getting close. But first, here we go:

On March 17, 1956, we were guests on the *Holiday Ranch* TV show broadcast from Toronto with Cliff MacKay as host. This was a hometown country show with musicians from the radio show of the same name, who were also part of the long-running *Happy Gang* radio show. It also included the legendary Gordie Tapp.

The next day I made a guest soloist appearance in Toronto with The Jewish Folk Choir, and sang several songs in Yiddish. This was no doubt approved by my early Naivelt muse, Fagel Gartner. She used to send me a message at the Naivelt pool in Yiddish, saying, "Zalman, men darf gayn zingen." Zalman was my Yiddish name, and her words meant, "We gotta go to sing." In all the years I sang with her, that was my siren call to show up for a rehearsal.

I rehearsed with Fagel and the choir, and was a great success in something I really hadn't planned on doing—singing only Yiddish songs as a career. But it was a great honour to return to my roots in Yiddish music, with Emil and Fagel Gartner. I've always enjoyed group singing and creating harmonies. To this day, when I go to a concert by other folkies, I always sing along in harmony, which for me is just second nature.

June 5 and 12 were the dates selected for the final two *Pick the Stars* shows, which would bring the contest to a close. In the previous semi-final, we were up against a new duo of comedians, one called Rich Little, with a friend from Ottawa. Rich went on to have a huge career as a mimic with many voices, mainly in the U.S. He was considered to be one of the best, appearing frequently on *The Ed Sullivan Show* and *The Tonight Show* with Johnny Carson. He returned to Canada to do many concerts with The Travellers, and I never stopped mentioning to the emcee at the places we sang, that Rich Little had finished behind us on *Pick the Stars*.

In the June 5 final, we did well, but the show ran longer than planned and part of our last song got cut off. With e-mail being still almost thirty-five years away, the audience had a week to send their votes by mail before the cut off date. The second week, each of the five finalists would appear with a new song or performance to be seen across the country. After the last performer had finished, the mail results would be announced. As I recall, we finished second or third to an English-speaking, bar act from Montreal. Years later, I heard they began drinking away their pay in bars, and soon left showbiz.

Even though we did not win, by appearing on *Pick the Stars,* we made our mark on the music scene as we thought we could. *Toronto Star* columnist Alex Barris wrote: "The Travellers should have won, with their ability to light up a crowd." Ron Poulton from the *Toronto Telegram* made a similar comment in his review.

That summer, we sang again in Muskoka at Camp Ogama, as we sharpened our ability to sing for young kids. This became part of a later career of singing kids' songs, before anyone else in Canada. But more about that later. As the year went on, we had several more events. In the fall, Yonge Street was finally reopened after construction was finished on the subway, and the ditch was filled in and paved over. On a sunny day in the fall, a rally was held at the south end of the Eaton's College Street store parking lot where The Travellers did an hour of celebratory songs and sing-alongs. In October, The Travellers appeared for the third time on *The Jackie Rae Show*, and two weeks later we appeared on a show called *Frigidaire Entertains,* hosted by Frosia Gregory. I have no idea where she went after that season, or where she ended up.

It was the end of a memorable year. I was in my final year at dental school, almost ready to graduate. Greta and I decided that next summer on July 1[st,] which at that time was still called Dominion Day[4], we would get married. How patriotic could we be? It was an omen that the date was great, which proved to be true because over the next fifty years a great many more happy events happened on July 1. The

---

[4] July 1st was originally called **Dominion Day** from Confederation in 1867. It was not until 1982 that Dominion Day was **renamed Canada Day.**

Travellers had become an established go-to group that everyone in showbiz said would have more success. Then, just before the turn of the year, we learned we would be recording our first album in 1957!

On February 1, I made my fourth and last appearance at the Faculty of Dentistry Show, *Dentantics*—appearing as an entr'acte. In dentistry, I joined the Alpha Omega fraternity, a Jewish organization of undergrad dentists. It later became a graduate society whose members would lecture for the undergrads in North America, Europe, and Israel. One of the main things the fraternity did was to lobby dental schools to stop their prejudicial attitude towards Jewish students, for instance having their qualified applications rejected in favour of non-Jewish students who were less qualified, as had happened in my case. The intercessions of this fraternity had lasting results. I truly did not have the time to be an active member, but my class that year was about thirty per cent Jewish, and many of my friends had been high school pals.

It was the last year that I took part in interfaculty basketball. My close and lifetime friend, Marvin Kopel, played basketball with me throughout high school and into inter-faculty sports. Our team finished second in the league; I made the first all-star team and Marvin made the second. At my graduation, I received a plaque for having appeared in *Dentantics* for four years, and for being on the basketball team and getting to the final. I also played one year on the football team, but as I was soon to have two careers—one in music and the other in dentistry, I decided to opt out of football because of the danger to my hands and fingers, which were very important for both careers.

In March, The Travellers got a call from the CBC to appear on *The Jackie Rae Show*, which again featured Moe Koffman and Peter Appleyard in the band, along with many other great musicians we'd met over the years. One of them was a great trumpet player named Bob Van Evera, who turned out to be the brother of a guy I'd coached back in the playground basketball league. He was just starting out as a singer and comedic actor, and had shortened his name to Billy Van. He appeared on many TV shows mainly from CHCH in Hamilton, Ontario, several game shows, and hosted on *House of Frightenstein* among many other credits. But he'd also played football against me in my last two years at Harbord C.I. Billy Van was one of Canada's most prolific performers, and we talked often at places where we shared the stages and screens. Our long relationship started in sports, and ended on Canadian TV history. He died young and I still have happy memories of his wonderful personality.

On May 18, 1957, The Travellers were invited to appear on a CBC Radio show, called *Junior Magazine*. On May 27, we were on a summer replacement TV show called *The Jack Kane Show*, and another Jazz-oriented CBC musical show called *Summertime*. In June, we sang for a B'nai B'rith Upper Canada Lodge party. I was now off school for the summer between third and fourth years of dental school. I was working at my summer day job at Coca Cola, lugging heavy wooden cases of glass pop bottles and delivering them to various locations around the city. I also got my driver's license, which enabled me to drive the big huge Coke truck when the head driver wanted a rest.

A Bridegroom and his Bride – Here's to the Couple

As July 1st approached, I was given time off work for our wedding day, and for our honeymoon. Greta and I were as poor as could be. My young bride-to-be was now teaching at Grace Street Public School in the south downtown area of Toronto. We used all the money we had to pay for the wedding, and any monies we received as gifts at the wedding we put aside for a honeymoon.

Pete Seeger had taught us an African song that he had translated, called "Here's to the Couple", which all our folkie friends knew. They sang it at our wedding, and many of our friends also used it when they married, and later their kids used it when they got married. Greta had always dreamed of palm trees as a honeymoon background, so we got tickets to Miami, ate the free rolls at the Jewish delis on Miami Beach, and enjoyed the sun and sand for almost a week. Then we flew to New York City to walk the streets of Manhattan, and see a few shows on Broadway at last-minute performance-day rates.

As young and poor honeymooners, we had faith that life would get better for us. The future looked bright, with only one more year of school for me to finish. When we got home, Greta bought a used British Morris Minor, the first car we ever owned. The only thing wrong with that car was that it stubbornly refused to start in our Canadian winters, which are much colder than those in Britain.

Our First Album: Across Canada With The Travellers

The Travellers had planned to make a recording that year, and finally a friend and musician from a left-wing Ukrainian organization scraped some money together for us to make it. Mitch Sago and Joe Wallace had written a song called "Making Hay" about two lovers on the back of a hay wagon, trying to make out. We eventually recorded it for Hallmark Records in the living room of a small house near Bay and College Streets owned by the son of Sir Earnest MacMillan. The only other studio in Toronto at that time was at the CFRB radio station at Bloor and Bay Streets. To say that the studio we recorded in was primitive would be an understatement. There was only one Telefunken microphone for five Travellers and our three instruments. In those days, it was not possible to record on certain tracks and then fuse them with other tracks later, because there was only one track.

Before the session, we prepared fifteen songs at Sid's home, and then completed recording the album called *Across Canada With The Travellers* in three, three-hour sessions. The album cover featuring Canadian fall-coloured leaves, was prepared by former Traveller Oscar Ross, who was now the art director for Jerry Goodis and Sam Goldberg's ad agency, Goodis-Goldberg. He had designed it in the shortest possible time. There was really nothing to compare it with because The Travellers' recording was a first in Canada. Produced on a shoe-string budget, it was released in Toronto by Eaton's department store, and was also available as a delivery item.

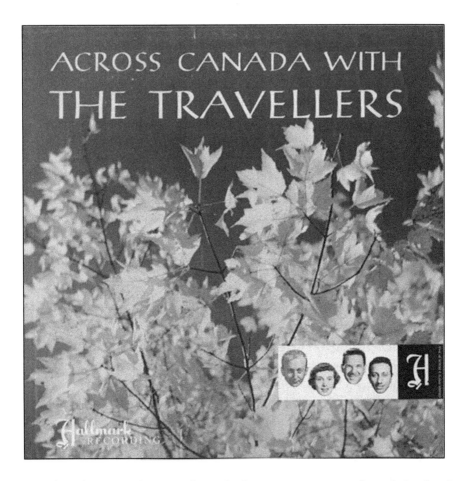

After the record was released, the company transferred the lead song, the Canadianized version of "This Land Is Your Land", to a 78 RPM recording as a single. I probably have the only known copy of that first single recording. Copies of the first LP recording of the album are possibly tucked away in many people's basements, waiting for it to increase in value. I have two copies, but they are in poor shape. Who knew we were going to be a hit?

Later in 1957, we sang again at the Hillel Foundation at the U. of T., chaired now by Stephen Lewis. In November, we were asked to appear at the Prince George Hotel night club for one week. This was the first time we had performed in a night club, and there were a couple of small problems. Jerry Goodis's wife, Carol, was still under twenty-one, as was my wife Greta. Due to the strict liquor laws in Ontario at that time, the club could not allow either of them in to watch us perform. For the first evening, they sat in the lobby, and we joined them between sets. But for the rest of the week? Greta returned each night wearing dark glasses, and sat in on the shows.

In early 1958, we travelled to Montreal and sang at McGill University's Moyse Hall for a sold-out concert. In March we sang again for a UJPO Convention, which had undergone some serious changes in the past year. In 1955, Joseph Stalin had died, and the world finally learned the truth about the atrocities he had ordered, and what he had been doing to Soviet Jews in the USSR. People were understandably upset and angry. The Soviet Union was still working with pro-Stalinist policies, and by 1957 this dogma had resulted in the UJPO splitting in half and many members quitting. A new organization called the New Fraternal Jewish Organization formed, with many of the leadership having come from the UJPO. The Travellers had made a commitment to appear at the UJPO convention, but that was the last time we sang for them, as most of us were opposed to the Soviet Union's pro-Stalinist policies.

The record company, Hallmark, having had some sort of success with our first LP, wanted us to do another. This time, we added several more instruments and a drummer to our arrangements. The recording company got the same "studio", and because of the cramped quarters, during the recording the drummer, Mickey Shannon, had to be placed in the nearby washroom, and muffled by several empty boxes. This second LP was called *Songs of North America,* as we passed Canadian boundaries into Mexico, the Caribbean, the U.S., and Puerto Rico, and created a fourteen-song album. The album was released in the summer of 1958, once again at Eaton's and Simpson's. Later in the year, we showed up at Eaton's for the official launch to autograph many of the records that were sold. These recordings, done in such primitive locations, were historical, but also hysterical when you consider how the recording was done. They are probably stored in people's basements now.

In June of 1958, I graduated with a DDS (Doctor of Dental Surgery) from the University of Toronto. At my graduation ceremony, now, with a degree in dentistry in hand, and acceptance as an upcoming Canadian music force, I asked my mother which career path I should follow. My mother replied in Yiddish about the music business saying, "Fun dos ken men machn a lebn?" Translated, it asked the question, "From this, you're going to make a living?"

As always, I took part of my mother's advice and, borrowing money from one of the dental supply companies, I opened my first dental practice in northwest Toronto at the corner of Keele Street and Lawrence Avenue. But I also decided to keep option two (music) around and see what happened.

So, at the end of my school career, I had a dental degree, but also many press clippings from the last five years of doing some twenty or so musical TV appearances. In August of 1958, The Travellers appeared at the CNE (the Canadian National Exhibition) for a two-week appearance at the *Toronto Star* Bandshell. Sponsored by *The Toronto Star*, we did several shows a day there, and sang free concerts every day. For a fledgling dentist waiting for his office to be constructed, it brought in some needed revenue to tide me over.

As the summer of 1958 came to an end, I thought back on these last five years of actually growing up in this troubled world. I had finished my schooling, become a practising dentist as well as a husband, and done much in my community. I had grown as a person, but I knew I had much more to contribute.

A European Adventure

Earlier, I mentioned that to me life was much like a merry-go-round. Sometimes when you had an opportunity to grab the brass ring and do something other than what was expected, or considered to be wise or correct, it might turn out to be a rewarding experience.

Greta and I had some close friends in Toronto who were part of a Ukrainian folk-dance group that Greta used to dance with. Much like the UJPO, they were a left-oriented group. They had heard there would be a world assembly of young people gathering in Europe in the coming summer of 1959. This World Youth Festival was usually held in countries like Bulgaria or Romania, countries that lay behind the Iron Curtain. But this year's mid-summer meeting would be held for the first time in the West—in the beautiful city of Vienna.

Jerry leads delegation to Vienna, 1958

That summer, Toronto had decided to widen both Keele Street and Lawrence Avenues. The resulting road construction mess created a kind of crisis in my new dental career, because for three months people could not easily get to my new office.

Guess what? Greta and I decided to go on an adventure. In mid-summer, we took a ship, (definitely not a luxury liner), from the port of Montreal to Le Havre, France. From there we took a train to Paris where we spent a day waiting for "The Orient Express" train to take us through France and Germany to Austria, and finally to Vienna. Once we arrived, we rented a room in a large house in downtown Vienna. I felt as if I was in the movie called *The Third Man*.

Near to where the convention would take place was a large park known as The Prater, with a huge and historic Ferris wheel with closed cars, just like in the movie. We took the streetcar often to get around, and exchanged pins with many delegates. Then we sang some songs about Canada and the dance group did some Ukrainian dances. As the four-day meeting was drawing to a close, we befriended a group of people from Poland who offered us a free trip to their homeland with them. We were scheduled to go to Italy, but the offer of a free trip to Poland was enticing.

We met at the Vienna train station for a trip that would normally take about four hours. However, the train had to go through Czechoslovakia with no stops, so it was sealed by police, with no one getting on or off. This was the Iron Curtain at its worst. We arrived at a town called Katowice, in a coal mining area in the southwest of Poland. It was the oldest coal mine in Europe, and they asked if we would like to go down into the mine. We said yes, so they gave us miners' boots and outfits, and a cap with a light attached. The ride down to the coal face was the scariest I have ever had and was at least a mile underground. As the oldest mine in Europe, it probably also had the oldest elevator. At the bottom, there was about four inches of water, and the ceiling was so low that we both had to bend down to walk, even though neither of us is very tall. We couldn't wait to get back to the top.

The next morning, we drove to nearby Auschwitz with our hosts. There were very few people visiting that day, so we walked the grounds ourselves to see the horrors of the barracks, the crematoria, the railroad platforms, the huge storage room filled with human hair, eyeglasses, shoes, and suitcases. We were sickened by the horror of the world's worst concentration camp. It had been only fourteen years since the war had ended, and not many people came to see this place. But we saw the gate signed with the phrase, "Arbeit Macht Frei"—the German words proclaiming that "If you work hard, you will be free"— the ever-famous lie about its very existence. At that time, few people in Canada had ever seen such a sight, except those who had survived the inexplicable horror of one of these concentration camps.

In silence, we boarded a car to travel to Warsaw where our Polish hosts and benefactors lived. When they left us, we stayed another day or two in Warsaw and looked for the sewer cover in Mila 18. But we found the city square did not have much remembrance of the Holocaust, or the Warsaw Ghetto. In the evening, there were no neon lights to light the city, and there was not much happiness about. After the horrors of the war, the Soviets had come in and spread their grey pall throughout all the areas behind the Iron Curtain.

We continued our European adventure with three days in Switzerland, and then continued on to Paris for three more days. It was startling just how life was so different in free Europe, with lights and food and laughter everywhere. We visited the normal tourist sites, and enjoyed walking the streets with a new appreciation of freedom.

The last part of our trip was spent in London. For three more days, we enjoyed playing Jerry and Greta Tourist and walking the streets. On our last day, we boarded a flight back to Montreal where our car was parked with Greta's relatives, who were anxious to hear about our trip, and very glad to see us again.

Once home in Toronto, I was glad to be back making a living in dentistry again, and back into showbiz, where we had left off a month ago. A lot of our friends took trips to Florida or the Laurentians or to the Catskills, but we'd had a world-class experience visiting Europe, both east and west, rather than just sitting around waiting for the road construction to be finished.

During Christmas week of 1959, our friends decided to go to the Concord Hotel in the Catskills, ninety minutes north of New York City. We joined them the last week of the year and took part in a "learn to ski week". In our beginner ski class was comedian Buddy Hackett who was entertaining there, and we spent our time laughing at both his and our efforts on the hills. But we all learned to ski and returned unscathed. Buddy was there with his dog, Laika (named after the Russian space-dog), who accompanied him up and down the ski hill.

One last bit of housekeeping, regarding "This Land", took place in late 1959. We got a letter from Pete Seeger and Harold Leventhal, Pete's manager and agent. They said they had started an agency to try and collect revenue for Woody Guthrie's songs, called The Guthrie Foundation. Woody had been in a care facility and unable to function well because of his Huntington's disease, for which there was no treatment and no chance of survival. We learned that the Canadian version of "This Land" was generating income because of all the television appearances The Travellers had made. Pete and Harold requested that the group cede all payments to the Guthrie Foundation. We agreed to do it with one proviso and it was this: that whenever the Canadian version was used in print or recordings, it should state that this Canadian version was written by The Travellers. When the sheet music was later published in Canada, it had a picture of The Travellers on the cover, and the statement we had agreed upon.

Several Canadian schoolbooks were published without that codicil, and they were ordered by the publisher to recall all copies and reprint them. Up to and including today's date, all royalties from the Canadian version of "This Land" have been sent, in perpetuity, to the Guthrie Foundation.

It had been an eventful five years of dental school, growing up musically and recording the first couple of Canadian recordings, getting married, and gathering a book full of positive reviews. I had also made a group of wonderful lifetime friends as part of the dental class of '58. In May of 2018, this class held a sixtieth anniversary reunion in Toronto. There were many faces missing, and many others were there at various stages of health, but those of us who made it, were able to renew the lifetime experience of our five years together at the U. of T. Dental School. I was very glad to be one of the surviving members, and walking easily, unaided by canes or walkers. So, let's keep going until the next reunion in 2023. I should live so long.

I once read a book of Jewish jokes and witticisms. There was a joke about a teacher who said that, if he was as rich as Rothschild, he would be richer than him. "How can that be?" he was asked. In response he said, "I'd do a little teaching on the side."

In many ways, I think that that's what the future held for me because, "I'd still be a dentist, but I'd do a little singing on the side."

CHAPTER 2:
I'VE TRAVELLED POOR AND I'VE TRAVELLED HUNGRY

1960

For the first seven years of The Travellers' existence, much happened that was important to us, as well as to Canada. During those years we had no one to guide us or show us the way, so we muddled ahead, just trying to make each year better than the one before. As this story will show, I think you'll be able to see how the number and quality of our engagements progressed. Our popularity with audiences grew but we always followed an original path by doing what we thought was right.

Alan Borovoy, the later forty-year president of the Canadian Civil Liberties Association, and I were both part of the Jewish Labour Committee in Ontario. Our province was growing up, and we were worried about fairness in housing, employment, and helping people in need. There were no groups other than people in the CCF party that cared. The Jewish Labour Committee stared down the ruling Conservatives in Ontario, and we asked if they could help out and back us, as we tried to help people who could not help themselves.

I had been singing for several unions, and rallies were often being organized to help people in trouble. Earlier I mentioned how my Yiddish music muse, Fagel Gartner, would call me and say in Yiddish, "We have to go and sing." (Men darf gayn zingen). Alan Borovoy knew The Travellers and I, had a deep feeling of compassion for the downtrodden, for workers, for human rights and people without fair housing Alan and his group knew that if a rally was being planned, either I or The Travellers had to be called. We would then lead the rallies with singing before the speakers came on to deliver the "sermons".

Alan would call me at my office and leave a short message like, "Rally tonight, Christie Pits Park, 7:30, be there." And we, or sometimes just I, would show up with voices and songs. This went on for years. In street singing, to help a cause, it was always good to have people at the front of the crowd to pick up the chorus and sing loud enough to drown out the naysayers. I knew the words to all the labour songs, so that helped.

Actually, this singing on wagons or street corners began in the 1940s and fifties, when the pre-Travellers group from the UJPO were asked to sing out for J.B. Salsberg in his early elections around 1950, in the Spadina-Kensington area. We wrote a song based on the Davy Crockett song, and changed it to "J.B., J.B. Salsberg, The King of Kensington." I had two copies of the Salsberg street song-sheets and, after he died, I donated one of them to a Salsberg retrospective at the library at Queen's University in Kingston, Ontario.

The Travellers' First Cross-Canada Tour

In 1960, the second Hallmark recordings by The Travellers were being sold around the country, mainly by Eaton's. There were very few actual record stores then, as long-time friend, Sam Sniderman, opened Toronto's first Sam the Record Man store in 1959. Sam's, of course, grew into a string of 140 stores right across the country. But at that time, Eaton's sold the most recordings because of its cross-Canada delivery network.

After being seen across the country on TV for the past six years, it was time for The Travellers to actually be seen on stage. So, we began planning a cross-Canada tour to publicize our new LP. We signed up to do a CBC TV show called *Youth '60*, where we sang with a group of younger singers from across the country. The show was broadcast live on January 25, 1960, and the very next day we left for performances in Winnipeg, Saskatoon, Calgary, Edmonton, and Vancouver. This was only the second time in Canada that a performance group made a cross-country visit to these large western communities—to sing songs originating from different regions across Canada; to show people what Canada was really about, both musically and politically. This time we went by plane.

Do you recall that some eight years earlier I was in the first Canadian group to go on a cross-country tour, by train with the Jewish Folk Singers directed by Fagel Gartner? Now here I was, eight years later with The Travellers, duplicating the feat of the Gartner Singers and becoming the second folk group to tour Western Canada. We enjoyed large crowds in university halls and local concert venues. It was as much about them learning from us as it was about us learning from them about teaching the songs. And of course, every concert ended with everyone singing "This Land Is Your Land" along with us.

Shortly after arriving home in Toronto, we were back on the road and heading east, this time to New Brunswick to play at the Mount Allison University Winter Carnival on February 10. We were to be the judges of the ice sculpture competition, and the students were hoping to impress us with the model trains, dog sleds, and personalities they had created from ice. I think we said it was a tie for all the amazing ice sculptures that were entered, and chose the school as the winner for being the first university in Canada to do this.

Speaking of doing it first, Greta and I announced that we were expecting our first child, to be born in early December 1960. Our other close friends were all expecting their first child during that same calendar year. Fortunately, we had no long-term tours going on then.

We Move to Columbia Records

Earlier in the year, we had severed our ties with Hallmark Records because of their lack of national publicity, and the inadequate recording facilities they provided. As luck would have it, Columbia Records of the U.S. was listening to the growing crowds of kids who were taking up folk music in the U.S.

Columbia Canada was given the job to sign up some Canadian artists. Very quickly, Frank Jones, a Columbia A & R man (artists and repertoire), signed us up to make a series of LP's over the next five years, beginning in the spring of 1960! This was a ground-breaking event—a major first for a Canadian artist to be signed by such a prominent international recording company, and to actually record in Canada. It was the early 1960s, and Frank Jones had the foresight to see what was happening as he looked at the rising start of the coffee houses and street hootenannies, and saw the need for Columbia to be part of this scene.

The best part of our arrangement with Columbia was that we were now able to record in the only recording studio in Toronto with proper equipment. We moved out of the kitchen studios of Hallmark (with only one Telefunken microphone) and into the RCA studios on Mutual Street. This was also a beginning for the recording industry in Canada. Most Canadian radio station playlists were prepared according to American charts, and the stations went along with that for many years.

The Travellers first LP with Columbia Records, 1960

Martin Bockner was our manager during the 1960s. He served on many committees and put a lot of effort into trying to get the federal government to help support the Canadian recording industry, by legislating Canadian content minimums for radio broadcasting. The chairman of the government commission was Pierre Juneau[5].

The Travellers were involved in another first, which was also a first for Canada. In 1960, Trans Canada Air Lines introduced their new McDonnell Douglas DC-8 jets, which were able to fly non-stop across Canada. To inaugurate these flights, and also to initiate the name change from Trans Canada Air Lines to Air Canada, the company asked The Travellers, "Canada's singing and recording stars", (as described on the record jacket) to make a record as a gift to every passenger who booked a cross-Canada flight on a DC-8 jet. We then recorded parts of ten songs— one from each province and territory, with jet noise between each track while an announcer read the name of the next province. I don't know how many they made or how many they gave out, but I have one playable copy of that recording. I should probably contact Air Canada to see if they have this story in their archives, or any copy of the recording.

As it turned out, the name change, from TCA to Air Canada did not actually happen until 1965 when a parliamentary private member's bill finally got it through the House!

With our first cross-Canada tour behind us, the summer of 1960 involved staying close to home and making our first Columbia recording. And summer was a great time for camps and concerts. We had a friend called Stan, "Sharky", Starkman, who attended Harbord Collegiate one year behind me, and who eventually got into Canadian book publishing. While he was at university, Stan served as director of Camp Kvutza, a Jewish summer camp on the shores of Lake Erie near Crystal Beach, sponsored by a Labour-Zionist group. The camp invited me to do a solo program as part of their End-of-Summer Program, a kind of international Olympics, much like what we'd done for Alan Borovoy six years prior at Camp Ogama. They could not

---

[5] The Juno Awards are named in honour of Pierre Juneau, first president of the Canadian Radio-television and Telecommunications Commission(CRTC) and former president of the CBC. Wikipedia.

afford the whole group, so I went alone. The repercussions of that performance have followed me all my life.

It was an amazing afternoon both for kids and staff, part of an important event in their lives. The camp was divided into international sections, and with songs, dances and costumes, the kids represented each of them. It was a cultural Olympics, and I was invited because I could sing songs in many languages. To this day, I am confronted by kids, now adults, who remember that camp program, and how it made a huge impression on them. Sharkey later played an important part in the life of The Travellers by helping us record the first children's album in Canada.

This summer of 1960, I was also invited to sing at a kids' summer camp in Starlight, Pennsylvania near the New York border, one of the many Camp B'nai B'rith's around the U.S. One of their Canadian staff members had said, "You gotta get this guy from Canada to sing for our kids." It turned out that, four years earlier, he had been at Alan Borovoy's Camp Ogama in Muskoka, and had seen some of our concerts. So, I did all the songs I'd been learning from Pete Seeger's records, as well as from my own history in Camp Naivelt. It was always a dream to eventually do a kids' album for Canadians—not an easy thing to sell to a record company.

As the summer ended, The Travellers' schedule began to pick up. The Canadian Dental Association was holding its annual convention on September 28 at Toronto's Royal York Hotel. Being a dentist now, I persuaded them to feature The Travellers as the entertainment at the final night's dinner dance. (Having one of their brethren on stage to entertain was a help.)

Many of the Toronto dentists who had gone to U. of T. remembered me from my entr'actes at the annual *Dentantics* show, so I was spurred on to do well for them, and we did. Several days later on October 1, we were invited to do a concert in Montreal at the Hermitage Hall. It was actually the first time we had played in Montreal outside of the UJPO. My wife Greta, large now with our first child, had grown up in Montreal, so she came along and spent time with her family and a few old school friends.

The next day, October 2, we returned to Toronto for a concert date at Hillel House on St. George Street to open their season, the sixth time we had appeared for them. Hillel House did not have an auditorium, but had a very large living room. The show could be seen from the hallway, the dining room, up the stairs nearby, and was piped up to the second floor and out onto the front lawn with an improvised sound system. It was a great evening, and not the last time I'd have an opportunity to appear for U of T. students.

The Final Weeks of 1960 – and a Birth

Here it comes. Two weeks later on October 14, the U. of T. held a huge Homecoming Show at Varsity Arena with Jerry Gray alone as the successful Homecoming star. This was likely a result of the popularity of the Travellers' hit song, "This Land" finally being heard on Canadian radio.

During my university years I'd spent a lot of time at Hart House, a multi-functional student building. It housed a theatre and full athletic areas including a basketball court, squash courts, a library, comfortable reading rooms, and a restaurant. Because of my involvement on the stage, and spending time there, after refereeing or playing in the athletic centre, I was well known at Hart House and by its head, the Warden, Joe McCulley. I had done a few gigs myself for him and we got on quite well. Now, I was two years past graduation and he called me to do a final concert at the theatre, for it seemed I had never finished off my undergrad years with a performance. It went well, with a large crowd that was happy with the free concert, although I did get paid. During that time, I was building a parallel, popular following for myself as a solo performer.

Although my first-born was due in early December 1960, we had a lot of upcoming gigs in November. On November 1, we were booked at the Royal York Hotel for the Canadian Manufacturers Association Convention. Because we were able to sing songs from across the country as well as from around the world, we could perform at these international conventions for about forty-five minutes to an hour, and drive back home without leaving town.

The agents who booked the dance bands were eager to hire us to provide the entertainment. And our shows really started to add up. On November 6, we were booked to appear on Wally Koster's CBC TV show. We had worked with Wally previously when he hosted the old *Cross Canada Hit Parade Show*. The other guest on the show was Peter Palmer, known for his portrayal of *L'il Abner* on the Broadway stage.

On November 9, we were booked to host a hootenanny in Toronto. A hootenanny was a concert where folkies would try out new songs, sing others' new songs, or just get together in a group to jam and sing along. Having seen Pete Seeger's ability, and having been a part of a hootenanny and playing a banjo like Pete did, hosting a hoot was easy. Everyone left with a song in their hearts and on their lips.

November 11 was Remembrance Day in Canada, in honour of the day the Armistice was signed and peace was declared, marking the end of the First World War. Accordingly, the Canadian Peace Congress planned an evening concert at Massey Hall called *Songs for Survival*, an apt preview of what The Travellers would sing. We closed with Wade Hemsworth's song of peace, "Last Night I Had the Strangest Dream".

On November 26, we were in Montreal, to entertain members and their wives of The Knights of Pythias, a men's fraternity at their annual banquet. Afterwards, we prepared to return to Toronto to sing on November 30ᵗ for Hillel at McMaster University in Hamilton. It was much the same as we'd done for many years at the Toronto Hillel, and we enjoyed it along with everyone else.

Oh, Oh! The month is up but we still had one more obligation before the year ended. On December 1, we wound up doing the *Tommy Hunter Radio Show*, along with Tommy Common and Gordie Tapp, where they'd been on the *Country Hoedown* TV show. This was a seasonal show before he took over TV country shows with his own name on it, and it ran for many years.

Greta and I had planned to keep the month of December open for the birth of our first child. Greta's doctor said she would require a caesarean section to deliver the baby, and it was scheduled for the morning of December 6. Our first son, James Alan, arrived safely that day, and of course he's brilliant.

Because Greta and I had gotten married on Canada Day, July 1, 1957, it meant I would rarely be around to celebrate our anniversary. It was now three years since our marriage, and we had lived in three different apartments. Now, with the birth of James, we had finally moved into our own three-bedroom ravine home on Finch Avenue East. The object now, as it turned out, was to try and fill the bedrooms of this new house! It, therefore seemed prudent to keep up with my two jobs in order to finance future expenses. Before I knew it, 1960 was over.

1961

After Jamie's birth, Greta had a temporary leave from her teaching Grade 1, and then life took a few more turns. The new year of 1961 began for the Travellers on January 26 when we headed to Montreal for another concert, and also appeared on the *Pot Pouri* TV show. Two days later, we returned to Toronto for *The Ross McLane Show,* a new CBC late-night TV show. We then took a couple of weeks off as we prepared to return to New Brunswick to be a part of the second Mount Allison University Winter Carnival. Again, they had amazing winter weather, and the sculptors were back at their creations. The event was photographed by *Maclean's* magazine and seen across the country. We did two concerts before saying goodbye to a joyful audience.

Folk music was becoming more and more popular in Toronto. New folk clubs were giving up-and-coming singers the opportunity to display their talents. I played a few of these clubs as a solo act, because they could not afford the full group of our four or five members. Some of the clubs opened on a Friday night, and by Monday they had closed down when faced with the reality of creating a financially productive music scene.

Actually, our first club performance in Toronto was in 1957 when Vivian Stenson (now Vivian Meuhling), booked us into The Piccadilly Club on Jarvis Street. On the first night as we prepared to sing, Jerry Goodis tried to move the piano across the stage and the leg broke.

Jerry, who weighed about 130 pounds, was left holding up the piano until a work crew arrived to free him. At the time of this writing, Vivian is still with us and living in The Performing Artists Lodge and still organizing concerts.

The early folk song backers in Toronto opened folk clubs in order to book acts into these new venues— centered mainly in the Yorkville area of Toronto. Some fifty years later, in 2016, the Toronto Historical Society created three plaques in honour of the clubs that survived the longest: The Purple Onion and The Riverboat and had a ceremony in Yorkville in the places where the first three folk clubs began.

Gordon Lightfoot and I were invited to perform and talk about those early clubs. As it turned out, Gordon had come without his guitar, so I ended up leading the throng in several songs including a mass singing of "This Land", while the words were projected onto a large screen behind me. Gordon talked about his early days in Yorkville, but I trumped him by revealing that not only did I play in a Yorkville club long before he did, I was also born on Yorkville! Most people don't know it, but the Mount Sinai Hospital was first located on 100 Yorkville Avenue before relocating to University Avenue. Gordon had no reply, but I have a photo with me leading the singing of "This Land", and Gordon clearly singing along with the crowd. You can also check You Tube to find the ceremony there.

In May 1961, the group planned a concert at Hart House Theatre with me as one of the emcees, and I sang solo as well. This event was one of the first occasions that a new duo sang together—Ian Tyson and Sylvia Fricker, later to become famous as Ian and Sylvia. The concert was both an artistic and financial success. On January 11, I was invited to sing at a political rally in Toronto for the Ontario Federation of Labour (OFL), with delegations from labour groups and farming folks. It was an opportunity to sing the songs I grew up with, as well as to entertain and educate.

On June 25, I was invited to Camp Northland, the YMHA summer camp near Haliburton, Ontario, to sing and work with the incoming counselors, waterfront, and cook house staff. I was to entertain and to teach them songs to sing with the kids when they arrived in about four days. My close friend, Irv Petroff, also a dentist, came along for the ride, as my friends rarely saw me entertaining and performing for outside groups. I had brought two vintage swim suits from the 1920s and I gave one to Irv to wear when we swam in the lake. Anything for a laugh! We slept over at the camp, and headed home in the morning. I recently spoke to Irv who mentioned that he still has that bathing suit.

Several days later, on June 28, The Travellers sang at an outdoor rally for the Ontario Federation of Labour and the New Democratic Party of Ontario. We were drawing close to another election, and that always meant work for The Travellers

The Mariposa Folk Festival

Early in 1961, a group of people in Orillia, Ontario, along with a broadcaster friend from Toronto, formed a committee to plan a folk festival for late summer of that same year. Canada had never had a folk festival before; this would be the first. Orillia had been the home of celebrated writer Steven Leacock, famous for his humorous short stories book about his home town, *Sunshine Sketches of a Little Town.* The planners decided to call the new event, The Mariposa Folk Festival. They then contacted The Travellers, who at the time were the most well-known folk singers in Canada, and asked us to be the headliners at this first Mariposa Festival.

The Travellers at the first Mariposa Festival, Orillia, 1961

The three-day event was planned for a weekend late in August, before the nearby summer camps had discharged their campers, and before the cottagers had returned to Toronto after the summer season. It was held in a downtown park right next to the armory, and went on well into the evenings of both Saturday and Sunday.

The committee's vision and wisdom were evident when it began to rain during the Saturday night concert and no one left. Jerry Goodis managed to move the people into the covered arena in about fifteen minutes. The Travellers headlined both evening shows, and also did a children's show on Sunday afternoon. By this time, The Travellers had four LP's in the stores with another coming up the following year. The other acts at that first Mariposa were groups and individuals who were part of the new "folk scene", occurring nightly on Yorkville Avenue. This was the era when folk music truly made an imprint on Canadian music audiences.

We sang at the first four Mariposa Festivals and appeared many times after that, particularly at anniversary shows, right up to the fiftieth anniversary. During Mariposa One, the CBC frequently interviewed the members of The Travellers. In one tape, you can hear Jerry Goodis and I talking about Mariposa becoming the folk music equivalent of the Stratford Festival, able to showcase both Canadian folk music and musicians. We believed that it would, and we were committed to supporting Mariposa any time they asked us to participate.

More Changes

After Mariposa One was over, our manager Sam Goldberg, and original member, Jerry Goodis, announced they would be leaving the group. They had realized they could not be advertising executives in Canada for their agency, Goodis Goldberg, and also remain involved in folk music. It was quite a loss for us. Sam was our original manager and, with his music degree, was often our musical director as well. Jerry Goodis and I had both grown up in Camp Naivelt where our mothers had also been close friends who sang in The Jewish Folk Choir. But they were leaving the group, and The Travellers had to find a way forward.

We knew a young man named Ray Woodley, who came from Sudbury. Ray played the guitar, and we'd heard him sing in a strong baritone voice at some early hootenannies in Camp Naivelt. When Goodis, left, Ray joined the Travellers and remained with us from 1961 to 1974, the years when The Travellers were at their peak, and probably at their best. Ray Woodley's baritone voice had a huge potential that developed the more he sang with us. The addition of his guitar made us sound more like The Weavers, and when Ray joined us, we made better records and also sounded better on stage.

During that busy summer, The Travellers became involved in more events, for we built upon what we'd been doing since we were founded eight years earlier. In October of 1961, a new Toronto folk club was opened on Church Street near Carlton, by two moneyed folkies. It was called The Fifth Peg in honour of the fifth string found only on five-string banjos. Bill Cosby played there many times in the early years when he was touring as a new young comic. Fittingly, The Travellers were the first act to open the new venue, and the only Canadian group that featured a five-string banjo as well as a guitar. That was a busy night for me because I'd already agreed to sing at the opening convention of the Ontario Federation of Labour in Niagara Falls at 6:30 p.m. When I was done, I jumped into my car and sped all the way back along the QEW, Queen Elizabeth Way and arrived at the Fifth Peg only a few minutes before we opened at 9:00 p.m.

On October 26, we answered a call from an area where we had never played before—Cape Breton Island. I'd never heard of Xavier College in Nova Scotia, but they had heard of us from the time we performed at nearby Mount Allison University. So, they hired us as part of the new trend of folk groups performing on university campuses.

One month later on November 25, we were at Queen's University in Kingston, Ontario to continue that new trend. Several days later, we appeared in concert at Eaton Auditorium in Toronto with Québec singer Jacques Labrecque, whom we had introduced several months earlier at Mariposa One. Several days later, we appeared with Jacques in Winnipeg's Playhouse Theatre.

When The Weavers first began, they played a night club in New York City for the last two weeks of the year. They were then held over for six months when they were finally "discovered" by Decca Records. In Toronto, The Colonial Tavern on Yonge Street near Queen Street was a jazz venue, where small groups like The Nat King Cole Trio would play several times a year. The slowest time in night clubs is Christmas week, but then, just like the club that had hired The Weavers ten years earlier in NYC, the Colonial Tavern hired The Travellers to appear during a similar time frame. We were far from being discovered there, but as a group with a lot to sing about, it gave us an opportunity to learn how to perform in rooms with clinking glasses. It also gave us the opportunity to sing Christmas and Chanukah songs as part of our program. The only losses in 1961 were two original members of The Travellers, but the change had little effect, and the product turned out to be better.

1962

The year began with a couple of days of R&R, as Greta accompanied me to Montreal for the Alpha Omega Dental Fraternity Convention while my mother looked after little Jamie at home in Toronto. In February, Greta announced another upcoming birth, this one due in October. Better start the count down again. But a lot of things were already on the books. In February, we had a trip to another Winter Carnival, this time at Acadia University in Wolfville, Nova Scotia. After a couple of concerts there, we were back to Waterloo University in Ontario for their first Winter Carnival. Then we headed across the border to sing at the University of Buffalo. Our first foray into the U.S. went well, and we heard about some possible upcoming gigs for the summer. So, we thought we should get some new repertoire to better incorporate Ray Woodley into the group.

I mentioned earlier some big events that were coming in our future. Well, for July 1,1962, Ottawa planned a huge festival on Parliament Hill. They then invited The Travellers to headline at Canada's first official televised birthday party! It was truly spectacular, an amazing experience! for us, and set the bar high for future July 1 spectaculars. This was another Canadian first! "Canada's Birthday Party on The Hill, starring The Travellers". It was a real awakening for us, having the opportunity to lead 100,000 of our fellow Canadians in the singing of "This Land Is Your Land"!

The Travellers Tour the USSR.

The next morning, July 2, 1962, the group met Toronto bass player, Jack Lander, at the Montreal airport as we flew to Amsterdam en route to Moscow for the first ever Canada-Soviet Union cultural exchange. While we toured the USSR, a Ukrainian tenor was supposed to tour Canada. At the same time, the U.S. announced their own cultural exchange: The Red Army Choir would tour the U.S. while The Benny Goodman Quintet toured the USSR.

Our tour in the Soviet Union began in Moscow, then we continued to Vilnius in Lithuania, Riga in Latvia, then Kiev and Chernovtsi, Ukraine. But before we began, we knew we had a dilemma. How does a Canadian English-speaking group, that often has comedic introductions to their songs, introduce those songs to audiences where few people understand English?

We requested a speaker who would prepare a translation of our intros, making the explanation of each song more understandable to our audience. Gosskoncert, the sponsoring Soviet producer of the tour, complied with all our requests about non-interference in our program, except when it came time to include several Yiddish songs. At that point we were told that Yiddish songs were not "appropriate". I replied, before the tour began, that what might be appropriate would be for us to complain to the Canadian Embassy, then get on a plane and return to Canada. After a small conference, they agreed to translate what we wanted, and made it possible to include at least three Yiddish songs in our program. I took a stand on the side of having the right to do what we wanted as outlined in our contract. But I also had a selfish and very personal motive. My mother's sister, my Aunt Lisa, had survived the war in Soviet Asia, and was once again living in Vilna.

When we first learned we would be doing this tour in the USSR, my mother got very excited. As you may recall from the first page of this story, my mother was born in Vilna, Lithuania, and was the youngest of five children. The eldest sister, Goldie, was twenty years older and had left Lithuania for Winnipeg and later to Detroit, in the first decade of the twentieth century. She and her family were the only relatives I had ever met, and we kept in touch until Goldie passed away many years ago.

My mother's two brothers had remained in Vilna, and both perished in the Holocaust. The middle sister, my Aunt Lisa, had married and also remained in Vilna, where her husband also was killed by the Nazis. Then the Soviets sent Lisa to live in mid-Russia. After the war, she returned to Vilna with her son-in-law who had been injured during the war, and a granddaughter. When my mother and Goldie discovered that Lisa had survived, they were overjoyed of course, and kept in touch by mail.

Once we learned I would be going to the Soviet Union, I contacted my Aunt Lisa to let her know my schedule. She and some friends met us at the airport, and we managed to arrange tickets for her to attend one of our two concerts in Vilnius. It was amazing to meet this woman, my mother's sister. I noticed quickly that, like both her sisters, she was feisty, so it was no surprise to me that she had survived the war. I took some pictures of her as part of my memories of this trip, and felt so fortunate to have had this opportunity to meet her.

On a side note, my wife Greta's aunt and uncle had also survived the war. They were living in Kharkov at the time, but we were not allowed to travel there. When we arrived in Kiev, they managed to meet us for a short visit, but because of their advanced age and inability to speak Yiddish or English, we could barely converse. They left for Kharkov on the next train, and passed away shortly after our meeting.

Jerry's relatives from Vilna with Greta (middle), Vilna, 1961

Aunt Lisa, Holocaust survivor, Vilna, 1961

While on tour, we sang a few Russian and Ukrainian songs. In one concert, after we did a Russian song, they kept clapping and wouldn't stop until we sang the song again in its entirety. In most places, we also sang several Yiddish songs from the WWII era. After each concert, we would find groups of Jews standing outside the concert hall, wanting to speak to us in Yiddish. Both Sid and I spoke Yiddish, and could understand their words.

The second concert in Vilna was very well attended by Jewish people in the area, and many waited after the concert to speak to us. One man told me it was the first time they had heard anyone singing a Yiddish song on that stage, since before the war, back in the 1930s. The day following our first concert there, we were walking along the streets of the Ukrainian city of Lvov. After seeing the concert, the night before, a Jewish man approached me on the street and spoke to me in Yiddish. A passerby stood and listened for a while, and then body- checked me while giving the Ukrainian version of "F-ing Jews." The truth is, many Jews were killed by Ukrainians during WWII, in all three of the Ukrainian cities where we sang: Lvov, Chernovtsi, and the capital Kiev (Kyiv). Each of these cities had graveyards full of Jews who had been slaughtered by locals during the war. It was now 1962, and anti-Jewish sentiments were still around, for only seventeen years had passed since the war had ended. So, even though it may have led to a few problems, I'm glad I stood up to the GosKoncert people and insisted that we include Yiddish songs in the program.

The Jews who waited to speak to us in Yiddish after the concerts spoke cautiously about the positions that Jews still held in Soviet society some ten years after Stalin's death. Sid took the side of our Soviet hosts, but I completely disagreed with him. My Aunt Lisa, who of course lived there, took him to task for his view of Soviet-Jewish relations, something he actually knew nothing about. He did not want to listen to, or believe her tales of both Russian and Lithuanian complicity in the murder of her family (my family), along with many other Jews.

The Travellers performing in Russia, 1961

The Travellers performing in Russia, 1961

The Travellers performing in Russia, 1961

While visiting in our hotel room, my aunt had pointed to a fan in the ceiling and warned us that the Soviets often hid microphones in hotel rooms. But Sid pooh-pooed and dismissed her words saying, and truly believing, that the Soviets would never do that. But three months after we returned home, Aunt Lisa wrote and told us they had been "interviewed" by the Soviet police about communicating with foreigners. After that episode, my family petitioned the Soviets to allow the three of them to go to Israel. We were successful, but sadly my aunt died shortly after arriving there.

I could write a whole chapter about that tour alone. It was a ground-breaking first for a government-sponsored tour in a country with which Canada did not have great foreign relations. After a few concerts in Moscow that received good reviews, we noticed we were being followed by a camera crew. They were filming us for what we later learned was to be part of a Soviet documentary. They were also recording all of our performances in Moscow. So, I called Columbia Records in Toronto and let them know. They tried to negotiate a deal whereby GossKoncert would send the audio tapes to Columbia to be included as part of our next LP, *The Travellers on Tour*. We learned that the concert tapes included the intros to the songs as well as the songs, but sadly the quality of the recordings was not good enough.

Russian concert LP on Columbia Records, 1961

When we returned to Toronto after the tour, we went to the studio and rerecorded some of the songs we had sung. We kept those that were good enough, along with the Russian intros, in order to produce a true replica of what we had done in the Soviet Union, and how we did it. In 2001, there was a documentary by the National Film Board of Canada about The Travellers, and I arranged to find the Soviet documentary from 1962 which was included in the new 2001 documentary.

We were truly glad to get back on Canadian soil because this was the time of the Cuban Missile Crisis when American President John F. Kennedy stared down the Soviets to remove weaponry from Cuba. The U.S. told the Soviets that their ships en route to Cuba with missiles would be met by the U.S. fleet and not allowed to proceed. This confrontation was considered by many experts as the closest the Cold War came to escalating to a full nuclear war. We travelled abroad many times, and were always happy and relieved to return home to Canada.

In late August, Mariposa Two in Orillia enjoyed even greater success than the year before. The Travellers appeared three times during the new festival, and then did the kids' concert again. At that time, few performers had begun singing songs for children. In early September, with an election looming, I sang alone at an NDP rally at the O'Keefe Centre to support Tommy Douglas. The next year, the federal government approved a universal medical plan for all.

A Second Birth

Greta had announced an early October delivery date for the birth of our second child, again by C-section. But all planning went for naught as the delivery was delayed by doctors for another two weeks, so it was back to work for me. When the UJPO broke apart in 1958, many people were unhappy with it and formed The New Fraternal Jewish Organization. They asked me to sing solo at their October 2 convention. After that engagement, I returned to Hart House for a concert, again for Warden Joe McCauley. My U. of T. roots were still deep and strong, and I'm glad they remembered me.

Our second son, Robert Gray, was born on October 26, with no complications. Several days later, on November 1, The Travellers did a concert at Dalhousie University in Halifax, and then returned to Toronto for a date at McMaster University in Hamilton. In mid-November, I did a solo performance sponsored by the YMHA and the United Jewish Appeal (UJA) at Bathurst Heights Collegiate in Toronto. Finally, we performed a full concert at the Plateau Hall in

Montreal. It had been a very successful year for me and for The Travellers, with plans for a new LP early next year, and talk of other important Canadian events that we might be a part of. The tour of the Soviet Union at the request of the Canadian government, and the beginning of an annual July 1st celebration on Parliament Hill were other firsts from 1962. The Travellers were invited to appear in Ottawa at the July 1, Dominion Day/ Canada Day Concert for many years after that.

1963

When 1963 began, it looked as if it was going to be busier than the last, with more exciting new firsts. In mid-January, there was a conference in Toronto on Human Rights in Canada, and The Travellers were hired to provide songs about the struggle for peoples' rights. It was a powerful protest evening, and we were booked to close the meeting. It was always nice to be recognized by them; to be the prime entertainers, singing songs on the subject.

In February, a group of folkies in Sault Ste. Marie[6] decided to have a winter folk festival— called the "Bon Soo" Festival. The Travellers and Alanis Obomsawin, an indigenous Canadian singer, headlined the show. It had a large attendance because let's face it, what else are you going to do in February in "The Soo?" Just joking. The head of the committee was a Jewish lumberjack, Max Iland, who had plans to create a similar festival in the summer. Max was a Holocaust survivor who loved Canadian folk music. He caught up with us in this initial and subsequent ventures.

On February 27, the group was signed to appear on *Hymn Sing*, a TV show from Winnipeg. We did the show, successfully, sang some gospel-type songs we'd always done, and the show was rebroadcast several times the following year. On March 16, a charity event for the UJA was held at the Oakdale Golf Club in Toronto, and I was asked to provide some entertainment. Then, on April 13, The Travellers did

---

[6] Sault. Ste. Marie – pronounced Soo Saint Marie – is commonly referred to by residents as simply "The Soo."

a concert at Massey Hall with Pete Seeger. As publicity for the concert, he and I did an instrumental duet at a Toronto TV station. The only instrument Pete had with him that day was his Israeli flute called a *chalil*. So, Pete played his *chalil*, and I played my banjo, and we did a French-Canadian folk song, "Envoyant". It was always great to be on stage, anytime, with Pete, and I'm pleased to have a video of that show.

The Travellers participated in a rare and unusual event on June 28. Throughout our career we'd always championed human rights. Holy Blossom Temple, one of the largest synagogues in Canada, organized a weekend event in Toronto to raise money for Dr. Martin Luther King's civil rights campaign in the U.S. The event would begin with a luncheon on a Saturday afternoon with Harry Belafonte, followed by a concert at the O'Keefe Centre on Sunday evening. The Oscar Peterson Trio from Montreal would join us on stage for that Sunday evening concert.

After we agreed, we learned that Belafonte would only be at the luncheon. We would sing "We Shall Overcome" with Harry, and then lead the crowd in learning the song and the next day. Belafonte would have to leave after the luncheon to join Dr. King at a rally in the U.S. This left The Travellers to headline the concert with The Oscar Peterson Trio.

Well, we closed the evening, leading everyone in singing "We Shall Overcome"— the first time this song was sung in protest in Canada. Holy Blossom Temple raised a lot of money and sent it to support the campaign. We received gracious thanks from Belafonte and from the Temple committee for a job well and powerfully done.

I have a photograph that was taken of The Travellers singing at the noon luncheon with Harry Belafonte. It's one of my most prized historical pictures of The Travellers at work, doing what they do best. This was certainly another "first."

Several days later, we were again booked into Massey Hall, for an NDP political rally.

Harry Belafonte and The Travellers sing at a rally for Dr. Martin Luther King, Toronto, 1964

Hold on! The year's only half over. The third Orillia Mariposa Folk Festival was held on August 10–12. It marked the first appearance for an unknown Orillia resident, Gordon Lightfoot, and for other artists like Ian and Sylvia, who were marching up the ladder of success in folk music. The Travellers appeared again, and I did the kids' concert, but with a newcomer from Camp Naivelt, Sharon Trostin, who later teamed with two others to form the children's entertainment trio, Sharon, Lois, and Bram. The Canadian National Exhibition[7] had taken place in the last part of August for many years. They used to get big American entertainers like Danny Kaye and Bob Hope to headline the Grandstand Shows, but a new patriotic spirit was growing, because of Canada's Centennial coming up in 1967.

On August 19, I was invited by the CBC to headline a children's TV show, *Vacation Time*, to be broadcast live from the CNE. I loved doing children's concerts, and this one felt perfect—a happy bunch of kids on vacation, and me acting as the singing emcee. A week later on August 26, the CBC hired us to perform a second time. I often

---

[7] The **Canadian National Exhibition** (**CNE**), also known as **The Exhibition** or **The Ex**, is an annual event that takes place at Exhibition Place in Toronto during the 18 days leading up to and including Canadian Labour Day, the first Monday in September, and dates back to 1879. Wikipedia

wondered if anyone was actually watching daytime television. But Frank Moritsugu, a TV writer at the *Toronto Star*, happened to catch the show and wrote the following review:

> "Talking about folksingers, I thought yesterday's *Vacation Time Show* was a bit of late afternoon fun. The CBC TV's summertime show for children was taped at the CNE on August 26, with Jerry Gray and The Travellers, and other folk artists firing up an enthusiastic CNE audience. This was my first exposure to banjo-strumming Jerry Gray, the spokesman and lead singer for The Travellers, and he came over very strongly. A warm mobile comedian's face, an arresting stage presence and assured control of the audience and singing ability, GRAY has them all."

Frank Moritsugu later headed the Ontario Pavilion at Expo 67 in Montreal, and we performed there for a full week. He clearly loved the Travellers, because at the end of that week he told us he'd be opening the Canadian Pavilion at Expo 70 in Osaka, and would be hiring us to appear there. He did, and we sang in Osaka, Japan, for the first three weeks of Expo 70.

The *Vacation Time Show* was a harbinger of kid's shows to come, and why? Very simply, The Travellers had an amazing ability to entertain and educate children when we sang. Later, in 1970, you'll read about recording our first kids' album, *The Travellers Sing for Kids*, which came from doing that type of concert, long before anyone else.

The next day, August 20, *The Toronto Star* booked a free concert for the public at the Bandshell at the CNE. They invited The Travellers to be the hosts, and included The Brothers Four to be part of a Hootenanny. This was indeed my return to "The EX". While I was in high school and college, I used to work at my summer job, and then would quit when The Ex started. I'd work for two weeks there, because I could make more money at The Ex than at my regular summer job. Well now here I was, back working at The Ex, but now I was actually appearing on stage at the Bandshell!

Regarding those two August 1963 CBC *Vacation Time* kids' shows that were so successful, I've tried many times to get a copy of them without success, and I actually have no idea if they were ever transferred to videotape. A few years ago, I noticed an ad for a concert by The Brothers Four who are still performing. I met with two of the original members, and they remembered their gig with me at the CNE in 1963. Glad they still can remember (as in their song of the same name, "Try to Remember") as well as I do, those wonderful concerts at the EX.

On August 29, The Travellers appeared on the same bill as Judy Collins, part of the second Hootenanny sponsored at The Ex by the *Toronto Star*. On September 2, again at the CNE Bandshell, The Travellers returned and sang with Oscar Brand. Oscar had left Winnipeg in the 1940s to become a main cog in the early 1950s and '60s folk music scene in New York City.

Folk music had certainly become the big thing in Canada, as evidenced by all the shows at the CNE. Because the Ex closed after Labour Day, The Travellers had agreed to perform the weekend of September 10 at The Purple Onion, one of the early coffee houses in the Yorkville area. Because of their relatively small size and space for patrons, these clubs could rarely afford a group of four or five. However, we reduced our fee because we knew The Onion deserved all the help we could give. The Purple Onion remained open from 1960–1965, a relatively long time for this era. I can also mention that Ted Roberts, a noted Toronto guitar player, lived upstairs at The Onion then. Six years later, Ted joined The Travellers, and was with us for forty years!

Back to work in Toronto and beyond. We sang again at St. Michael's College School at U. of T., a typical college concert ending in a sing-along. September 29 and 30 found us in Regina and Edmonton singing at two conventions. While out west, we were booked at the University of Alberta in Calgary for a student hootenanny. Several days later, we returned to Toronto and drove to Owen Sound to do a benefit concert for the local YMCA. It was very successful, so we knew we'd probably get invited back the next year. On October 17, we were booked to do a high school concert in

Richmond Hill. After the concert, we met a pair of student brothers, who told us they were forming a folk and country group on their own, patterned on The Travellers. This was our first meeting with The Good Brothers, whose family are still performing today. In 2017, I met one of them as the City of Toronto Historical Committee was raising those three plaques in Yorkville on the sites of the original coffee houses.

In October of 1963, an unforeseen event struck from nowhere. The Travellers were booked in Chicago to sing at the Great Lakes Orthodontic Convention after singing for them last year in Toronto. We hit the road and slept overnight in Windsor. The next morning, after driving through the tunnel, we were stopped by U.S. immigration who told us that some of our group were not allowed to enter the U.S. They could not tell us why. We were informed that, if we decided to not enter the U.S. then, but simply turned around and went home, all the problems would be gone. But if we decided to ask to enter then, we would not be allowed in, and there would be a mark on our record which would bar us from entering for five years!

We called our manager in Toronto who agreed to take care of cancelling our performance. He also said he would call some political friends in Ottawa to investigate and discover what this was about. We'd sung several times in the U.S. before and had had no problem crossing the border, and we'd recently represented the Canadian government on our tour of the Soviet Union. Our sources in Ottawa could find no reason why we were stopped at the border; there were seemingly no problems. We had no other upcoming dates in the U.S., so we let it go until we had another U.S. date booked. We would look into it further then.

As the year's end approached, on November 22, The Travellers were booked to appear at Mount Allison University in New Brunswick. We got off the plane around 1:00 p.m., loaded our instruments into a rented station wagon, and headed to the university. As I was driving, I turned on the radio and heard the dreadful news of the death of President John F. Kennedy in Dallas. I stopped the car at the side of the road and we talked about not cancelling the concert. Having been to the Maritimes many times, we knew of the close relationship that eastern Canadians had with the residents of the northeast U. S.

When we arrived at the university, we discussed what to do and how we could mark this significant event. We decided the concert should go ahead as planned, except for ten minutes of silence right at the beginning. Then we would proceed with a regular Travellers concert that would include songs of right and wrong, and humour as well, for although we had all lost a friend, life had to go on. This was one of those times when one has to carry on.

Upon our return, we were back in the studio for two three-hour sessions to finish up our Columbia recording of *The Travellers on Tour* LP from the Soviet Union. We had also been speaking with singer Oscar Brand and TV producer Sid Banks about a new Canadian Hootenanny type TV series, called *Let's Sing Out*. Oscar Brand would go to many Canadian university campuses and record two and sometimes three shows in one day. The first show was at the University of Toronto, and Oscar wanted us to sing the new theme song he'd written called "Something to Sing About". In 1964, we included this song on our fourth Columbia record. Over the next four years, the eleven taped shows of *Let's Sing Out* that we appeared on, were seen both on CBC and then CTV.

I also did a children's show alone with Oscar and the Beers Family that was seen on December 23, 1965. There are far too many shows to list, but they can all now be "googled". Sid Banks held these shows privately and only released copies of the fifty or so shows he had filmed when I was halfway through writing this book. Then he released them all. *Let's Sing Out* was the best show of its era, much better than the American Hootenanny series on ABC.

1964

We began the new year on January 10 with a concert in Hamilton for the Alpha Phi Pi Fraternity at McMaster University. Hamilton is close to Toronto, so we had a good night's sleep at home. On January 16, we appeared live on *The Juliette Show*, produced by old friend

Paddy Sampson. The next day, we flew to Halifax, and did the *Gazette* TV interview show to advertise the next day's concert in Charlottetown, PEI, hosted by Jack McAndrew.

We were now getting repeat bookings from places where we'd performed before. On January 24, we drove to Waterloo University to appear at a concert associated with their Winter Carnival and Ice Show. The next day, we drove north to Owen Sound for a repeat of last year's concert at a fundraiser for the YMCA—again to a full house. We returned to Toronto and caught a flight to Sault Ste. Marie for the second edition of the Bon Soo Winter Carnival, which we had helped start the previous year. Returning also was Canadian artist, Alanis Obomsawin. Max Iland was again running the festival, and said he would call us about singing at the Summer Soo Festival. Then on March 15, The Travellers had booked our own concert at Massey Hall. A large crowd was there to welcome us back to our home town. The reviews in the paper were great!

In early April, we were booked for a three-day excursion to Wilmington University in Ohio. This university had a very good history of supporting folk music, particularly with regard to Canadian music. The previous year, we'd had a problem entering the U.S., so we were a bit concerned as we approached the border. But we had no problem this time and assumed our immigration problems were over. What a relief! We spent three days doing demonstration seminars followed by a concert, which was the best way to showcase The Travellers.

On April 9, we returned from Ohio and drove to Ottawa to sing at Glebe High School, where Sid Dolgay's brother, Len, was a teacher. On the way back to Toronto, we made a stop in Peterborough to do a public fundraising concert on April 10 for the new YMCA building. Then we did a concert on April 16 for long-time friends at the Orillia Opera House. By this time, there'd been trouble at Mariposa III, and the town refused to permit them to return for Mariposa IV. But we'd made a lot of friends at the first three Mariposas and continued to sing in town every summer for many years.

Then in May, The Noshery Restaurant in Toronto planned a hootenanny night to cash in on the folk boom, and hired me to appear alone. As I mentioned earlier, I often opened a folk club on a Saturday and by Monday, it was closed. After singing both Saturday and Sunday, I think that may have happened there. On June 20, we were off to Brantford, Ontario, for a public concert at their arena.

After a few days at home, and no bookings for July 1, we caught a flight west to be marshals at the Calgary Stampede, and to take part in the Stampede Parade. We were in a convertible, waving to the crowds as the parade wound its way through Calgary's main streets. On the last day of our trip, we did a concert at the prestigious Oilmen's Club. The food was amazing and the concert went well too.

Back in Toronto, I was invited to sing solo at Camp Naivelt on July 25, and to speak about our trip to Russia several years before. The Naivelt people were mainly those who had stayed with the ultra left-wing UJPO. I told them what I liked about our trip, and also what I was not happy about. I sang and spoke from my heart, but some people were not pleased with my criticism of the Soviet treatment of Jews

Dusty Cohl had been the sports director of Camp Naivelt in his youth, and was about five years older than I. He became a lawyer, and was one of the people who started the Toronto International Film Festival. He was also a master bridge player, and brought the Bridge Olympiad to Toronto's Royal York Hotel. He wrote a special bridge players' song for us, and afterward we did our normal post-dinner show to great acclaim, for a "A Grand Slam Show", they said.

We left Toronto the next day for Sault Ste. Marie to appear at the second Algoma Folk Festival, where we'd appeared the year before. Then it was back to Toronto for the CNE. On September 4, we again appeared at the Bandshell for a series of concerts with Theodore Bikel, the Simon Sisters (including Carly), and other folk people. After a month at home in Toronto, on October 5 we drove north one hour to Barrie to do a concert for the Y's Men's Club, to help raise money for a new pool. Guess what? We returned twice more to repeat the fundraising, the last one being very humorous. It's worth waiting for.

We Meet a Prince, and Have a British Adventure

The next day, October 6, we flew to Charlottetown, PEI to begin what turned out to be one of the greatest adventures of our musical lives. In three more years, it would be 1967, the Canadian Centennial Year, the hundredth anniversary of Confederation. But Confederation actually began in 1864 when Canada's premiers all met in Charlottetown to discuss and plan the new confederation.

The current Liberal government mirrored that historic event by creating the Confederation Centre for the Arts, to be completed in 1964. At that time, a Command Performance was planned at the new theatre, with Queen Elizabeth II and Prince Philip in attendance. Canadian actor Lorne Green would be the emcee, Howard Cable would lead the orchestra, and Dave Broadfoot would provide the comedy. The organizers also chose The Travellers to close the first half, and then to close the whole show as well. We were honoured of course, and very pleased, but also surprised because by now, Gordon Lightfoot and Ian and Sylvia might have become more well-known. However, The Travellers were the seasoned veterans and had written the Canadianized version of "This Land is Your Land" which the organizers wanted, and with which we closed the show.

After the show, there was a press conference where Prince Philip was asked what he liked on the show. He said he was quite taken by the song, "This Land", and by the exuberance of The Travellers. And then he asked us directly, "Why don't you come to Britain while the Beatles are away?" Well, certain members of the press mis-heard and thought he said, "while the Beatles are on the wane". The British press raced to the pay phones (cell phones had not been invented yet), and reported what they thought he had said. The next day, everyone wanted to see this new group that the prince had raved about.

Booking agent Joe Collins took over. He contacted our group to come to Britain in a week, do some TV and radio interviews, and then to perform at the Palladium! We invited bass player Terry Quinn to accompany us to Britain, booked our flights, and were there within a week. The British press headlines read, "Philip's Group Arrives!" Joe Collins was the father of actress Joan Collins.

After that initial one-week visit, Joe Collins, who was as smart an agent as I'd ever seen, arranged a second three-week visit for January of 1965, with radio and TV appearances in Britain and Scotland.

Following our first return from Britain in 1964, we had a gig on October19 at a convention in Niagara Falls at the Park Motor Inn. Playing in the bar at a hotel next door was a group of friends called The Chanteclairs, who'd been with us at the last CNE Bandshell. Their new bass player, Joe Hampson, had just arrived in Toronto and had married ex-Naivelter and singer, Sharon Trostin. We enjoyed their set, and I made some notes for the future.

On October 21, our group was invited to the Royal York Hotel to close the meeting of a group celebrating the anniversary of the start of the United Nations. Years earlier, I had learned the words to the U.N. song, which had been sung at its inaugural meeting back in the 1940s. The rest of The Travellers didn't know it, so I sang it myself, accompanied by the rest of the group. Two days later, singer Oscar Brand and I were invited to sing together at the U. of T. Home-coming Weekend. On November 27, The Travellers flew to Montreal to entertain at a convention of Kraft Food employees at the Airport Hilton. Back in Toronto again, the group appeared at the Royal York Hotel in a concert against Apartheid, a cause we had often sung for. It was marvelous to have been invited to sing at this huge meeting. We were inspired by the many people who attended this meeting to fight for a just cause.

There was one more event that took place at Toronto's Royal York Hotel on New Year's Eve. I had joined a dental Fraternity group called Alpha Omega, and this year the international convention was held in Toronto. I had rehearsed a group of performers I had worked with during my *Dentantics* years as an undergrad. So, I helped produce a ninety-minute show which everyone thought was spectacular. This ninety-minute show had several numbers that I was a part of, and required many rehearsals during the year that had to be fit into the schedule of 1964—as if I had nothing else to do— that you've just read about. As usual, I had someone tape the performance, and I still have it. It was a great way to end the year, enjoying the company of my wife and friends, at a convention of dental colleagues following a succession of events I was thrilled to have been a part of.

CHAPTER 3:
I'VE TRAVELLED HERE, AND THEN
I'VE TRAVELLED YONDER

1965

We were now entering the busiest period of time we ever had, with ground-breaking appearances and events. The year began with a quiet week, followed by a week of performing two shows a night at The Purple Onion Folk Club in Yorkville. The week was interrupted by one night in order to tape the opening of the new CBC TV show, *Take Thirty*, where we were the only guests on this new show, hosted by Paul Soles. One week later, on January 19, we taped two *Let's Sing Out* TV shows with Oscar Brand at the University of Toronto.

Now we began part two of our Command Performance British Adventure, following Prince Philip's misquoted remark about The Travellers the previous November. Sid Dolgay was in charge of making the arrangements and, on January 20, we flew to London. Two days later, we appeared on *The Joey Loss Pop Music Radio Show* in London, followed that same day by a late-night TV show, *London Tonight*, with Dick Amery. On January 24 and 25, we recorded two *Hoot* shows, a London sing-along TV show. Next day, we did *The Radio Show* and *The Five-O'clock Show*. On January 27, we were in Wembley where we taped another TV show, *Carnival*. The next day, Winston Churchill passed away, so Great Britain entered into an official mourning period of one week and most TV shows only showed video of the former PM.

We sang again in London on February 2 at The American Club. On February 4 and 5, we journeyed by train to Glasgow and Edinburgh to sing at a folk club, and to tape sessions of *The Andy Stewart TV Show*. The shows were quite rewarding as Andy was a great performer, and we sang some songs together.

When we returned from Scotland, we got ready to record our next Columbia album at a London recording studio. We were delayed several times by poor planning and studio cancellations. We finally did the recording on the evening of February 10, going overnight into February 11 after which, a few hours later, we boarded a plane home to Toronto. Because of these delays, we were not too thrilled with our London adventure.

We were fortunate to have stayed in a hotel right across the road from the London Museum. Because we had nothing to do and no gigs, I spent many of my off-days there. Ray Woodley was always mischievous and, during the first night in our London hotel, he noticed that hotel guests left their shoes outside each hotel room door. Well, Ray started switching the shoes around, causing cries of anguish in the morning when people awoke to clean, but mismatched shoes. When Ray saw the chaos in the hotel corridor, he wisely chose to not repeat the mischief.

When we returned to Toronto, Ray confided to me that he was very unhappy with the arrangements Sid Dolgay had made for us in London where we had no extra income and nothing to do. Ray was therefore thinking of leaving the group. We decided to have a meeting to discuss the future of The Travellers.

Meanwhile, on March 7, we were off to Sudbury to sing for old friends from the Mine, Mill and Smelter Workers' Union. On March 10, we performed at a convention at the Royal York Hotel for Office Overload. One week later on March 17–18, we appeared at the Winnipeg Boat Show, and shared the bill with Ricky Laine and Velvl, a U.S. ventriloquism act. Back in Toronto, we performed at an anti-racism concert for the Student Non-Violent Co-ordinating Committee (SNCC). I was not too happy with a lot of the things they advocated, in contrast to Dr. King's teachings, but we did the concert anyway to great response and acclaim.

That week, we held a meeting of The Travellers' Production Company, the corporation we had started three years earlier for business and tax reasons. At that meeting, with the encouragement of our manager, Marty Bockner, we held a vote about Sid Dolgay's long-term position in The Travellers. Ray Woodley was not the only one unhappy with how Sid's arrangements in London had turned out. There were other issues as well. For example, while we had been in the UK, we were trying to move ahead, but we paled in comparison to The Seekers who were in Britain at the same time that we were there. Sid had not been aware of this situation.

It was now the mid 1960s and there were huge shifts happening in popular music. I knew the popularity of folk music was already reaching its peak and would soon be changing. If the Travellers were to remain successful and continue moving forward as we always had, we needed to change as well. And Sid had indicated he was unwilling, or maybe incapable of making any changes.

Our lawyer, Muni Basman, ran the vote and we four —Simone, Ray, Sid and I agreed to support the outcome. Three members voted to remove Sid Dolgay from The Travellers and from the company, and the results were recorded officially by our lawyer. My vote was based on my concerns for the future wellbeing of the Travellers, and I knew I would rather give up Sid than lose Ray. But Sid countered by asking for the three of us to depart, and that we leave the group to him. This, of course, was voted down.

As a group we decided that Sid's last gig with us would be on May 1st in Port Hope, Ontario. Our formal contractual agreement was clear in stating there would be no recompense for anyone who left the group, under any circumstances, including dismissal. Sid and his wife were the signing officers for The Travellers' bank account. He rarely showed us the books or updated us, especially after the British trip. So, as recommended by our lawyer, Sid was instructed and required to turn over to us all documents, contracts and financial records of the group in his possession. Our ensuing investigation revealed that our bank account had been emptied.

It was now time to complete, with Sid, the performances that had been booked, and try to find someone to replace him. On March 28, Oscar Brand, Jean Ritchie and I did an Easter TV Special for the United Church of Canada. (I've not yet been able to track down a copy of that film, but the reviews were very good.) On April 3, we returned to the Maritimes for a concert in Fredericton, New Brunswick and, two days later, we returned to the Charlottetown Theatre (where we now had great connections) for a concert. The next day, we returned to Moncton for a concert, and three days later on April 9, we were back in Toronto for a concert at Massey Hall. At this event, we introduced and shared the stage with popular American folk singer, Judy Collins, for her first concert appearance in Toronto. As you might expect, this memorable evening was sold out. (I am still in love with those blue eyes.) On April 11, I did a concert for Toronto's Holy Blossom Temple at its Spring Arts Festival. Then, on April 23, the group headed east to Whitby to do a concert for the local Rotary Club.

By this time, we had arrived at an agreement with Joe Hampson to replace Sid Dolgay. Joe was an American bass player who was newly-come to Canada, after he'd married Canadian singer Sharon Trostin. Joe had had a successful career accompanying many folk groups in the U.S. But now, through Sharon's connections to Camp Naivelt, it was great adding Joe to the "Naivelt Alumni Singers". Sid would appear with us for all those remaining dates. It was difficult for him, as well as for us, but we persevered. On April 28, we appeared a second time at the Barrie Y's Men's Club, at a fund-raising concert for the new "Y".

On April 29, we made another concert appearance in Orillia, to great success. Even though Mariposa was now long-gone from Orillia, we continued to be invited back as we were clearly remembered from our appearances there at the first three Mariposas.

The Travellers' last gig with Sid was on May 1, in Port Hope, at their wonderful stage. It was certainly the end of an era for both us and for Sid; he was the last original member of the group along with me. Admittedly, there were some logistical problems in ending Sid's tenure with us. But getting Joe Hampson into the group was going to bring us a different, more versatile look and sound. So, we rehearsed some old numbers with Joe and found ways to incorporate him into our music. By doing so, we created a new sound with different instrumentation and vocals.

The New Travellers Begin

The "new" Travellers did their first gig on June 25, at a Spring Fair in Listowell, Ontario. Thirty minutes before the show began, we were served with a writ from Sid Dolgay's lawyer, claiming that Sid's removal from the group was illegal, and demanding we "cease and desist" all activities. We phoned our lawyer in Toronto, Muni Basman, who told us to deposit the writ in the nearest garbage receptacle. The show went on to great success with Joe's inclusion.

At that time, I looked ahead at our schedule, and the rest of the year looked as full as it had been before, and then some. It was heartening to hear the views of Toronto columnists who looked forward to The Travellers continuing their rise up the ladder in Toronto's music scene. To give Toronto a way to see the "new" Travellers, we had signed on to appear at The Riverboat Folk Club in Yorkville for the first time! Again, it was expensive for them to have a four-person group appear at that venue, but they had good crowds that were anxious to hear the new sound. The week went well for us, for the Riverboat management, and for their audiences.

On July 17, the NDP (New Democratic Party) was holding its national convention in Ottawa. The Travellers were invited to sing some traditional songs related to labour and the NDP campaign, and to perform just before the main speaker, the celebrated Pierre Berton. A large audience enjoyed the show. Backstage, just before the show began, I started doodling some union songs, and soon discovered that Pierre Berton knew the words to many of them. It turned out that his father had been a union organizer in Yellowknife, and he had grown up on all the labour anthems.

On July 27, The Travellers sang at an event at the Oakdale Golf Club in Toronto. Two days later, we did a hootenanny concert on the hillside at Riverdale Park in Toronto. There was a large crowd, and it turned out to be a great sing-along concert. This event marked the beginning of a long series of annual hootenanny concerts for the Toronto Parks Department. One week later, on August 7, I returned to Mariposa which was now being held at Innis Lake, and I did the children's concert alone. On August 12 and 13, we finished another Columbia record using American, Jim Kweskin, and Canadian friend, Amos Garrett to sit in with us. It worked well and, years later, when I was singing at the Edmonton Folk Festival, I asked Amos to sit in during my part, singing with Emmy-Lou Harris and Arlo Guthrie and his family.

That summer, a Young Peoples Conference was held in Toronto, and several university professors were on the board of what was called, Assembly '65, a Protestant Church Assembly. At this event, certain intellectuals were to speak and provide information on the world's problems. I was asked to conduct and sing at a "Coffee House" set up at CFTO TV in Toronto, where I would sing and introduce a song. The assembled students would then discuss the song and what it meant in terms of the world's affairs. The show lasted an hour, and was successful. I was then asked to attend another session at the University of Saskatoon from August 14–21, where I discussed politics and the songs that were written about current events. From these experiences I knew that someday I would return to academia, and use songs to illustrate political and social causes.

It was now nearing the end of August, and every Torontonian knows that that means it's time once again for the CNE, the EX. The Travellers were hired to perform on August 21 at an event they called a "Foodenanny", a folk sing-along concert for food handlers and CNE staff.

On August 27 and 28, *The Toronto Star* concerts returned to the Bandshell, hosted by The Travellers and including both local and out of town performers. On September 3 and 4, we hosted two more shows at the Bandshell. *The Star* sent some photographers and journalists who were writing a story about The Travellers' twelve-year history. The resulting six-page story appeared in *The Star Weekly*, their weekend magazine that was seen nationally, with pictures of the group along with a full-page colour photo of us on the cover.

The following day, I drove to Kitchener where I did a show of Yiddish and Canadian songs at a local synagogue. The next day, The Travellers joined me in neighbouring Waterloo for a full concert at Waterloo University. We slept over, and drove the next day to St. Catharines to entertain at a convention of Medical General Practitioners at Prudhomme's Restaurant, on the south-east shore of Lake Ontario. And the dates kept coming.

We had signed to appear on the Tommy Hunter TV show on October 1. It was great fun meeting up with a lot of old friends in the cast, including Gordie Tapp. On October 7, we returned to Owen Sound for the third straight year to do a concert for the local Y's men's group. Although it was our third time there, the addition of Joe Hampson gave us a few new songs, and the new sound seemed to work. A week later, it was an easy one-hour drive to Guelph University for a Hootenanny concert there. The next day, October16th, found us on the road to Lindsay for a concert sponsored by a local charity.

The rest of October was filled with busy evenings. On Oct. 22, I returned to Hart House to close an Ontario Social Workers convention. I knew a lot of them from my undergrad years, and it was good to see them all again. I guess it was also good for them, as the concert was a resounding success with several encores. The next day, Oct. 23, I drove to Hamilton to sing at a church meeting. Then, on October 27, the whole group performed at a meeting of the Hamilton local of the Teamsters International, who were hosting a national convention for their members. That was the first time we had sung for the Teamsters, and we felt we had gone back to our roots.

On October 31, we performed in Toronto at a national convention of the B'nai B'rith youth groups. Our old friend, Alan Borovoy, was the main speaker, and The Travellers were the main singers, making this event a special night of reunion for all of us.

There were still two months to go during that year, and here is what we did: First, we went to Ottawa for an NDP convention where they were planning for the next election. On November 26, we sang at a meeting of The Oshawa Builders' Association. You see, we could sing as easily for building executives as we could for labour organizations! So, by the same token, on December 2–3 we did two Christmas concerts for the Sudbury Mine Mill and Smelter Workers' Union. On December 5, we were at Toronto's O'Keefe Centre in Toronto to do a benefit concert for the nearby St. Lawrence Centre for the Arts. And, on December 6, I drove to Hamilton to sing at the Hamilton YMHA, for long-time friend, Bill Stern. That ended the shows for the year, but on December 18, everyone was invited to the Gray household for a seasonal party.

It had been an eventful and successful year for us as a family and for The Travellers. We had successfully incorporated our new member, Joe Hampson, who stayed with me for forty-four years as a member of The Travellers. Sadly, Sid Dolgay would not go away and threatened to keep suing us. So, we made him an offer to pay him ten percent of our fees from dates already signed with him in the contracts, for the next year. Because of several bankruptcies by Sid, we had to make the payments to his wife. I had a feeling that we would see more of the vindictive Sid Dolgay.

During the past year, we had taped two TV specials and did five other TV shows. We also recorded two albums for Columbia— one in London and one in Canada. That's a lot of productive work for the group, but it was nothing compared to what the next two years were to bring.

1966

In 1965, we had begun performing for a week at The Purple Onion Folk Club. In 1966, we started off with two weeks, January 4 to 16, at the Gate of Cleve Folk Club, a fairly large venue in East Toronto. Several days later, we were off to Ottawa for a concert at St. Patrick's College.

We had been offered the opportunity to be part of a series of commercials involving Molson Canadian. It was to look as if it were part of a concert performed on the stage of The Royal Alexandra Theatre. Several other Canadian performing artists were involved as well.

We began on February 10 at the TV studio, and then moved to a recording studio. We did a thirty-second recording, and then a sixty-second version as well as radio commercials of various lengths. We then went to the Royal Alexandra Theatre and made a video of the performance scene. We made the most money from these short commercials than from any other performance we ever did. In fact, our version of the "Molson Song" was the most watched version of all the others made." The song ran for about five years, and then the radio versions were sliced and diced and reissued.

Let me explain about commercials: Every time the contract is renewed for a different time cycle, we would get paid, as if the commercial had been redone. The commercial often ran during the Maple Leafs' televised hockey games. The commercials ran with the header that it was The Travellers singing, so each time it was played, we got national recognition. That publicity alone made the project worthwhile.

On March 2, we were invited to sing for The Labour Committee for Human Rights at a testimonial for Eamon Park who had been their president for many years. He, along with Alan Borovoy and I, had been a part of the Ontario Human Rights group for years.

We were also about to finish what would be our seventh and last recording for Columbia Records. Frank Jones, who had signed us in 1959, had moved to Nashville in 1963. He invited us to record a couple of new tracks there with him. We took guitarist Amos Garrett with us, and headed to Nashville to do a recording session with guitarist Grady Martin and piano player, Floyd Kramer. It was quite an experience recording four songs in Nashville for the first time! It was still March and, when we returned, we did a concert at The Collingwood High School at the behest of folk music and Travellers' fan, Mike Kirby.

On March 28, CTV carried a rerun of an Easter TV show that Oscar Brand and I had recorded a year before. Again, I never had the opportunity to view this show. On April 10, we recorded a TV show with long-time CBC singer, Juliette, on her new TV show, which followed the hockey game on Saturday night. *The Juliette Show* appeared on TV, on a night that our Molson commercial was being shown, so we were seen first in the commercial during the hockey game, and a little later on *The Juliette Show*. It was great timing.

On April 20, we were invited to do our third concert for the Barrie Y's Men's Club, as they were finally ending their campaign efforts, and had successfully built a new swimming pool. This concert was ground-breaking for us, because we had been involved twice with this group's fundraising efforts.

Our new bass player, Joe Hampson, was "follicly-challenged" (he was bald), but that day he was wearing a new hair piece for the first time. He was told he could even go swimming while wearing it. After the show, people were invited to take a look at the new swimming pool, and The Travellers were invited to try it out before we went to the reception which followed. Well, our Joe bounded forward and dove into the pool. Within seconds, a wad of hair was floating beside him! He rescued it, of course, and once he was out of the pool, tried to comb and dry it. Joe was last seen that evening in the locker room, still trying to comb out and dry his hair piece, as the reception continued without him. Later, we hustled him back into our vehicle for the trip home. The next day, Joe called his hair person, who said, "I told you you could swim with it, but not DIVE!" Lesson learned.

On May 7–8, we appeared at the Ottawa folk club, L'Hibou, owned by Harvey Glatt who did much for the Ottawa folk scene. The next day was Sunday and we were invited to sing in Arnprior at the Grace Church on the Hill. We delayed our return to Toronto, and sang as part of the Sunday morning service. Another first for us. On May 17, I performed solo at York University in Toronto. On that same day, Columba released two of the songs we had recorded in Nashville.

On June 2, we sang at a Graduation Day concert for the Royal Military College in Kingston Ontario. On July 2, we drove to Orillia for a performance at Owaissa Lodge on Lake Couchiching. This place had a curling rink on its property, and there were plans to turn the rink into a hockey school. But the owner's kids wanted to turn the place into a coffee house during the summer, so we sang at the opening of the coffee house. During the performance, I noticed an old friend from U. of T. sitting in the audience. Alan Eagleson and I used to hang around the Hart House gym when we were undergrads but still keen on sports, so it was a nice reunion.

CHAPTER 4:
THE LONGEST ALL-CANADIAN TOUR
BY ANYONE

1967

Since our beginning in 1953, The Travellers had now been together for fourteen years. For a variety of reasons, we had replaced all the original members, except for myself. Some of our friends and fans were saying that it seemed the group now mirrored solely my ideas, but maybe that wasn't such a bad thing. With my recent guidance, and by enlisting some replacements, the musical stature of the group was now better than ever. The group had also demonstrated its ability to change its sound as well as its on-stage appearance. We were hoping to go beyond our storied past, and beyond what people thought the Travellers might ever attain. In 1967, Festival Canada chose The Travellers to be the prime attraction in the celebrations being held in every province and territory in Canada, as well as at EXPO 67 in Montreal for this significant year marking Canada's 100th birthday.

The 1967 Tour Begins

On Monday January 2, the group prepared for its first engagement of 1967 in Brockville, Ontario at the Brockville Civic Auditorium. Toronto Entertainment writers, Blaik Kirby, Sid Adilman, and Joe Lewis were there to review the show by Catherine McKinnon and The Travellers.

One reviewer said that The Travellers were there to sell Canadian music, songs, and history to Canadians, noting "the group seems to be up to the challenge."

The first show in Brockville was sold out, ending in a celebratory mood with a reception party following the show. Several days later, on January 6, the group appeared on *The Elwood Glover TV Show* in Toronto, and we discussed the coming tour. On January 11, we appeared again on CBC TV, the *In Person Show,* for producer Mark Warren.

The next day, we were booked for three days of shows in Orillia, with songs about Canada. We have a lot of friends in Orillia from the first three Mariposas. So, after Mariposa left Orillia in 1963, we were invited about ten more times to do a summertime concert in Orillia—but not as part of Mariposa.

The busy month continued with an appearance at Toronto's Queen Elizabeth Theatre to sing for the Toronto Jaycees and the Toronto Board of Trade. On January 23, I appeared at a luncheon meeting of Hadassah at the Shaarei Shomayim synagogue and, by evening, the whole group was on its way to nearby Port Credit for a celebration and the crowning of Centennial '67's, Miss Port Credit.

On January 26, we were booked to entertain the Ontario Conservative Party caucus before the return of the members to the Legislature. Bill Davis was premier at that time. Even though he knew The Travellers were definitely left of centre, he still invited us to appear at many of his Conservative Party functions.

The next day, we were back on the road to Queen's University in Kingston for a centennial concert. The day after that, we were off to the University of Western Ontario in London, where we did one concert in one location, followed by a second one with Gordon Lightfoot at the Thames Hall concert area. That was the last gig of the month, for Greta and I had booked a vacation in Mexico for the first two weeks of February, before the year got too hectic. Our time in Mexico City and Acapulco was a welcome respite after only the first month of this busy year. My mother looked after our kids back home and, to our joy, the end result of this Mexican adventure was that Greta got pregnant after we had been trying vainly for two years.

It was back to work on February 27 and 28, for two shows in Galt, Ontario, (now part of Cambridge) with jazz singer, Phyllis Marshall, on the bill with us. After a night in a motel, we continued west to the Cleary Auditorium in Windsor for performances on March 1 and 2.

Back in Toronto, we took ten days to record an album of labour songs. This album included some Joe Hill songs and included "Solidarity Forever". This was a new partnership between The

Travellers, The Canadian Labour Congress, and Arc Records. It was the first recording of labour songs ever produced in Canada. Later, when CBC TV planned a TV special called *A Century of Song*, we sang many of these songs from the recording on the show. This was definitely one of the highlights of our year.

The Travellers LP salute to 100th anniversary of
7yCanadian Labour Congress, 1967

Popular Toronto radio station 1050 CHUM rarely invited The Travellers on the air, but we were invited to do a live call-in show with deejay Bob McAdorey, where we talked about the group, and this ground-breaking tour. After a week off, we got a call from the Iroquois Hotel in London, Ontario, to appear from March 27–31. This was our first time there, and we had good appreciative crowds. On April 13, a recording of the *Gordie Tapp CBC Radio Show* followed. We were well into spring now, a fact which was significant, because as part of this Centennial Tour, a lot of appearances were planned for locations in northern Canada and involved flying daily to each area. These gigs had to be delayed until we were sure the winter was really over and flights could be made safely.

On April 16, the Penny Farthing Folk Club hired Jerry Gray and Sharon Trostin to do a children's program in the afternoon. That was the first time a coffee house had opened in an afternoon for kids under eight years old. Good crowd, good program and well received. On April 19, The Travellers sang at the convention banquet of the Ontario Dental Association in Toronto. It was only April, but already I'd almost forgotten I was still an Ontario dentist on a semi-sabbatical break for this year.

On April 22, The Travellers headed to Chatham, Ontario for a Centennial Concert, and then returned to Toronto to pack. On April 24, we flew to Quebec City to entertain the people from Festival Canada—those who are actually planning many of our upcoming appearances. We then flew to The Lakehead[8], rented a station wagon and toured daily. At many of the places we visited, as well as an evening Centennial concert in the school auditorium, The Travellers did an afternoon children's concert in the same location.

On May 8, we left Toronto for our flight to The Lakehead. We then proceeded to: Geraldton, Nipigon-Redrock, Atikokan, Fort Frances and Dryden (the black-fly capital of Canada). Our last stop was Rainy River, the farthest point you can go in Ontario before you arrive at Minnesota and Manitoba. Our trip to this remote part of Ontario reminded me of my first tour of that area with the Fagel Gardner Singers back in 1952. After our concert in Rainy River, we returned to the Lakehead Airport, unloaded the rental station wagon, loaded the gear onto the plane and flew back to Toronto where my station wagon awaited us. We loaded the car, and finally, home.

It had not been an easy week of performances, because of all the travel involved and performing two different concerts each day. We

---

[8] "The Lakehead" refers to the geographic area at the head of Lake Superior, composed for many years of Fort William and Port Arthur, with a municipal airport in Fort William. The two cities officially merged in January 1970, to become Thunder Bay, and the airport was known as the Canadian Lakehead Airport. In 1997, the airport was handed over to the Thunder Bay International Airports Authority, a non-profit organization.

didn't have a crew of "roadies" to set up and break down our sound equipment. So, when we arrived in town, we unloaded our station wagon, set up the sound for the kids' concert, did the show between 3:30 and 4:30, had a quick rest, found some place to eat, and then showed up for the evening show. After the show, we took down the sound equipment, loaded it back into our station wagon, drove to a motel and slept over. The next morning, we ate breakfast, drove to the next town, and then repeated the process.

For the next group of performances, we travelled along the Trans Canada Highway, from May 22 to May 27. We began by flying again to The Lakehead, but this time we headed south to Manitouwadge, Wawa, Sault Ste. Marie, Espanola, and Sudbury. Many of the towns are mining or mill towns, with the smell of seasoning wood and sulphur warning us that we were getting close.

In one of those remote towns, I met Whitey Myers from Oakwood Collegiate in Toronto— whose team I swam and played basketball against back in high school. After high school, Whitey became a "worker priest" in these northern mines. It was so interesting to meet someone from my non-musical past in one of the remotest areas of the province! Whitey was surprised to see me there. He thought I was still an athlete but didn't know I was a singer and entertainer.

In addition, here in this same area, folk singer-songwriter Wade Hemsworth wrote many of his songs like "The Blackfly Song" and "The Log Driver's Waltz" while he was working for Ontario Hydro, The songs he wrote reminded us of people working in these remote areas and their struggle to survive. As we travelled on, we reflected on how great it was to be Canadian.

The next week, we returned home to see our families, do laundry, and check the schedule ahead. It was now time for the main event. We drove to Montreal and appeared, from June 5 to June 10, for three shows per day at the Canadian Pavilion and Theatre at EXPO 67. CBC radio and TV were there to interview us daily and ask us how our travels had been so far and about the impact that our tour was making on the country. (I have all of the radio interviews on my home tapes.)

Because Greta is from Montreal and had relatives there, she came to spend the week and take in the fun and excitement of EXPO. We were now expecting child number three in late November. After a week together in Montreal, we returned to Toronto. On June 14, the group drove north to Haileybury, near Timmins, for a one-town concert. That was one heck-of-a long way to drive for one concert. And then home again.

The next segment of the tour we did for Festival Canada 1967 was again ground-breaking. It was the first concert tour ever planned for "North of 60" or north of the Arctic Circle, part of Canada's far north. The tour involved our travelling to twenty communities, most of which had never seen a live performance before. None of these communities can be reached by road, only by plane, as there are few roads here.

Fortunately, the tour organizers waited until late in June to start scheduling these concerts, but even then, some of the landing places still had snow or ice on the ground—or on the water—where we might have needed to land. With the Internet still over thirty years in the future, there was very little knowledge of the places we were going to, so it was a real leap into an area of the unknown—even to this day. But the tour was fascinating, and so rewarding to learn first-hand about this area of Canada.

Twenty-one Days North of the Arctic Circle

From Toronto we flew on Air Canada to Edmonton on June 17. Then Pacific Western Airline (PWA) flew us to Yellowknife, in the Northwest Territories[9]. We gave our first concert in the schoolhouse in the town of Hay River, the most northern spot that the train lines went to. From there, you could actually travel on a paved road to the Mackenzie Highway, where you might drive north to Inuvik on the shore of the Arctic Ocean, if you had over a month to do it, one way. This was not recommended.

In the town of Hay River, we did a show to a mixture of local indigenous people, and transplanted southern Canadians who were there working for the nearby mining or shipping companies. This was

---

[9] In 1999, the Northwest Territories was divided into two territories, the other of which is now called Nunavut.

the first live concert given by anyone in most of these disparate Arctic communities. There was no hotel in Hay River, so we flew back to Yellowknife the same day to sleep over in our hotel. The next day, June 18, we flew to Fort Providence, a mainly Inuit and Métis community on the southwest shore of Great Slave Lake. There, most of the town showed up for our afternoon concert at the local school. After the show, we packed up and flew back to the Yellowknife hotel. The next day, we followed the same routine as we flew to Fort Rae, also a mainly Inuit community. The show at the school took place when we arrived, as we were now in "The Land of the Midnight Sun"—with twenty-four hours of daylight at this time of year. Again, we returned to our Yellowknife hotel and, on June 20, we awoke and did an evening concert in the Yellowknife Hotel meeting room. Because there were no motels or restaurants in any of the small communities we travelled to, we had to return each night to Yellowknife.

After the Yellowknife concert on June 21, we flew on a regularly-scheduled PWA flight three hours north to Inuvik, probably the second-largest community in the North after Yellowknife. It had streets, several hotels, and an airport and, because it was summer, it was 26° Celsius (80° Fahrenheit) when we arrived. Then, while walking from the plane to the terminal, we were attacked by large mosquitoes, and our initial slow gait shifted rapidly to a quick run to the terminal.

We did our first show on June 21 in Inuvik with a pretty urbane crowd. We slept in a nice hotel that night, and ordered a plane to fly us to Tuktoyaktuk for the afternoon concert the next day. We loaded the equipment onto the plane and arrived in an almost entirely indigenous community. We flew back in the daylight and slept in Inuvik. The next day June 23, we boarded a plane to take us to Aklavik.

Partway there, we encountered some bad weather, and the pilot decided that we had to turn back. The next day, the weather was better, so on June 24 we flew to the small hamlet of Fort McPherson down the Mackenzie River, and then we continued south back to Yellowknife for an overnight there.

For the next seven days, we worked out of Yellowknife, as all the places we visited had no adequate overnight accommodation and no restaurants at all. On June 25, we flew north again up the Mackenzie River to Norman Wells, a petroleum town with nearby oil wells. To get there we had to fly at noon to reach Norman Wells, and then return to Yellowknife to sleep. We ended up flying about 1,000 kilometres (about 620 miles) all day each day. We saw mainly "Southerners" at the concert, for they were transplanted oil workers and their families.

We returned to sleep at our Yellowknife hotel. The next day's trip was an unexpected treat! We were heading to Fort Simpson, again on the Mackenzie River. That day there was no plane available in town that could take all of us and our equipment up the river to Fort Simpson in one trip. But they offered to make two helicopter trips to get us there. There was no room for five-foot tall speakers in the passenger cabin of a helicopter, so on one flight they put two passengers in the chopper and tied the speakers to the pontoons, since we would be landing on a gravel strip, not water.

The extra treat? They said they would take us into the Yukon, to the South Nahanni River where the Virginia Falls are located. These falls are twice as high as the Niagara Falls, so on our way to Fort Simpson, we diverted and flew over them. Then it was back to Yellowknife to put the rest of our instruments in the cabin, and another flight back to Fort Simpson again over the Virginia Falls, simply a spectacularly breathtaking "Canadian scene". We left the helicopter in Fort Simpson, and managed to charter a plane there to take us back to Yellowknife in one trip.

Next morning, we flew to a Dene village on the shore of Great Slave Lake. The town was called Pine Point near a mine of the same name—the only reason for its existence. Five years later, the mine closed down and the town was abandoned. Nothing remains there now but a spot in the forest. The interesting audience for our show included local indigenous people who had never seen a live show before, plus transplanted miners and their families from the South. Again, we returned to Yellowknife and then repeated our trip the next day by flying to Fort Smith—another community that has since disappeared from the map, with the same history as the town the day before. On all of these trips, we had to take a lunch with us as these two towns had no restaurants and only a Hudson's Bay Company grocery store, with very high prices.

It was now June 29, and we flew from Yellowknife to northern Saskatchewan near the border of the Northwest Territories to the town of Uranium City. The uranium mine was in full operation at that time, so they had a hotel and also a pub. As unlikely as it seems, in the bar there I met one of my dental patients from Toronto, who was working that summer with Atomic Energy Canada. We again had a mixed audience, but it was a good concert, and well appreciated by the audience. Uranium City closed ten years later when the mine ceased operation, and the town virtually disappeared from the map.

The next day, June 30, we travelled to Fort Resolution, or "Fort Rez" as it was known. This was an entirely indigenous community with a church, a Hudson's Bay Company store, a school and not much else, but the show was well appreciated. Then it was back to Yellowknife for July 1, Canada's 100th birthday. Yellowknife was holding a 24-hour golf tournament because of the "midnight sun" and the twenty-four hours of sunshine. It's difficult to grow grass in the Arctic, so in place of greens they had "browns" which were oiled sand and flattened earth. The non-stop drinking feature at the 24-hour golf tournament truly made the day.

Canada Day in Inuvik 1967

We had a concert date in Inuvik, so once again we boarded a plane and flew up to Inuvik to do our "Canada Day" concert. As you may recall, Inuvik had a hotel, so we checked in. I had been attempting to reach my wife by phone at home in Toronto, for this July 1 was our tenth wedding anniversary. As we were leaving the hotel for the school to do the concert, Ray Woodley emerged from his room and hung his clothes bag on a hook in the hallway, not realizing the hook was attached to the fire alarm. Well, the alarm went off and caused much panic, as a fire in a wooden hotel was dangerous to the whole town. I had finally reached Greta, but had to say hello and goodbye quickly because the fire alarms were blaring. We proceeded to the school where we did a well-attended concert to an appreciative audience.

It was now July 2 and we flew to the community of Coppermine on the south shore of the Arctic Ocean. We boarded a large old DC-3, with a sloping floor. Then we discovered we had to make two unscheduled stops. Along our route were two NORAD bases, staffed with mainly American crews. But because of local flight problems, a number of specific planes had not been able to travel from Inuvik to either of the local air bases, CAM 1 or CAM 2. Both bases had run out of beer! So, we loaded up with beer in Inuvik, and the pilot made two stops to deliver beer before taking us to Coppermine. As a consequence, we were now known as a "Mercy Booze Bomber."

Coppermine was near where the *Terror* and the *Erebus* vanished in 1845 while seeking the Northwest Passage.[10] When I realized where we were going, during the flight I sang a song I
knew about the lost Franklin expedition and the lost ships.

Coppermine was the home of many Inuit carvers who carved whales, animals, and birds, and we were hopeful of bringing some carvings home. But it turned out that, several weeks earlier, they had sent their winter carvings south to be sold. There were only a few, left in town. Even so, they generously gave us some souvenirs to take home and, during our performance, our all-Inuit audience was very appreciative.

We returned to Inuvik, and next day flew to Aklavik, a small hamlet nowhere near the NORAD Beer Drop. Our concert started at noon, once again for an all-Inuit audience. It went well, and we finished at 3:00 p.m. With twenty-four hours of daylight every day, it could have been 8:00 at night because the kids went to sleep when they felt tired. People did not use a clock much at this time of year.

On July 4th, we headed north to Holman Island,[11] a small hamlet on the west coast of Victoria Island on the Arctic Ocean. The town had

---

[10] Recently, in 2014 and 2016, Sir John Franklin's ships from that lost expedition were finally found, exactly where Inuit reports said they would be. But back in 1967, no one knew this yet. Diving crews are now trying to salvage artefacts.
[11] Holman, or Holman Island is a small hamlet on the west coast of Victoria Island in the Inuvik Region of the Northwest Territories. On April 1, 2006, the name was

no airstrip and the bay still had too much ice, so around two o'clock in the afternoon, we landed on the main street of the town and we performed for an all-Inuit audience. Again, it was the first time they had ever seen a live show of any kind. After we had performed three songs, they did not even clap as this custom was unfamiliar to them, and they did not know what to do. So, their teacher told them that if they liked the songs, they should clap their hands when the song ended. After that they became very enthusiastic, and as a result the concert went about twenty minutes longer than planned because of the extra length of the clapping!

Our last day in the far north was July 5, and our flight took us to adjacent Banks Island to visit the town of Sachs Harbour, very close to Alaska. After our concert, we returned to Inuvik to pack everything and prepare for one last trip to the Yukon, and later back south to Edmonton. On July 6, after checking out of the hotel, we took off for the Yukon, and the town of Fort Liard on the Liard River. There was no airstrip and no road, so we landed on the river to be then faced with a twenty-minute walk to the town. So, they got an open horse and wagon, and loaded us and all our equipment onto the cart and drove us into town. Fort Liard was an all-indigenous community of First Nations and Métis heritage that in 1967 had had very little contact with the outside world.

After the show, we said goodbye to everyone, loaded our gear, and went back on board the horse and open wagon. Full of feelings—sad to leave, knowing that we would never return, but looking forward to getting back to what we called "civilization". We headed back to the river where our plane was waiting. As we boarded the plane and took off, we knew we would not return to Yellowknife again, for we were heading directly south to Edmonton. The very same plane that had landed on the Liard River in the Yukon now flew us south into Alberta and, after a four-hour flight, we landed safely on the airfield at the Edmonton airport. After making our way into the terminal, we checked all our gear and luggage with the airline and, after a short wait in the

---

returned to **Ulukhaktok** (<u>Kangiryuarmiutun</u> (<u>Inuit language</u>) spelling *Ulukhaqtuuq* [ulukhaqtu:q̄] as it was known to the local indigenous people.

terminal, boarded a regularly scheduled flight with other people and flew back to Toronto. We were filled with thoughts, and oh-so-many memories of our twenty-one days north of the Arctic Circle, and the twenty concerts we had performed there. Who knew if we would ever return to the "North of 60" area of Canada? We had the satisfaction of knowing that we had done the very first of this type of tour of Canada's far North.

We were now about halfway through 1967. We had just finished the longest tour of the Arctic and Subarctic communities that had ever been made—a record that as of 2018 still stands. Apparently, the number of consecutive performance dates we did has not been equalled, or even attempted, by any group or even by an individual. That tour could only have been done by air using planes like Beavers, DC-3s, and Otters, and we had had to rent a plane in each location to meet the heavy performance schedule drawn up for us by Festival Canada. It was masterful to even attempt to complete that schedule, but it's a credit to the members of The Travellers—Ray Woodley, Simone Taylor, Joe Hampson and Jerry Gray—who did fulfill that schedule, and did Canada proud. Yet for some reason, there really has never been any official designation by any federal body, to recognize or even thank The Travellers for doing this, We fulfilled a commitment to the country to educate and entertain the people who live in largely unknown and forgotten areas of Canada, and to help them feel that they are part of the country and share its promise and ideals. Why has no one ever done anything to honour this achievement that certainly went above and beyond what any group or individual had ever done.

The Canadian federal government asked for our help, and we succeeded beyond anyone's expectations. Yet it was still early summer of 1967, and our schedule was only half done. We now began the second half of our commitment to Canada. We returned to Toronto on July 7, reacquainted ourselves with our families and recharged our batteries for what lay ahead. Some of the future tasks we had agreed to had also never been done before.

There is one thing we must apologize for to those people who live "North of 60." We wrote the new words to "This Land" in 1954, and in the chorus, we sing, "From the Arctic Circle, to the Great Lakes' waters". But for most of a month, we had been singing to Canadians who actually live far north of the Arctic Circle. It's hard to circle back now and change the lyrics, so we simply have to acknowledge that much of Canada lies north of the Arctic Circle, and is filled with heroic people who live and survive north of the 60th Parallel, in Canada's far North.

The Last Part of 1967

As you may remember, when the year began, Greta and I had two boys, James and Rob. We had been trying for over a year to increase our flock, and in February we took a vacation to Acapulco in Mexico. Several months later, we were thrilled to find we were expecting another child, to be born before the end of the year, and hopefully when I was not on tour.

After one week at home, The Travellers rented a car and drove for an hour west of Toronto to the town of Guelph. Like many of the events we did, this one was co-sponsored among the local, provincial and federal governments. First, we did an afternoon concert for kids in a local school, and later, an evening concert for university students and adults. Then we packed up and drove home. Three days later, on July 17 we were driving north again—back to North Bay for another locally sponsored show, and then back to Toronto that same night. On July 19, the Toronto Parks Department had us booked for our annual Hootenanny in Riverdale Park. We set up at the base of the hill. The audience was sitting on the hillside and looking down on us, and participating in a singalong performed as only The Travellers could do.

On July 21, we rented a car and drove to Wallaceburg in southwest Ontario, and returned the next day. After a couple of days in Toronto, we began a small tour around central Ontario starting on July 24 in Midland. The next day, we headed to Collingwood on the other side of Georgian Bay and slept over. While I was there, I visited some friends at the Collingwood High School. At that time, teacher John Kirby at Collingwood High began a long friendship with The

Travellers. On July 28, we found ourselves in Walkerton, and the next day in Goderich. These are similar communities with similar crowds, enjoying the music and history of Canada as taught by The Travellers. We finished our last concert of this small tour on August 1ˢᵗ in nearby Kincardine.

After a few days of relaxing at home, on August 5 and 6 we were invited back to the Ontario Pavilion at EXPO 67 in Montreal. There we did a program that included songs such as "The Black Fly Song" and Ontario's theme song, "Give Us a Place to Stand". It was two days of three shows per day. Greta and the boys joined us there to visit with her family. Then again, we headed back home to Toronto.

Two events had happened earlier that year. First, we changed record companies, leaving Columbia for our new label, Arc Records. Since we first began, both The Travellers and I had performed many times for labour unions and on picket line rallies. There was no other person or group in Canada with a similar history. So, to mark their 100th anniversary, The Canadian Labour Congress asked us to create an album of songs. Earlier in the year, we'd recorded an LP of Canadian labour songs under our joint sponsorship. Then, CBC-TV decided to produce a TV show based on our recording, called *A Century of Song*. Between August 11 and 13, we videotaped a new colour TV show of those songs based on our LP, with a studio audience of workers who were on strike at the time. The show was scheduled to be broadcast three weeks later on Labour Day. But before that, The Travellers returned for a fifth appearance at Mariposa. With that show, we returned to our roots. It's important to note that no group ever made as many appearances at Mariposa as the Travellers.

What happens in Toronto at the end of the Summer? Why, the EX of course! That year, the city of Toronto and the province of Ontario hired The Travellers to do our all-Canadian show at the CNE Bandshell. After so many years, we returned to our almost second home, the CNE Bandshell.

On August 27, we fulfilled an obligation to the town of Parry Sound, which is about three hours north of Toronto on the eastern shores of Georgian Bay. As the end of the summer approached, we travelled to Ottawa and did a TV show where we were interviewed about what we'd done so far that year. But our real reason for being in Ottawa? The Conservative Party of Canada Convention was being held there on September 3, and The Travellers were booked as the main performers. To date, we had sung for the Provincial Conservatives, but never for the Federal Party. That same week, our Labour Day TV show was broadcast nationally on CBC TV.

While The Travellers had performed throughout Ontario as well as toured the north during the year, we'd not yet gone east. But it was time. We'd been to PEI many times during this decade, but now the group had been booked for an unusual tour. It was a six-community tour of PEI without performing in either Summerside or Charlottetown! Is such a thing even possible? Watch!

On September 11, we flew to Charlottetown and registered at a hotel which would be our home for the next week. Ahead of us was a circular tour of the Island through small rural and coastal communities; our concerts were booked in schools and church halls. The towns were all similar, but each community has its own character and history. We were bringing the rest of Canada to these small communities. That evening, our first stop was in the small town of O'Leary. We returned each night to our hotel rooms in Charlottetown and headed to the following places in order as we rotated around the island from September 12 to 16: Miscouche, Kensington, North Rustico, Montague, and Souris.

These concerts were co-sponsored by the PEI and the federal government's Centennial Commissions, and each night was sold out. What a lucky bunch of communities they were, invited to share in the Centennial experience, virtually for free! We delivered a full concert experience in every community, and if there were kids in the audience, we did specific songs for them, which oldsters took a part in as well. On September 16, we flew back to our Toronto homes. We'd set an Island record though, of performing six concerts in six days, and none in Charlottetown or Summerside! Can anyone duplicate it? I doubt it. And that is still so.

On September 19, we appeared at a sold-out Maple Leaf Gardens, singing for Bell Canada's Telephone Pioneers Association. We shared the stage with Guy Lombardo and his Royal Canadians and with old friend, Rich Little. Later, we headed home to pack for a long eastern tour. We'd been booked by the New Brunswick provincial government and the federal government, to do thirteen concerts in fourteen days, all in New Brunswick. We asked ourselves, "Has anyone ever done such a tour of New Brunswick before?" The answer was that no one knows!

The next day on September 20, we flew to Saint John, New Brunswick and did our first concert. The next night, we packed the car and drove to Fredericton, the provincial capital. Then on September 21, we sang at the U of NB, and the next night for the city of Fredericton. Travel distances were not great, so we criss-crossed the province while covering eleven more venues.

On September 23rd, we were in Moncton, and then we had a break with two days off. As I often do with two days off, I grabbed a late flight out of Moncton after the concert and flew back to Toronto. I then spent a couple of days sleeping at home, and working in my dental practice. On September 26, I returned to the airport for a flight to Fredericton to do a concert at the Oromocto Army Base. But when the Air Canada flight attendants discovered there were no wine glasses on our flight, we were delayed by two hours! I told the captain of my need to be in Oromocto quickly, and could we drink wine from paper cups? But my plea fell on deaf ears. Even so, the captain contacted the army base, and they arranged to have an army vehicle waiting for me. I arrived at the base about fifteen minutes before concert time.

The next day, we left for northern New Brunswick—an area not seen by most tourists because it's off the regular Trans-Canada Highway routes. We started on September 27 in Edmundston, and then followed performances in Campbellton, Woodstock, Dalhousie, Bathurst, and finally St. Andrews on October 3, my birthday. On October 4, we packed up to return to Toronto. Just like our tour of the Northwest Territories, this was the longest concert tour done by anyone ever in New Brunswick, or since. It was only made possible because of the Festival Canada funding given to provinces to help defray the costs involved in bringing a four-person group to tour the whole province. The federal funding made it possible to provide these events to communities that would otherwise never have seen anything like it. But sadly, once again there was never anyone from either the provincial or federal governments that made mention of The Travellers' tremendous efforts in fulfilling these record-breaking tour schedules. To this day, there has never been any recognition of this tour by anyone! Hard to believe isn't it? Thirteen concert dates in fourteen days by a four-person group (with no crew) who prepared their own stage set-ups and took them down, and then travelled on. We certainly lived up to our name THE TRAVELLERS more often than not.

The Travellers go East

We were home on October 4, then on October 6th we drove to Simcoe, in southwestern Ontario near Lake Erie, for a date there. The next day, we flew to St. John's for three concerts in the Newfoundland capital, our first visit to the Island known as "The Rock". My wife had negotiated a deal and found a babysitter to care for our two children, while she joined me on this tour of Newfoundland and Nova Scotia. When we arrived at the Holiday Inn where we were staying, they gave us a welcome sign on behalf of our TV sponsor, Molson Canadian, after seeing our TV commercial after the game on *Hockey Night in Canada*.

We gave one concert at the university and another the next day at the new Concert Hall. The next day, we were on the road for a concert at Grand Falls, a town we could smell the sulphur before we get there because of their pulp and paper mill. We arrived at 4:30 for an 8:00 p.m. concert, and decided to eat first and then set up and do the concert. Ray and Joe went into the hotel dining room when it opened at 5:00 and ordered the "Special of the Day" for dinner. Greta and I followed about ten minutes later. There was no one else in the dining room, and we also ordered the Special. But the waitress said she was very sorry, but they were now out of the daily special! With no other restaurant around and no one else in the dining room, after we stopped laughing, we decided to eat something else, anything. The concert went on as planned, and we had a real "Newfie" joke to enjoy later.

After Grand Falls, we drove to Corner Brook, at the other end of the island for the last part of our Newfoundland trip. We saw a beautiful area of the country for the first time, and it was great to share it all with Greta. We also gave a memorable concert and, after the show, we flew to Nova Scotia for the next leg of our tour.

The first stop on October 11 was Antigonish on the mainland. It was not a university gig, but one for the whole community, and it was a great success. Now we dove into a series of one-nighters: Truro, followed by Digby on the north shore. In Digby, we stopped at a restaurant for a lobster dinner, and were amazed at the sight of a huge five-pound lobster in the restaurant tank. We didn't have the heart to have the giant creature killed to make a dinner for us, so we each ordered smaller ones. After dinner, we headed out to our concert. It was very interesting for The Travellers to make this Canadian tour. Our musical repertoire includes songs from every region of Canada, allowing us to perform songs that are native to each area, and Nova Scotia was no different. The audiences appreciated our including these songs in the program, and always applauded with appreciative gusto.

On October 14, we arrived in Halifax for another show, and then took a day off to be tourists in some of the nearby sights, like the area of Ecum Secum on the Eastern Shore. On October 16, we flew to Sydney on Cape Breton Island, and arrived as a black cloud hovered over the city. In Sydney, they call this day "Black Friday"— the day when the local mines were ordered closed forever by the government. We recognized the misfortune of the community, and tried to do a more upbeat show to raise their spirits. Our Nova Scotia songs and our Cape Breton tunes were well-appreciated by the audience, and the next morning we departed for home. We sang "Farewell to Nova Scotia" as this lengthy tour came to a close.

Back in Toronto, we did a concert at Sir Francis Fleming Collegiate on October 25, and a private convention at the Royal York Hotel on October 28. On October 29, we returned to Brockville, Ontario where we had started the year on January 4th, for a performance in the home city of Ontario Minister of Tourism, James Auld. this concert was set to officially be the last stop, but we had some last-minute commitments to honour. On November 1, we went to the

CBC radio department and recorded a small album of Christmas songs for a radio show to be broadcast at Christmas time. The show was called *Once in a Year*, a tribute to The Weavers who had recorded *We Wish You a Merry Christmas* sixteen years earlier.

On November 9, we went to Lakehead University for a Centennial-based program. While we were preparing to return to Toronto, we were invited by the university pub to extend our stay and perform there for five days. But I declined, telling them that my next child was due soon and I needed to get back. Our friend, guitarist Amos Garrett who is a fine musician, was in town, and we asked him to fill in for me for the week. That was the only gig I have ever missed with The Travellers, but I knew I had to get home to Greta, and I also knew that Amos would fill the bill perfectly.

The last official gig of the year was on November 24 at the University of Windsor. Similar to our first concert of the year in Brockville, we shared the bill with Catherine MacKinnon, who was again accompanied by guitarist Ted Roberts. Ted agreed to play the second half of the concert with us—and just like that, a new person joined The Travellers. Ted joined the group as a lead guitarist, official musical arranger and good friend, and has remained with The Travellers for almost forty-five years. Two days later, Kevin Gray was born on time in Toronto. a third boy to our home. Both mother and son were fine. Early in the year, we had purchased an empty lot near Bayview and Hy 401, and hired a builder to design our dream home. So, as this monumental year came to a close, it was marked by the birth of our third child, and moving into our new home.

It had been an amazing year when you consider the feats we accomplished. Several years later, our guitar player Ted Roberts, wrote a song about the British North America Act being returned to Canada in the 1980s, and he included several verses about The Travellers' tour of Canada's small towns. He said we often had to wait outside town until Bobby Gimby had left, singing his "Ca-na-da" song. He said that Bobby Gimby had been to a nasal specialist and had his horn elongated so he could play and sing CA-NA-DA.

The1967 tour should be appreciated for what The Travellers did for Canada. It has never been noted in any official federal or provincial publication, nor were The Travellers ever sent a letter of congratulation or even thanks for our huge efforts. My hope is that, after reading this memoir, someone like you will now remember. I sure do. The official record for that Centennial year of 1967 is 186 performances! Someday I'll find the time to tally up the number of miles or kilometres we travelled by car, horse and cart, airplane, helicopter, and regular airline. If you have the time, perhaps you'd like to do it after finishing this long history of Canada with The Travellers.

1968 and 1969

When 1967 ended, our group was wondering what our future looked like. Actually, we began hearing from convention bookers, as well as government bookers. There were always things happening in this country and, as we headed into 1968, it looked as if we were again going to be part of the changing history of Canada. During 1967, we had made Canadian history by the number and quality of Canadian concert appearances we had done, as well as their impact on Canadians. We recorded three record albums, did three TV specials, and made 186 concert appearances, sometimes three times in one day, often including a kids' show in the afternoon and an evening adult concert.

At home, my family moved into a new home to make room for our new member, son Kevin. (The new house had a room for one more permanent guest, so we would see.) Our new, custom-designed home is in the Bayview and York Mills area of Toronto. We will end up living there for twenty-five years, with many memories and more additional kids.

Early in January, the CBC called us to participate in a radio program. A new show called *Folk World* wanted our input about the state of folk music in Canada. We taped the show on January 26. Several days later on January 29, one of the B'nai B'rith lodges in Toronto invited me to a Sunday morning meeting to sing a program, and speak about our folk future. On February 11, I was invited by CHUM Radio to be interviewed about the past year, and about the future. It's not often that we were heard on CHUM Radio, so I gave them my experienced view that the cycle of political songs would change, and young people would be involved in global rather than local problems.

On February 15 we were asked to do a concert at Ryerson Polytechnic Institute (later to become Ryerson University) with Ian and Sylvia. It was a warm folkie evening for an upbeat audience in our home town. On March 18, CBC TV rebroadcast The Travellers' Labour Day TV special from the previous year. The next day, the group appeared at Eaton's to play at a fashion show. On March 26 we appeared at the King Edward Hotel, at a convention of North American optometrists. We had recently appeared at conventions for smaller optometry groups, and this, was finally the "big" one.

The year 1968 was an election year, so on March 27, The Travellers were invited to be the main entertainment for the Conservative Party of Canada's Convention, with Robert Stanfield being the main speaker. On April 1 we were back in the main ballroom of the Royal York Hotel to again provide entertainment for Bell Canada employees. So far, all these gigs were easy because they were in Toronto, and we didn't need to bring our own sound system or travel overnight. But soon we were on the road again. On April 4, we headed to Ottawa to provide two days of entertainment for the Liberal Party of Canada's Convention in a large arena. Several days later, on April 9, we were back in Toronto at the Inn on The Park, for a banquet meeting for McLaren Advertising.

The Savarin Tavern on Bay Street in Toronto announced the appearance of The Boss Brass, beginning April 1st for two weeks. Beginning on April 15, for the first time, also for two weeks, The Travellers would be performing, The Savarin turned out to be the very best local drawing place for us and, as a group of four or five, the financial remuneration we received was much more than we could eke out at folk clubs, as they simply didn't have the volume in patronage or revenue to pay us as much.

We were well received, and we realized it was because many folks in these new Bay Street audiences had seen us when we played at their universities, and were simply renewing their relationship with us. In fact, many people in the audience came up between sets to tell us they remembered us from their college days. During those two weeks, we also spent the afternoons recording our next album for Arc Records, finishing it all up by May 1. The album was called *The Travellers Salute Canada,* and contained songs written by Canadians Joni Mitchell, Ian and Sylvia, Gordon Lightfoot, Wade Hemsworth, Leonard Cohen, and our own Ray Woodley. We chose those songs from a new show we were preparing for that year's CNE, less than four months away. More about that later as it loomed as a big event for us.

On May 4 we returned to our roots by singing at the national convention of the Canadian wing of the United Auto Workers Union, held in the Ballroom of Toronto's Royal York Hotel. On May 7 and 8, we appeared on *In Person,* on CBC TV. Two days later, it was off to Orillia, for two nights at the Orillia Boat Show. On May 13 we headed back into the Arc Records studio for three days to record a sound track for an upcoming show at the CNE. (I'll share the details of that ground-breaking event as we get to August.) On May 24 we did a show for a Molson's salesmen meeting in Toronto. June 6, we were off to Montreal's Bonaventure Hotel to do a show for the Canadian Institute of Underwriters, then were back in Toronto the next day for a CBC radio show—part of the Ontario School Broadcasts where we sang and talked about songs of Canada. On June 10, we were still in Toronto, this time to sing at the Funeral Directors' Convention at the Royal York Hotel. We cover you coming and going!

I mentioned earlier that that was a month leading up to coming elections, so listen to where we went. On June 11 we sang in Hamilton at the Palace Theatre, an event sponsored by the Steelworkers' Union for the Hamilton NDP. Tommy Douglas was the main speaker and, later, I was sent a video copy of that event. It was certainly a big loud crowd, but on June 19 we sang at a rally for The Liberal Party of Canada at Nathan Phillips Square in front of Toronto City Hall. The elections were nigh and, on June 21 we were invited to sing at an NDP picnic at Toronto's Kew Beach. On June 23 we did a picnic for the Toronto NDP Committee, and on June 26, for the fifth year in a row, the Toronto Parks Department had us singing and leading a Hootenanny in Riverdale Park. It was always a great success because we'd performed at Hootenannies since we began fifteen years earlier. I don't think that Lightfoot or Ian and Sylvia or Anne Murray ever did Hootenannies.

During that month, we sang for all three major federal political parties, doing the same program for each—songs from and about Canadians. For July 1st that year, we were in Sudbury at the Bell Amphitheatre for a public Canada Day event. Some performers do their best work on recordings, but aren't able to live up to them at a live concert. The Travellers were the opposite. We sang to all types of audiences, to all parts of the community, and we were at our best in live public performances. That is where we truly shone.

We were soon on the road again, this time heading east, back to the Maritimes. On July 10 we were in Shediac, New Brunswick for the Lobster Festival where we did two shows per day. On July 15 we flew to St. John's, Newfoundland, for two days of shows at the new Arts and Culture Centre. Next, we stopped in PEI for the Summerside Lobster Festival where we sang between races at the race track events. That was not a great week for intimate concerts, but the food was amazing—especially the lobster!

While we were in Shediac, we were feted at the Moncton Yacht Club with a luncheon. When we showed up, we noticed that all the members were dressed in shirts and ties while we were in summer wear. With permission from the yacht club, we had invited our friend David Silverberg to come and see us as our guest. David was an ex-Montrealer, a former classmate and friend of my wife, and now the Artist Laureate of nearby Mount Allison University. He arrived with his brother, Nachem Silverberg, and another friend, David Kolokovsky. All three of them had beards down to their belt buckles; they actually looked like escapees from a Jewish shtetl in Poland! Two of The Travellers, including me, were also Jewish, and each time the Silverberg brothers were introduced, as well as David Kolokovsky, we were amused to hear the MC struggle with their names as he attempted to introduce these bearded, artistic individuals. The members at this exclusive yacht club in Moncton had never seen nor heard anything like them. We all had a good laugh at this before returning home to Toronto for a few days. My wife, Greta had also been there to watch her Montreal artist-friend Silverberg astound the yacht club. Greta has always been a great storyteller, and she tells that story to this day.

It was now July 24, and CBC Radio had invited us to Winnipeg to be on their syndicated show, *Hymn Sing*, done at the University of Manitoba. The show was called the "The Gospel According to The Travellers". Our originally all-Jewish group had performed many gospel songs in concert, as well as on our recordings, so it was easy to come up with enough gospel songs to fill out a half hour on the radio. We actually had so many it really came down to what to leave out.

The next day, July 25, we flew to Lakehead University for a concert there. On July 29 we were invited to appear at the Academy Theatre for the Kawartha Summer Festival, in Lindsay, Ontario. Next in line was that year's Mariposa Folk Festival, August 9–11. Singing for the sixth time in their eight-year history, at the Festival we had helped start, was like returning to our backyard family to show them what we'd been up to since they'd last seen us.

On August 14, we returned to Toronto. The Richmond-Adelaide Centre was officially being opened to the public, and we were asked to sing appropriate songs for an opening. That same day, Arc Records released an album of our next project—a show which would open at the CNE Grandstand on August 16 and run for two full weeks. Shows at the huge CNE Grandstand venue were usually reserved for the likes of Guy Lombardo or Bob Hope or Danny Kaye, but, since Canada's Centennial, the Grandstand shows were undergoing a change. This year the show was a review of Canada's history including a depiction of the Riel Rebellion and the building of the trans-continental railroad, all on the huge CNE Grandstand field. Howard Cable wrote and arranged the music; Don Harron wrote the lyrics. John A. Macdonald was played by Robert Christie. Catherine McKinnon sang some of the songs. The Travellers also suggested some significant songs, and sang "Farmer Is the Man", Lightfoot's "Great Canadian Railroad Trilogy", and the theme song to the production, called "Sea to Sea".

Those two weeks of daily performances made it impossible for the Travellers to do any other shows at the CNE that year. It was a huge production which included a hot-air balloon, a railroad engine, and actors and dancers who reproduced the Riel Rebellion. The Travellers sang the songs of the era, as well as those written for this huge event.

When the show ended after Labour Day on September 8th, for the tenth year, we were invited to return to Hillel House at U. of T. On September 10th, The Travellers were invited to sing at Toronto's Metropolitan Church at the memorial for Dr. Martin Luther King. This was truly a great honour for us, to be invited to help headline the event, which ended by us leading everyone in the singing of "We Shall Overcome".

On September 12 we sang at the Ryerson Theatre for a group of kids with cystic fibrosis, where we delivered our original children's show. One week later, on September 21, we returned to do a concert for Ryerson students. On September 26 we finally did two children's concerts at Toronto's St. Lawrence Centre Hall and, on October 7, CBC Radio, asked us to do a children's show on the School Radio Program. For the second time, we did a program for the Ontario Funeral Directors Association at their Toronto Convention at the Royal York Hotel.

We had been in negotiation with the CBC all summer to do the pilot for a new TV series. The show would be set in various festival locations across the country, with The Travellers performing songs that fit the appropriate festival. The pilot would be done on October 16–19, at the International Ploughing Match held, that year, in Guelph, Ontario. The TV show was to be called *Movin' On with The Travellers,* a very appropriate title. We wrote a tune for the series' theme song, and taped the pilot in colour. We were told it was "a sure thing to be picked up by CBC TV", which Arts and Entertainment writer Sid Adilman wrote in the *Toronto Star.*

But early the next year, there was a change in upper CBC management and, to our disappointment, we learned the show had not been picked up. We were left with a terrific pilot that was shown on TV to great reviews. Sid Adilman wrote that he could not fathom why they had cancelled the series. And neither could we.

After the pilot was shot, on October 25 we returned to the Maritimes, this time starting in Charlottetown. On the 26th we went to Acadia University in Wolfville, Nova Scotia for the first time. On

October 28 we recorded a TV and a radio show in Halifax, both for the CBC. We finished the tour with two concerts in Fredericton on the 29th and 30th. All the places where we had sung on our 1967 tour were now calling us back.

We returned to Toronto and, on November 8, played at the Skyline Hotel for a meeting of the Advertising Club of Toronto. On November 14 we taped a TV show called *River Inn*, hosted by singer Catherine Mackinnon. Done at CFTO for CTV it was shown in the new year. On December 1, the TV show we'd done in Winnipeg was broadcast on the CBC TV Network. On December 3, Norman Alcock, founder of the Canadian Peace Research Institute, had invited us to appear at his group's convention at the Galaxy Club in Oakville. The Travellers had long been on the pro-peace bandwagon, and one of the first three songs we ever learned was "The Strangest Dream".

Looking back on 1968, it was certainly another productive year for us. We sang for all three major political parties, and returned to some places where we'd sung before. We recorded the pilot for a TV series that almost happened, and were a part of a huge stage show at the CNE about Canadian history. We recorded two record albums and about five TV shows that were shown over the next few years. We did a lot of conventions in various places, and were still able to spend more time with our families, as many of these shows were done in and around Toronto. I also began a new sport for me, squash. A few of my close friends had begun playing squash in college, so I had lots of people to play against to learn the game. I also began to ski in the Collingwood area of Ontario, and you'll hear about that as we progress.

1969

Faced with the loss of our potential TV series, as a group we needed to decide which way we should go, and what was available to us. The first gig on the books was January 14 at the London Ontario Fairgrounds, for the United CO-OPS of Ontario. Following that, we had a return two-week engagement at the Savarin Tavern. During that gig, a reporter asked us about the TV series, and interviewed Simone about her plans. When the article from that interview appeared in the paper, we were startled to learn that Simone had told him she was about to leave the group because of the loss of the TV series. She had not mentioned this to us, and when we asked her about it, she confirmed it was true. She was leaving the group.

Over thirty years later in the year 2000, Simone was interviewed for a documentary being made about The Travellers. During that interview, she said that in 1969 The Travellers were in the process of removing her in the same manner that Sid had been removed in 1965. Sadly, Simone seemed to be suffering from loss of memory. First of all, in 1965, Sid had been voted out by the other three members of The Travellers, including her, in a vote that was supervised and documented by a lawyer. Secondly, in 1969, Simone gave an interview to a *Toronto Star* writer and said she had decided to leave the group because of the disappointment of The Travellers losing the TV series. This was news to us, but when we asked her, she confirmed it was true. So naturally at that point, we began seeking a replacement. I'll talk more about that documentary when we reach the year 2000.

Once our gig at The Savarin was over, we began searching for a replacement. Ted Roberts, who had been working occasionally with us, suggested Pam Fernie, who had sung for several years with an Ottawa folk group called The Couriers, and had recently moved to Toronto. Ted had worked with her recently in Toronto, and said she would be great. So, we tried her out, and it went well. Pam is a real pro, with good rhythm and stage presence, and her experience with the Ottawa folk group made her a good fit. Whenever a new person joins a group there is a lot of work involved to reset all the harmonies and the stage gestures, and to teach the basics of what we do, and how we do it. We had a date on April 25 for Trinity College School in Port Hope, Ontario, so we began to work on a program for that date.

In the early years, when we had had to replace someone, it wasn't a problem, but in a now well-established group with a particular sound it was much more difficult. Any group is the sum of its parts, and we knew that with Pam we were going to be different, but better suited to the changing song culture. Once people in Toronto involved in bookings heard we were now available to return to the stage, the invitations started arriving.

On May 10, I was invited by Toronto's Holy Blossom Temple Young Peoples' group to do a show of Yiddish and other songs. It went well, and we began preparation for a new season for The Travellers. The Lindsay Lions' Club invited us back for the third time on May 31 at the Academy Theatre. We were underway again. On June 8, we went to McMaster University in Hamilton to do a concert to support the Police Union's Chorus. The summer was relatively quiet, so we kept rehearsing a new sound for the group. The folk music world was changing, and the audiences were looking for new sounds. So, we were changing too.

One big summer event: on August 6, Greta gave birth to our fourth son, Michael. Maybe you were like us, hoping finally for a girl! But four of a kind is a good poker hand, so with four boys we are winners, and time will prove that!

As a group we had started to recover, and headed to Ottawa for a concert on August 25 for a convention of radio program planners at the National Arts Centre, and hosted by the CBC. We accepted a gig in Brantford for September 1st at the Graham Bell Hotel, doing three shows a night, and rounding out the new repertoire and songs. On September 8, The Canadian Union of Public Employees (CUPE) was meeting in convention at our old stomping grounds, The Royal York Hotel. This event was Pam's first test at singing all the old union songs we had grown up on. The excitement was high, and the response was truly uplifting for us. On September 18 we did a concert in London, Ontario. We'd been there many times before, and they remarked positively on the "new" sound. On September 22, we sang to an International Brewmasters' Convention. Since 1967 international convention planners had begun using Canadian venues for these events, and The Travellers filled the bill by providing true Canadian entertainment. Three days later, we were at the Skyline Hotel for a convention of Canada Packers employees. Then, on September 27 we drove to Teeswater, Ontario, for the Teeswater Agricultural Fall Fair. The next day, we were back in London on the campus of the University of Western Ontario to do a concert at Alumni Hall for the London

B'nai B'rith. October 3 found us at the Sheraton Hotel in Niagara Falls, Ontario, for the World International Convention of Patent and Trademark Lawyers Association. The event planners that booked these hotel conventions enjoyed hiring The Travellers because of our repertoire of Canadian and international songs, and because we did not require a band to back us up. We were self-contained and reliable. Then on October 21 we did another convention at the Royal York Hotel for the Association of Canadian Real Estate Boards.

November 2 was a "watershed" experience for us, as we were booked to do two children's shows at the St. Lawrence Hall that day. This was the first-ever real concert for kids in Toronto, and the reviews were superb. That same month, we did another radio show for the CBC at the Toronto Press Club. We finished up this comeback year with another week at the Savarin Tavern starting December 15. The year ahead was filled with new bookings, with a special trip planned to sing in Japan to open the Canadian Pavilion at the Osaka World's Fair. We were also scheduled to finally record an album of kids' songs, plus there were some Christmas bookings in Europe coming later in the year. 1970 looked like it was going to be another "olde tyme" Travellers' year with bookings everywhere.

There is a post script I must add to this chapter about an event that happened during 1967, the year when we sang "This Land Is Your Land" 186 times. We had word that another group called The-Brothers-in-Law, who had recorded two albums for our Arc Records partners, had also written songs for a third album in 1967, which included a parody of "This Land". Woody Guthrie's music publisher was notified that the album had been recorded, but not yet released. The publisher of "This Land" then sought a ruling to stop the release.

A Canadian Exchequer Court heard several days of testimony, and ruled against a parody of "This Land". The main evidence was that in Canada, The Travellers' recording of "This Land" was considered as sacred as an anthem, and a parody was considered similar to parodying Canada's national anthem. I actually looked that up in the pages from the Exchequer Court. The Guthrie family was not aware of the trial, nor of the judgement in their favour, but I have apprised them of what happened and will be sending them the trial minutes to be placed in the new Guthrie museum in Oklahoma. The court ordered that all copies of the recording of the parody be destroyed, and I was never able to even track down the words to that song. Several years later, the Arc studios and building was destroyed by fire, and there appear to be no copies. I did look it up recently and found the version to be there on the internet. An interesting project might be to contact the now disbanded group, The Brothers-in-Law, in Windsor, Ontario to see if they have any copies. The group was so named because they were all ex-policemen.

Very few people know of this event, nor that The Travellers' recording of "This Land Is Your Land" is considered to be sacrosanct by the Canadian courts. It's another example of our record having played a part in Canada's history. It's ironic that there have been several incidents where this song was not allowed to be part of the "best song in Canada" voting at all, whereas a Canadian court has found, and ruled, that this song is indeed part of Canadian heritage! As such, it is part of our legacy as well.

This decade of the 1960s was earth-shattering for us, and all the Canadian events we were part of. The future ahead looked to be a continuation of what we had been doing—continuing to sing at the same events as before, as well as beginning a singular series of concerts and recordings specifically for children. It'll be interesting to find out!

CHAPTER 5:
TRAVELLED IN THE MOUNTAINS, TRAVELLED DOWN IN THE VALLEYS

1970

As the new decade began, it looked again as if it would be another successful year ahead for The Travellers. On January 4, we travelled "around the world" to do two performances that night at The Bohemian Embassy in Toronto. I had sung at this local club several times myself, and listened to music and poetry as a paying guest. The next day, we taped a CBC Radio show to be broadcast later. On January 10, we appeared at a Yiddish Festival at Lawrence Park Collegiate, and the following day I appeared solo at the YMHA as part of the Toronto Jewish Music Festival. On January 14, we appeared at The Inn on the Park for a convention, and later at their banquet.

On January 18, the Alpha Omega Dental Fraternity, of which I am a member, rented out Burton Auditorium at York University to have The Travellers do a two-concert day called *The Travellers Sing for Kids*, with both houses filled to overflowing. At this point, The Travellers were the only people doing specific concerts for children. It was still some eight years before either Raffi, or Sharon, Lois and Bram appeared on the music scene. In a recording studio, we piled some mats on the floor and began a concert for children. We'd been doing these songs for so long that not much rehearsal was necessary. It was fun to look out into the audience and see my own children, along with the kids of many of our friends. They can all be seen on the album cover. The kids were so great, everyone had fun, and the album was recorded in one take.

This special recording was sponsored by "Sharky" Starkman, who had previously sponsored me back in 1961 when I appeared for him at the Labour-Zionist Camp Kvutsa on Lake Erie. Sharkey is now working for a publishing company in Boston, part of D.C. Heath

Canada. It was recorded for Caedmon Records, a company more used to recording talking books and Shakespearean plays. We were short a couple of songs, so the next day we returned to the studio and recorded three more songs.

Dodi Robb, a children's music producer at CBC Radio, wrote in her liner notes: "When The Travellers do a concert for kids, they sing songs and tell stories, too. and for once, you don't have to do the telling. Of course, I'm sure your child won't mind if you stay around and listen and he might like it if you took a minute to sing along with The Travellers, too."

The Travellers Sing for Kids was Canada's first live concert recording for children

The reviews of this new recording were excellent, and we began accepting many bookings for children's concerts. When Ray Woodley joined The Travellers, I knew he had the ability to sing some of our kids' songs. But on this record, he came into his own with his version of "The Foolish Frog" and "B-I-N-G-O", and the kids were mesmerized by his ability to sing the story. Joe Hampson also had a natural ability to sing a story easily, and Pam Fernie learned on the job. By the time we made this recording, we were more than ready to record the songs that had been proven on concert stages for the past ten years.

January 19 found us back at the Savarin for two weeks, still trying new songs with Pam and updating many of the old ones. From the number of times The Travellers had appeared at the Savarin, it was obvious we were attracting the volume of business needed for them to hire our five-piece band for two weeks. It was Jewish Music Month, so we sneaked off one afternoon to do a concert at the Adath Israel synagogue. In early February, we were back on the road for three days in Espanola, Ontario, playing at a winter carnival. The legendary play-by-play hockey announcer, Foster Hewitt was the emcee host, and the audience received a resume-type summary from him of The Travellers' historic appearances. Foster Hewitt's comments about the show were, "They shot, and they scored!"

After a few days home in Toronto, on February 12 we headed to Ottawa's Skyline Hotel and appeared at a banquet sponsored by the Canadian Government Travel Bureau, for whom we had done many appearances over the years.

Back when we had appeared at Expo 67 in Montreal, we spoke to Patrick Reid who was slated to be heading up the Canadian Pavilion at Expo 70 in Osaka Japan. Patrick decided The Travellers would be perfect to open the Canadian Pavilion's showcase area by appearing there for the first three weeks. Our start date was March 15—cherry blossom time in Japan and it was supposed to be warm. But it snowed those first two weeks, so Pam Fernie had to wear her Canadian fur coat at every appearance. Her coat added a great appearance factor, as we performed three shows per day including an eight-verse folksong, in Japanese, at every performance. It turned out that the Canadian

Pavilion was one of the most popular venues on the site, so when the Japanese Emperor paid us a visit, we did a command performance!

Expo '70 World's Fair, Osaka, Japan, 1970

Also performing at the Canadian Pavilion for a week was a choir from Collingwood, Ontario. The leader was John Kirby, whom we'd met at Collingwood High School back in 1966 and '67. The coincidences kept coming, and we met John Kirby again later when we were invited to sing at a public school near Collingwood. At that time, we learned that he had become principal of the school.

Representing Canada in Japan was both uplifting and educational for us, as we toured the country on our days off. Patrick Reid later sent us a plaque thanking us for our "great work in the first month of EXPO 70".

We were on a twenty-one-day plane ticket with three days left, and Joe Hampson and I had both brought our wives along. So, on our way home, we stopped off in Hawaii to rid ourselves from the cold of Osaka. As soon as we arrived, Joe rented a raft for our three days in Honolulu. Being a very pale person, he returned home with second-degree burns from lying on that raft in the sun for 3 days. (Everyone else had been smart enough to not do as Joe did.)

After a few days of rest and reconnecting with our families, on April 12 we were off to Wiarton, Ontario, north of Owen Sound, to do an Easter Seal benefit show for CBC Radio. On May 9, we appeared at Toronto City Hall for "Pollution Probe", an early group investigating pollution on our planet. On May 14, we were back at The Inn on the Park where once again we provided the keynote musical entertainment at a convention.

It was May 30, and, where do you think we were performing? Why, we were back in Charlottetown, PEI! Jack McAndrew, a former CBC announcer in the Maritimes, was now head of the Charlottetown Theatre and kept inviting us to return, to our great pleasure both financially and gastronomically—because of the lobster. Then something funny happened. PEI's new provincial premier had instructed the police to watch out for out-of-province hippies who might be hanging out on the beaches or piers. With lobsters on our minds, Jack had sent us to the pier to pick up some fresh ones. Suddenly, some RCMP officers approached us and asked us what we were doing on the pier. They were obviously looking for "mainland hippies" who fit our description. A quick call to the theatre verified our identities and our presence. That night at the evening concert, we told this story to great laughter from the audience, and with some embarrassment to the new premier.

Back in Toronto, I had a solo booking on August 7, but I have no record for whom or for what organization. If someone accuses me of a crime on August 7, 1970, it couldn't be me as I know I was singing somewhere!

On August 25, we were back in Winnipeg at the Centennial Concert Hall doing a program for the Boy Scouts of Canada. Unlike a well-known American politician, Trump, in 2017, we avoided any political commentary. It was just a fun afternoon of singing along, with no politics.

Whenever we had no gigs for a while, we would get another call from The Savarin, this time for September 7–21. Singing there was always a great opportunity to rehearse on stage, and get paid for it. The only problem with working in a bar is that smoking was still allowed then, so after each gig we went home reeking from cigarette smoke and beer. We had to have our clothes cleaned often. Each evening, I hung up my smoke-filled clothes in the garage.

The day after we finished at the Savarin, we did a performance at the Park Plaza Hotel, and who was it for? The Ontario Brewers' retail stores! We made enough money to get our clothes cleaned again, but we also had some new songs ready for performance.

At that time, Canadian folk singer Ian Tyson had a new half-hour show on CTV called *Nashville North*, and on October 8 we joined him as his guests. His wife Sylvia was also there, along with their band The Great Speckled Bird. We did some songs along with Ian, and some by ourselves. Ian had always wanted to be a true country singer, so it was good to see him fulfilling his dream of hosting a Nashville-type of show. He ended up living on his ranch near Calgary, singing cowboy songs, and recording albums in Nashville.

It was November 1, and we were back at the St. Lawrence Centre for the Arts doing two children's concerts in one day. Some of those kids went home very happy, as their parents bought some of the kids' LPs we offered after the show.

The next day, we were invited to do a performance at the Rosedale Golf Club, a place I had never performed before, and doubt I'll ever do again. The event was a dinner for Consumers Glass Company executives. It was still 1970 and, by design, the Rosedale Golf Club had no Jewish members. At the same time, the Granite Club, another private Toronto club, had about three Jewish members—a change from when we had performed there earlier. The Travellers were invited to sing at the Granite Club to an international group of orthopaedic surgeons. The two individuals who hired us to be the entertainment were from the Toronto chapter of The Great Lakes Orthopaedics Society, and I happened to know them. Being Jewish themselves, they were well aware that The Travellers were originally an all-Jewish group, yet they hired us to appear at the Granite Club anyway.

Marvin Tile is an Order of Canada recipient for his innovative work on hip replacement surgery, and Irv Grosfield was head of orthopaedics at a Scarborough hospital for many years. When we took the stage, the two of them stood near the door watching us perform our first song—our version of "Go Tell It on the Mountain", in which the chorus repeats many times, "Let My People Go". They both burst out laughing. They still talk about that night, but there were no questions from the people at the Granite Club. I have since performed there many times, and I know their membership policy has obviously changed. Maybe we had something to do with it.

That year, the Grey Cup game was being played in Toronto on November 27, and the Cup Committee hired us to sing at the banquet the night before the game. In addition, we took part in the Miss Grey Cup presentation in a live ceremony and radio show from the Royal York Hotel. Even the sports crowd knew about The Travellers!

We Travel to Europe and Sing for Canadian Peacekeepers

There had been talk of The Travellers being part of a CBC Radio group that had started in 1967 to visit Canadian Peacekeeping militia serving around the world. This year, we were invited to join this performing group.

On December 7, we all assembled in Trenton, Ontario to board a military flight that would take us to Lahr, Germany, and then on to Nicosia, Cyprus for a one-week tour. The show would be taped by CBC Radio, and then broadcast on Christmas Day. Canadian comedy legend, Gordie Tapp, would be the MC. He would interview some of the soldiers and play their responses to audiences back home. In Lahr, we had a marvellous time doing four shows for both American and Canadian troops. In Nicosia, we did one show in an old Roman amphitheatre, and then we did a performance for kids in an orphanage. The CBC thought our performances, which included songs from all over Canada, was very effective in bringing a bit of Canada to these troops serving so far from home at that time of year. The Canadian Army also sent us a letter, thanking us, and lauding the Canadian musical Christmas cheer we had brought to the troops.

While on Cyprus, we were invited to have dinner at a hilltop restaurant outside of Nicosia, on the Greek side of the island. The only way to get to the restaurant was to ride up the hill by mule. I have an aversion to riding animals, and the mule I was on ran away, so I walked up. All the way, I could smell unplowed mule dung. When we got there, we ordered dinner, and then we saw some young men near us who began throwing their plates into the fireplace. We had heard this was a popular local practice, so, when we finished eating, we also threw our plates into the fireplace. We were instantly surrounded by three locals sitting near us, and some of the staff. They knew no English, and we knew no Greek, but somehow, they managed to convey to us that if you want to throw plates, you have to order special cheaper plates. Which of course we had not done. As quickly as we were surrounded, The Travellers all stood up. We were fortunate that Joe, Ted, and Ray are all over six feet tall—and towered over all the Greeks. We apologized as best we could, left a large tip, and quickly exited before sparking an international incident!

The Travellers perform for children, Cyprus, 1970

While in Nicosia, we stayed at the beautiful Leidra Palace Hotel, filmed two concerts for a CBC film celebrating one hundred years of the Canadian Army, and spent the rest of the time lounging around the pool. It ended up as a paid vacation, but we still did a good job singing with, and for, our Canadian peacekeeping forces and at an orphanage for children.

I often summarize the events at the end of year. Between 1960 and 1970, The Travellers were represented on several committees trying to get recognition for Canadian recordings. The Travellers were the example: In 1960, we had already recorded three LPs, with no national recognition, and by the end of the 1960s, the group had recorded seventeen LPs, again with no organization standing behind them to recognize their contributions and accomplishments.

The Junos began in 1970 and, in 1971 when The Travellers recorded their LP, *The Travellers Sing for Kids*, we submitted a bona fide nomination for that LP to be considered. We got a letter back from the board saying that, since there were no other nominations for best children's recording, a Juno would not be offered.

Two years later in 1973, when a new category for Children's Recordings was established, we again submitted *The Travellers Sing for Kids*. This time we got a letter back explaining that because that album had not been recorded in the present year of 1973, it was therefore, again, rejected. My relationship with the Juno Awards committee has never been great, and The Travellers have never been recognized by that body as a "builder", or of any the other categories necessary for mention in their Hall of Fame.

As 1970 wound to a close, it ended another year— among all the preceding years—of un-recognition by the Junos, However, at least we got R-E-S-P-E-C-T from the press and from all our audiences, including the kids.

1971

After a relatively quiet year, including the changeover from Simone to Pam Fernie, it looked like 1971 was going to have some more interesting performances. The previous year, we'd done a recording for the CBC, and it seemed the contract between it and the Toronto Musicians' Union had some unused funds, so the CBC said they'd like to have The Travellers do a new recording using a string orchestra and a whole new selection of songs, with a musical director to run the recording. Over the years we had made many shoestring recordings, but this was the first time we would have an orchestra behind us. CBC's David Bird, an accomplished musical director, was at the helm, and it was truly something special for us. This would be the first time we would be recording an album with none of The Travellers playing a single note!

CBC LP with orchestral backing

I really want to share some of those new songs, and some of the reviews by jazz music Critic, Gene Lees: We did Bruce Cockburn's "Goin' to the Country", and Pam Fernie sang Judy Collins' song, "My Father" and Joni Mitchell's song, "Morning Morgantown". Gene Lees called her singing "a heartwarming experience." I sang Tom Lehrer's "Pollution" and also Gordon Lightfoot's "If You Could Read My Mind". Joe Hampson sang his own song, "Talk About Peace" and also the theme song for our cancelled TV pilot, "We're Movin' On". Joe and Pam did a country standard, "Silver Threads and Golden Needles"; the whole group did Jimmy Webb's "MacArthur Park", as well as Peter, Paul and Mary's song, "The Song is Love". This album was the best recording we ever made.

Shortly afterwards, Dave Bird left the CBC, and started a new company called Kanata Records. He then bought the rights to our record, *The Travellers*, from the CBC.[12] After the CBC had finished the recording, they submitted it for a Juno Award, but can you guess? They refused to enter it, because it had been recorded by the CBC! What? Is that a valid reason? Once the recording had been subsequently purchased by Kanata Records, I submitted it again to the Juno Committee, and it was again refused entry. This time, they did not bother to even give a reason. I think no further words are required. The actions of the people on that Juno Committee speak for themselves. But the songs we did on that recording were the basis for our programming for the next twenty years, for we were now appealing to a whole new generation of fans.

Now let's look ahead to 1971 which looked like the busiest year for us in the past five years. In early January, we were invited to perform in Huntsville, Ontario at the first Muskoka Winter Festival. The main street of town, Highway 11, had been flooded and frozen into a rink, and people were invited to skate up and down the main street. We did several concerts in the arena and, on January 22 and 23, performed both adult and children's concerts. Almost frozen solid from our gig in the cold arena, we returned the next day to the Royal York Hotel to sing for the Canadian Construction Association banquet. One week later, we were at the O'Keefe Centre taping a concert for the Canadian Heart Association—always a worthy cause to sing out for. The next day, we were at the Seaway Hotel on the Lakeshore (now gone) for Golden Foods. I told you it was going to be a busy year!

On February 5, we recorded a radio and TV commercial for Firestone Tires, a commercial which ran for about six months. On Valentine's Day, we appeared at the St. Lawrence Centre for two afternoon kids' shows, with those wonderful kids following our

---

[12] This LP was reissued as a CD in 2000.

requests exactly. Four days later, we were in London for a convention gig for London Life. We returned to Toronto that night and, the next day, I headed in the other direction to Oshawa to do a concert/lecture at Eastdale Collegiate for their University Women's group. After several days off, on February 19, I did a solo gig for the Beth Tikvah Synagogue for the United Jewish Appeal (UJA), Toronto.

We took a month off to do what we wanted, and then from March 29 to April 10, we were at the Town and Country Restaurant, doing three shows a night. It was much like the Savarin except they have food instead of drinks. One perk was that we got a meal every night. On two afternoons, we were invited to sing at two employee awards' luncheons on April 6 and 7 at Molson's headquarters on the Lakeshore.

There must have been another election coming up, because on April 2 we headed to Ottawa to appear at the NDP leadership convention, once again with Pierre Berton as the main speaker. Then after a full week off, on May Day we travelled to Cold Lake, Alberta, to tape a radio show for the Canadian Forces. Cold Lake is right on the Saskatchewan-Alberta border, and is a prime site for the Canadian Air Force. I have a picture of me at the controls of a Canadian Air Force jet. They never gave me the key, but I still have the photo. Singing for our forces that come from all over Canada was an easy and fun show for us to do.

Mid-May found us back at The Inn on the Park singing at a banquet for the Canadian Booksellers Association. On June 6, we were at the Ontario Science Centre for the Canadian Manufacturers' convention. We later received a lovely letter from them congratulating us for "an amazing performance". We hadn't been on a plane for a while, so on June 11 we flew to Thomson, Manitoba for both an adult show and a kids' show in the Steelworkers of Canada union hall. I guess word about our prowess with kids' shows had been getting around— even in the north Manitoba tundra.

On June 18, we appeared in Orillia's Geneva Park Centre for the Canadian Woodworkers' Union. It was the first time we performed for this small union group, and I don't think we ever sang for them again.

June 29, we were at the CBC to tape *The Weekend Show*, a local TV show.

I said earlier that we had not been on a plane much during that year. But that situation all changed when the Canadian Armed Forces asked us to appear on another film about the army, to be shot in Cyprus and Lahr, Germany during the summer. It was later broadcast on Armistice Day, November 11, but I never got to see that film either. That'll be my next project—to track down all the missing films we did. While in Germany, we had time to tour in the Lahr, Schvartsvald area, and again through to Cyprus.

Through his wife, Joe Hampson had relatives who lived in France and, as we were nearby, he asked that I make a call so he could speak to them. Now Joe is unilingual, speaking only American English. I can speak a little French and some German, which is very close to my Yiddish. Here's the picture: I was in a German pub in Lahr and, using my limited German. I got through to a French operator, who put me through to Joe's relatives. These relatives spoke only French and Yiddish and no English at all. So, for ten minutes in a German pub, I was going back and forth in Yiddish and French and translating it into to American English for Joe who was standing beside me. It was a strange scene, with the German publicans (I'm sure) wondering what the hell I was doing.

July 12 found us back in Toronto and doing the CBC TV's *Drop In* show. I guess we were always able to drop in. We then went to London, Ontario for several days with Rich Little at the Hotel London, in order to advertise a new product—two shows each day, July 21 and 22. I returned to Toronto that night, as July 23 is Greta's birthday and I didn't want to miss it.

When the Travellers were invited to appear in Halifax and PEI in late July, I saw a great opportunity to visit the Maritimes with my family. So, I loaded up our station wagon with my wife and four children and all our stuff. After the long drive, the group appeared first on July 26 at Dalhousie University at the Halifax Festival of the Arts— always a great place to perform. Then we took the ferry to PEI. (In 1971, they were still only talking about building a bridge.) Our Charlottetown deal was that we would sing at the Cabaret Pub from

Monday thru Friday, and Sunday night we would do a full concert on the theatre stage. Singing at the pub gave us time to rehearse the songs for the concert, which would be recorded by CBC Radio for broadcast later in the year. I was given a pristine tape of the show as a keepsake, and as I still have it, it's easy to say it was the best concert we ever did. After all, we'd been rehearsing it every day the previous week in the pub!

During the week, I visited beaches on the island with Greta and the boys, and enjoyed a long-awaited family vacation. After staying an extra day, we packed our belongings and memories and left on a 6:00 a.m. ferry for the mainland, and the long drive home. We took our time, for we had planned to sleep over in Quebec City. But when we arrived, there were no hotel rooms available, so we continued on to Montreal, arriving at about 9:00 p.m. A trade show had just opened in Montreal, so there were no rooms available there either. Then someone said we could get a room in Kingston. If we were sleeping in Kingston, I figured, I might as well go right on to Toronto. We ordered coffee, and I kept driving with the kids asleep in the car, bypassing Kingston. I was the only driver, and I made it in twenty-four straight hours of driving. It wasn't by choice, but I was known to do things like that when necessary. It would not be my last twenty-four-hour drive.

In mid-August, we sang at the Royal York Hotel for the Canadian Farm Equipment Dealers, followed by a slow time until after Labour Day. In late September, we headed ninety minutes north to perform at the Lindsay Fall Fair. We'd sung in Lindsay many times, and there were a lot of old friends present. September 29 found us in a CBC Radio studio to record an extended play disc with four Christmas songs on it. Doug Riley and Peter Appleyard were on this seasonal disc. I do have copies of that, which I use in Christmas lecture/shows.

On October 4, 5 and 6 we did some private afternoon concerts for a Toronto advertising agency. It was an easy gig because it was local. We didn't have to put up or strike our sound system, and I was home in the evenings. On October 17, we sang at an NDP election rally with the audience in a festive mood, and two days later we were at a similar NDP rally in Hamilton. We had recently done a lot of work for the Canadian Armed Forces, so they asked if we would do a singing tour of some bases in the north. We agreed, and on November 10 we flew to Timmins to sing at three air force bases: one in Timmins, one at Ramore near Timmins, a NORAD Base, and then in Chibougamou, in Quebec. I love that last name! We sang for them as a pre-Christmas pickup for these servicemen in remote areas. We were very happy that the military thought so much of our programs to invite us to entertain the troops. And we were happy to sing, and to see their smiles.

As the Christmas season approached, on November 29, we did a children's Christmas Carnival appearance at a Toronto store. Earlier that year, we'd done a singing commercial for Firestone Tires and they had enjoyed what we did. So, they invited us to sing at their company Christmas party in early December, in Hamilton. We could do a concert for any type of event. To close the year, Kanata records, who had purchased our CBC recording, had a record-signing event on December 17 in a Waterloo shopping mall as the last official event of the year.

That was a very busy year for us with over sixty appearances, some repeats, and a lot of new events. We already had some events booked for next year, so stay tuned.

1972

At first, it looked like this year would not be as busy as the previous one, but sometimes things happen to change our minds. January was always Jewish Music Month in Toronto, and The Travellers appeared at the Adath Israel Synagogue to do a program of appropriate songs, as we'd done on five different occasions. It was always a welcome stop on our schedule.

Soon afterwards, we were contacted by the Canadian Federal Department of External Affairs, who asked if we would travel and perform on their behalf in Panama at a meeting of the Pan-American Nations Conference. We were told to bring our own sound equipment because they were not sure if Panama would be able to provide adequate sound reproduction. We left Canada on the morning of Friday March 15 and changed planes in Miami to arrive in Panama late in the afternoon. We were sponsored by the Government of Canada, but would sing at the Saturday evening dinner as the guests of all the nations. We took the stage and did an international program of songs singing in French, Spanish and English, including "Guantanamera" in Spanish. The Travellers have always done well by getting the feel of their audiences with little knowledge of Canada, as well as showing them what our culture was all about.

We received a very nice thank-you from the Canadian Government saying all the nations present enjoyed our program. There are few groups that have the experience of singing folk songs in the many languages of such a disparate audience group, and also singing about Canada.

On March 17, we left for Miami and headed back to Toronto with all our sound equipment and instruments. At that time, Panama was infamous as a key transition point for drugs entering North America. So, when we arrived back at Pearson Airport in Toronto, we ran into problems. The customs crew began taking apart our sound equipment and looking for drugs. I recognized one of them as someone I'd known years ago, and I told him The Travellers were the straightest group ever regarding drugs, and we were in Panama as official Government of Canada representatives. He called, and then told his crew to reassemble all our sound equipment. We were told that it would take several hours.

I told them to reassemble everything, and I would be back the next day to pick it all up. I was reminded of the Mel Brooks movie, *Blazing Saddles*, when a Black family wanted to ride a trail blocked by an Indian chief, played by Mel Brooks, and he let them go through with the Yiddish words, "Loz im Gayn" which means, "Let him go." I was able to find a little humour here at the end of a very special trip to Panama, for Canada, and for The Travellers. To be asked to represent Canada at such an important meeting told us that the government had enough faith in our ability to do a good job. It was truly heartening to know how well we were regarded by Ottawa.

One week later, we boarded a flight to Winnipeg to tape a CBC radio special called, *Talk About Peace: The Gospel According to The Travellers*. We had sung many songs of peace, freedom and brotherhood at many gatherings, so our problem was not deciding what songs to include, but what songs to leave out, because we had so many: "Go Tell It on The Mountain", "We Shall Overcome", "Paul and Silas", "The Strangest Dream", and Joe Hampson's song, "Talk About Peace" were some of those we chose. I have an audio recording of this ground-breaking radio show from the CBC.

Our drummer, Don Vickery's wife, Fay Olson, was in the Canadian advertising business. She hired The Travellers to join Rich Little on a tour of Ontario in order to publicize products to select private audiences. We were there to entertain the audiences with our now patented program of "Canadiana" songs. This tour ran for most of the month of May. We opened in Ottawa for appearances on May 1, 2, and 3, but Rich Little was not available so they used comedian Pat Paulsen instead. On May 4, we were in Kingston for two shows, and there we were joined by Rich Little. The tour carried on with appearances in Peterborough, Sudbury, Sault Ste Marie and Windsor—most appearances two shows a day, and all with Rich Little.

The tour would end with three days at the Royal York Hotel Ballroom in Toronto, but when we showed up, we learned that Rich Little would not be there, and in his place, they had hired an "up-and-coming" comedian. When we went backstage into the Green Room we came face to face with the legendary Jack Benny! He then told us he'd be with us for the final three days of the tour in Toronto, May 22, 23 and 24. Between shows, we had a photographer come to capture a photo of The Travellers with Jack Benny. He was professional, humorous, and obviously nearing the end of his career, as two years later in December of 1974, he passed away. Our three days with Jack Benny definitely go into our bio, as well as onto our list of firsts!

Backstage with Jack Benny, Toronto, 1972

It was quite the tour! We visited communities where we had sung before and we were reunited with old friends. We had definitely earned some time off. For me, personally, it was an opportunity to share the stage with a legend, Jack Benny. This was an easy tour with the near distances for travel and many familiar faces and places. The bonus was that a tour company crew took care of all the travel, on-stage expenses, and set up. It also provided some extra money for some needed work on my house.

Our home was built on a large pie-shaped lot, with a wide backyard and many elm trees. That year, all the elm trees had to come down because of the danger of Dutch elm disease spreading. After all the diseased trees were removed, we were left with a vacant backyard. I thought we might put in a pool. But when I surveyed and measured the land myself, I found we had one of the few places in suburban Toronto that could contain a tennis court! So, I used some of the money from the Rich Little tour to pay for the court and a fence. Later that year, I myself built a wide viewing and entertainment deck attached to the house, in order to view the tennis court.

I also wondered about putting in court lights. Since we couldn't get a truck in to change the bulbs when needed, I had a firm install TV towers which could be climbed, and my electrician friend, Marty Kane, could climb the towers when it was necessary to change the bulbs. This tennis court and deck became the place to be—for us, our kids and their friends, and also for many of our personal friends. Over the years, Sam Sniderman, (the Record Man) and Alan Eagleson would come as guests, as would all of our close friends and our kids' friends. The Gray backyard became an inviting destination for the next twenty years.

During that year, there were a number of other "firsts", which soon followed. Our drummer, Don Vickery, was an instructor member of the drum section in the jazz program at Humber College in Toronto. The Travellers were invited to sing for their Faculty of Music program at Humber on June 13—a peer review performance.

June 20 was the opening weekend of the Ontario Place Forum, a circular stage that rotated once per hour during performances. The Travellers were selected to perform for the three-day opening weekend. This was indeed an honour and another first. Two weeks later on July 5, the group was invited to do another concert-in-the-round at Ontario Place. The director of the Forum was Drew Crossan, an ex-CBC TV producer who, during the early golden era of TV in the 1950s and '60s, had used The Travellers on many shows like *Pick the Stars*. He used the group many times again after that opening weekend at Ontario Place. We worked well on many shows for Drew, and neither he, nor the Travellers ever forgot our long common history.

Ontario Place Forum, Toronto, 1972

On August 6 and 7, The Travellers were invited to the National Arts Centre in Ottawa, as a part of *Summerfest.* It was a two-night gig that included sharing the stage with Sergio Mendes and Brazil '72. A quiet September was followed by a date on October 6 at Toronto's Sheraton Hotel for our third performance at the National Convention of the Canadian Dental Association. Clearly, my dental community friends must have enjoyed our previous appearances, as they kept inviting us back.

It was election time again, and October 16 found us performing at Maple Leaf Gardens in Toronto at a Liberal Party rally for Pierre Trudeau—in front of 22,000 people! We were on with the band Crowbar, and we closed the rally with "This Land Is Your Land". Truly an historic event for all!

On October 23, 24 and 25, CFTO hosted the final program of the song contest called, *I Can Hear Canada Singing*. Ted Roberts, our guitar player, had written one of the contending songs called "Something I Love About This Land", and we sang it as a part of the contest. We were very proud when Ted's song finished second, and the show was aired on December 5.

Then another first came to The Travellers on December 6. Johnny Cash had done a concert for inmates at an American jail, Folsom Prison, but no performer in Canada had ever done anything like that. But during the summer, I received a letter from an inmate at the Collins Bay Penitentiary in Kingston asking if The Travellers would consider coming at Christmas to entertain the inmates, similar to what we had previously done for servicemen.

Ken Dalziel, from CBC Radio, had been booking Christmas trips overseas to entertain Canadian servicemen. But then he told me that, due to budget issues, this year there would be no trips abroad. When I suggested it might be interesting, and within the budget, to make a trip to one of the Kingston penitentiaries, he began to consider it. Not long after, he called to invite The Travellers to take part in a Christmas show at Collins Bay Prison. With us would be Miss Canada, and singer Catherine MacKinnon, along with an appropriate accompanying band. So, instead of taking a bus to CFB Trenton, Ontario, the jumping off point for the RCAF to fly us overseas, the bus took us to Collins Bay Prison just outside Kingston.

For those of us who had never been inside a prison, it was quite an education. After passing through two sets of gates to get inside, we accompanied the crew as they set up the sound for the concert, as well as for the radio recording. We then had a run-through for the show. The other musicians had also been on these touring shows, and when the rehearsal was over, the warden took us to dinner in the mess hall with all the inmates. During dinner, the warden made his announcement to everyone about the Christmas show that evening around 7:00 p.m. He said that he expected them all to enjoy it, and maybe meet the entertainers after the show.

The concert went off without a hitch and was well received and appreciated. I have an audio tape of this concert that was broadcast on

Christmas Day across the CBC Radio network. We left around 9:00 p.m. to return by bus to Toronto. We had an extra passenger both ways on the bus. One of my closest friends and classmates, Dr. Marvin Kopel, said he'd like to go with us, if he could get clearance. That was no problem, so he sat in the audience and spoke to the inmates before the performance. One person he sat with told him he was in prison because, several years ago, he had been convicted of killing his wife and two children. He said he had no memory of doing it, but knows that he must have. It led to some sobering thoughts on the bus ride home, about life in prison, and how much good we had done by doing this show, both for the inmates and the guards, as well as for ourselves. I think that this was another "first" for Canada—for a group to do a live concert in a high-security federal prison.

The next day, we were booked in a new place for two weeks— the Royal York Hotel's Imperial Dining Room—to do two shows per night for the dining patrons. Wendy Michener, a *Toronto Star* artist and columnist, made a caricature drawing of the four Travellers, which was used in all the publicity in the papers. I treasure this drawing because she seemed to capture us so well. We were performing every evening, but CTV called us to see if we were free on one of the days to tape *The Ian Tyson Show* again. So, midway through the first week, on December 11, we spent the day out at CFTO, and then headed back downtown to the Royal York for our two evening shows.

The year was almost over, but we found time to book the 900-seat Seneca College Concert Hall for two kids' shows on Sunday afternoon, December 17. We entertained two full audiences—that's 1,800 kids and parents—in a typical Travellers' children's show. With smiles on both the kids' faces and on ours, we bid goodbye to another year with a lot of "firsts": Going to Panama, taping a Gospel Show in Winnipeg, a two-week tour of Ontario with Rich Little and Jack Benny, opening the Ontario Place Forum, singing at a rally for Pierre Trudeau at Maple Leaf Gardens, and doing the first concert and radio broadcast from a Canadian Prison. WOW! What a year. Hope we can duplicate it next year in 1973.

Meanwhile, we had been assessing the songs we did in our concerts, and making changes. People were used to us singing the early

Canadian and Newfoundland songs, like "The Black Fly Song" and "I'se the B'y", but we needed to update our songs as we updated our image. We had appeared at Charlottetown again, and rehearsed an almost entirely new repertoire while appearing at the theatre nightclub for a week. Here was part of our new line up:

- "Up on Cripple Creek" from The Band
- "Read My Mind", Gordon Lightfoot
- "Leavin' on a Jet Plane",
- "Early Morning Rain", Gordon Lightfoot
- "United We Stand" from Brotherhood of Man, written by Tony Hiller & Peter Simons
- "My Father", Judy Collins
- "MacArthur Park", Jimmy Webb
- "I Shall Be Released" and "Fire and Rain" by James Taylor

These new songs were a change from our early years. They were up to date, and had a positive impact on our continuing and long-term future.

1973 – The Twentieth Year of the Travellers

Because of everything that had happened in 1972, I was still tired going into '73. So, after finishing in 1972, Greta and I and the boys drove north of Toronto to ski in Collingwood, for about thirteen days. We are a skiing family. With four boys of all different ages, we had to make a choice of either enrolling each son into four different, time-consuming individual hockey programs, or trying something else. So, we began skiing, purchased a ski cabin in Collingwood, and we skied together for all their growing-up years, and beyond. It was a great decision, and we always enjoyed our four-season place in Collingwood.

At the beginning of the year, it looked like we would have some concerts as well as a few radio shows. We started on January 19 with a benefit concert for the Canadian Cancer Society at The Inn on the Park. We'd done benefit shows for many groups and societies as part of our commitment to the life of Toronto, and we rarely said no. On February 17, we agreed to be part of a new CBC TV show called *Drop In*. In early May, we returned to Winnipeg to tape another edition of the *Hymn Sing* shows. We continued on to Calgary for a May 21–23 date at a Calgary night club, three shows per night, followed the next day with a concert in Vancouver. This book began with events that happened on October 3, 1973, when all my friends feted me with a bus ride around Toronto and a show about my hectic life to mark my fortieth birthday and the twentieth year of The Travellers.

Here's what else happened that year.

It was May 28, and, guess where we flew to again? Why, it was Charlottetown to do another concert at the theatre we had opened with a Command Performance back in 1964. It was now a quick return flight to Toronto for the next day's gig at the Sheraton Hotel for an international convention group.

Murphy the Molar

On June 15, we recorded two thirty-second commercials for the Ontario Government. Here's how it happened. Sam Green was a Toronto dentist working for the Toronto Department of Health. Sam met with some Ryerson students, and then talked their Radio and Television Arts faculty into producing a short, animated film about dental health. They put it into two singing commercials called *Murphy the Molar*. Sam then asked me and The Travellers to sing the commercials. I did the pilot myself, and later the whole group came to the studio to record it with me. These commercials ran for about twenty years—the first one advising you to brush your teeth every day, and the second one as an instruction to wear a mouth guard when playing hockey. I was the voice of the singing tooth, dressed like a Beaver, who gave the instructions. You can still see these commercials on YouTube, just by requesting *Murphy the Molar*. This was called a public service announcement, intended to fill in time when the network had a gap between shows. The audio was recorded at a Toronto studio in less than an hour, and we were not paid, nor did we ask to be.

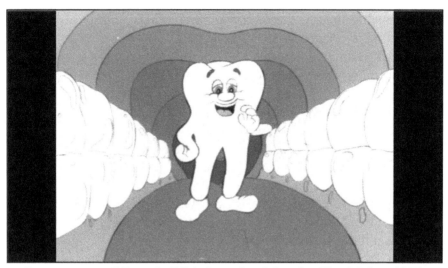

Government of Ontario PSA featuring Murphy The Molar, 1973

On June 22, we sang for another international convention at the Sheraton Hotel in Toronto, and we noticed that this new venue seemed to be taking some of the events we used to do at the Royal York. On July 21–23 we recorded three kids' radio shows for the CBC. After that, we were asked to fly to Vancouver and record two TV shows with The Irish Rovers. They had previously recorded in Calgary, but had all moved to Vancouver to do these shows. After a short break, we were back in a Toronto studio on August 17 to record a commercial for the United Way Appeal's Toronto fall campaign. They insisted we be paid the union scale fee for our work, and I believe we donated that fee back to the United Way.

The next day, we were back in a CBC recording studio to record an EP of four Christmas songs, and we were joined by veteran musician Peter Appleyard. (An EP is an extended play record of four songs, two on each side.) This EP was called *We Wish You A Merry Christmas*, and included an Italian carol along with three others, as part of the CBC's Christmas programming. I managed to get several copies, which are in my collection of memorabilia.

Now it was October 3, 1973, my fortieth birthday. In the introduction to this book, I recounted the events that happened that day. As well as being my fortieth birthday, it was the twentieth anniversary of my years with the Travellers. A landmark year—all marked so wonderfully by my friends with the bus ride around town, and a show about my hectic life.

Once again on November 3, we leased the auditorium at Seneca College for two afternoon kids' concerts with at least nine hundred kids for each concert. In addition to the ticket sales, we sold hundreds of copies of our *Sing for Kids* album. At this point in time, there was still no one else in Canada doing kids' concerts or making recordings for children.

You may remember the story of how, back in1963 for some unknown reason, The Travellers were turned back at the U.S. border. Since then, we entered the U.S. about ten times, with no problems. In 1973, we were asked by the Canadian Government Travel Bureau to represent Canada at an international travel meeting in Atlantic City. Mid-November is not a great time to visit Atlantic City, and at that time there weren't any casinos there. But we sold Canada from the stage with a bevy of Canadian songs and entertainment which, we heard later, appeared to have made a big increase in the next year's travel to Canada. The good news for us was that we never heard anything further about difficulties in travelling to the U.S. or being denied entry.

On November 21, we were part of an entertainment at the Royal York Hotel for the Toronto Musicians' Association's Christmas dance. It's always nice to be appreciated by your peers, and we were truly honoured to have been asked. It was an opportunity for us to finally share our whole show with many musicians we had often worked with and have them be a part of the audience.

Then we had a wedding! Before moving back to Canada, Joe Hampson and Sharon Trostin were married in a small ceremony in the U.S. But friends here in Toronto decided they should have another wedding to give all their Toronto friends a chance to help them celebrate. About thirty people were in attendance including The Travellers, and other mutual long-time friends and relatives of Sharon. I grew up in Camp Naivelt, so I knew Sharon's family. We all sang Pete's translation of the Bantu song that had been sung at our wedding called "Here's to The Couple", known by all, and led by The Travellers. It was a lovely event, and everyone enjoyed it.

Like most performers, certain things we do on stage are sometimes remembered for the wrong reasons. Fortunately, we've had very few of those unfortunate events. Other happier events, however, that may have happened many years ago, live on in history even to this day. One I am most proud of occurred late in this year. The Toronto Teachers Association had changed its name to the Toronto Teachers' Union and they had been taking a strong position in contract talks with Bill Davis's provincial Tory government. On December 18, they held a rally at Maple Leaf Gardens (which seats almost 20,000) and we were invited to sing. With an overflow crowd, the events were broadcast into the arena lobby and even out to the street. The Travellers closed this huge meeting with three union songs, ending with "Solidarity Forever". That date is emblazoned in the minds of the 25,000 public school teachers who were there. As the song ended, the teachers all marched the three blocks to Queen's Park to confront the premier with their demands, all singing the words to "Solidarity Forever" on the lawn in front of Ontario's Legislature. Several days later, the premier capitulated and gave a new contract to teachers—now members of a full-fledged union. Even now, I am often thanked on the street by teachers who were there, saying, "That was the day the teachers' union was born." And it was. And I am proud to have been a part of it, and of this being remembered, in union lore, as a significant event in Canadian union history. It was also our last formal gig of the year.

It was noteworthy that James Alan Gray was born in December, thirteen years prior, to Greta and Jerry Gray. Because he was now thirteen years old, we opted to celebrate his bar mitzvah. And, as the Grays do, we had it filmed. In that process, we formed the Gray Family Singers to provide extra entertainment for the many guests who attended. With three more sons to go, the tradition went on, until Michael's bar mitzvah nine years later. The year 1973 was not quite as busy for The Travellers, but sometimes it was cyclical. The year was noteworthy for the *Murphy the Molar* video, travelling to Atlantic City for the Canadian government, and of course, the rally for the Ontario Public School Teachers' Federation (OPSTF).

1974

The performance schedule for 1974 looked busy and different. Early in January, we were contacted by the Canadian Government Travel Department to travel to Roanoke, Virginia on January 15 for a meeting of travel agents where we would sing songs about Canadian events and sites. But winter travelling in Canada and the northern U.S. is precarious and unpredictable, and there are no direct flights from Toronto to Roanoke. One must fly to Washington D.C., and then try to get a connection to Roanoke. Our flights were booked, but the night before, we learn that, due to bad weather, the Washington airport would be closed on January 15. So, I called the representative in Ottawa to explain the difficulty. The rep then instructed us to charter a plane in Toronto big enough for all five of us, our sound equipment, a set of drums and all our instruments. We knew how to do that! It sounded just like what we had done in the Arctic—having to charter a plane each day. After all, we are The Travellers!

We made the calls and chartered the aircraft, (with the bill sent to Ottawa). We left early in the morning and flew directly to Roanoke, stopping only in Erie, Pennsylvania to clear American customs and immigration. The trip on regular flights would have taken us about five to six hours, and we did it in less than three—flying direct and bypassing the bad weather in Washington. The show was a great success, as most of these events were and, after we finished, we packed up our stuff and headed back to the airport where the plane was already fuelled and warmed up. We loaded up and climbed aboard, and then flew directly back to Pearson Airport in Toronto. At the private hangar, a Canadian Customs Officer pulled up in a car and checked us through. We loaded the cars, and were back home a little after midnight. That was the way to travel!

Two days later, we were back at The Inn on the Park to provide entertainment at a large benefit banquet for the Canadian Cancer Society. We felt we had to do our part. Then, in late January and early February, my three closest friends and I decided to travel to Vermont for a week of skiing. My Alpha Omega dental friends had all started skiing at the same time, and we skied as a group all over the world. We made other trips both as couples and as families. Our wives could all ski, but that year, while the guys travelled to Vermont, our wives opted to take a cruise.

After my return, The Travellers had been hired by the Leukemia Association of Canada to do two concerts for children at the Seneca College Auditorium, on the afternoon of February 17. Both concerts were sell-outs, the kids had a great time, the charity pocketed a large sum of money, we made our fee, and we also sold a lot of recordings. It was a win-win-win all around.

There was nothing on the books for a couple of months, and then on May 13 we were signed to appear at the Royal York Hotel providing after-dinner entertainment for the International meeting of Shopping Centre Managers I must comment here that these events at the Royal York, and other downtown hotels, were quite easily done: We drove or took the subway to the hotel, the mikes were already set up, we awaited the hotel staff to serve coffee, and that was when we were on. We took the stage, the show lasted about an hour, we packed our instruments, collected the cheque and headed home, often by subway.

It was May, lovely weather in Toronto, and time for The Forum at Ontario Place to reopen for the season. Beginning on May 18, we appeared for three consecutive days on this outdoor stage, as it revolved in a wonderful circle on Toronto's waterfront. We felt honoured to be singing again at this Ontario landmark. The very next day found us back at our home away from home—The Royal York Hotel. We provided entertainment for the Retail Council of Canada.

On June 3, we were at the Sheraton Hotel for the inaugural convention of the Paperworkers' Union. For this event we had been asked to sing a program of union songs. We ended the evening with "Solidarity Forever", with all the members singing with us. Over the next twenty years, we sang for this union some ten more times as they met in convention at various places around the country. These shows were always uplifting. At the end of this evening, we went straight home, for the next morning, we flew to Ottawa for a meeting of Federal Government employees at the Skyline Hotel.

Burton Auditorium, at York University is an amphitheatre in the round where we often did our kids' concerts. This time we were booked to sing for the World Craft Council as they met there on June

14. One week later, we were back at the Royal York to perform for an international fraternity, Beta Sigma Phi. Two days later, we were back at Ontario Place, invited again by program director Len Casey, to share the Forum stage with other performers. It was always such a great place to sing, as the stage rotated under the warm skies beside Lake Ontario. Four days later, on June 27, we were at Varsity Stadium at the U. of T. for a federal Liberal Party rally. Must be election time again! In July, we had no dates and declared it a vacation week for us all.

Ontario Place Forum, Toronto, 1976

As the August long weekend approached, we were booked to help open the new Harbourfront Centre—planned to be a key cultural organization and waterfront park on Queen's Quay in the center of Toronto's harbour area. This exciting new facility includes a wonderful outdoor stage, and there we sang a short program on each of the three days as part of the opening weekend. Our guitar player, Ted Roberts, was on staff in the early days of Harbourfront. Once again, The Travellers had been asked to open a new venue for performance in Canada.

The next day, we were off to Ottawa for five days of performances at the National Arts Centre. I took my whole family with me, as we are put up in a hotel right across the street from the Arts Centre for the entire week. On August 6, 7, 8 and 9, we did a concert every evening with Ottawa native, Rich Little. On the last day, we did a children's concert, which was a sell-out. My family had a great time seeing the sights of Ottawa before we headed home.

Back in Toronto, Ted Roberts, who worked for Harbourfront, invited me to do a French-Canadian Hootenanny there. The people who came were "well-oiled," and as I was arriving, a drunken attendee was already leading them in song. By the time I was ready to go on, he had already led them through my whole French-Canadian repertoire of fifteen songs; so, I did not go on, a bit of a disappointment for me, but Ted made sure I was paid anyway.

As we approached late August, my kids were starting to get ready for school. So, it must have been time again for the EX! On August 19, we did two shows at the CNE Bandshell all by ourselves with no guests. Then the Ex was over, the kids were back at school, and on September 14, there was an outdoor rally in Toronto for Cesar Chavez and the United Farm Workers of California, a boycott publicizing the grape boycott in Canada. This event played a large part in the banning of California grapes from being sold in Toronto. This was a real old time union rally allowing us to sing many of the union songs we had grown up with. Cesar Chavez was later honoured by the American Federation of Labour with the Lifetime Joe Hill Award. At the end of October, we were back at the Royal York where we sang at a convention for the Canadian Safety Council.

I looked at the calendar and saw Christmas was coming, so, in early November The Travellers performed for four days at SNO-GO-74, a pre-Christmas event held at the CNE Automotive building. We also did three shows a day for kids. On November 8, we were at

Toronto's Constellation Hotel to provide entertainment for a meeting of the Canadian Cancer Society, and mid-November found us in a studio where we recorded two commercials for the Bank of Nova Scotia. The series was called *Grow With Us* and ran for about a year. They paid us union scale, and there was no extra cash from the bank!

On November 21, the Toronto Musicians' Union threw a Christmas party for members at the Sheraton Four Seasons Hotel, and the featured singers were The Travellers. Then on December 6, we were back at the Royal York Hotel where we provided entertainment for the Transportation Club of Toronto, and then again, for our last gig of the year, we were back at the Royal York for an unknown convention. I guess I was so tired after all these gigs in 1974 that I didn't record who we performed for. These dates are generally booked about a year in advance, and the Royal York was fighting competition from the new Sheraton Hotel in the city a hotel which had a more central location, just across from City Hall Square and the Eaton Centre.

At home, our son James was accepted at a Michigan Music Camp the following summer, in order to further his own musical career. This past year, Greta was elected as President of the Ladies Auxiliary of Alpha Omega, and she and I had travelled to Israel. In the summer, Greta went to the Canadian Open Tennis matches, and was photographed by me, with Romanian tennis great, Ilie "Nasty" Năstase.

For the Travellers, 1974 had been one of the most financially and culturally rewarding years of our lives. During the past five years, the group had been composed of Jerry Gray, Joe Hampson, Ray Woodley, Ted Roberts, Pam Fernie, and Don Vickery. We'd recorded both a children's album and another album for the CBC, and had done several commercials and many children's concerts. But there were problems and dangers lying ahead! You may have noticed that when I warn you, something inevitably happens.

1975
More Changes in The Travellers

At the beginning of the year, both Ray Woodley and Pam Fernie decided they wanted to leave the group. Ray was our long-time guitar player who had joined us in 1961 after Jerry Goodis, left. Ray had divorced, and then in 1968 he met a woman who was a dancer in the Railroad Story *Sea to Sea* that we had done at the CNE in 1968. She was the sister of film director David Cronenberg, and her mother was the rehearsal pianist for the National Ballet of Canada company that had supplied dancers for the CNE show. Ray and his fiancée married several years later. She was not too friendly with us. Later we learned that she thought Ray should be more of a star than he was within The Travellers, and had been urging him to leave and form a career of his own.

So, Ray left us and did a radio show and one TV appearance on CBC—to not much acclaim. Then he and his new wife moved to Los Angeles where she got a position as a set director in Hollywood, while Ray got a job as a linotype operator, giving up his career as a singer and musician altogether. Just tragic. I was sorry to lose Ray as he was very close to all of us. I'll tell you more about Ray and what happened a little later. I always felt he had made a mistake in both his career and his marriage.

Pam Fernie was another story. I never learned exactly why she was leaving, but she used to record jingles for the radio, and told us she planned to restart her career as a "jingle lady". She also opened a dress shop downtown, and then began a problem relationship, going in and out of town with her new boyfriend, and I'll tell you more about that as the time progresses. Over those past five years, we had attained an ease of performance together that only true performers have. For example, we did all those gigs at downtown Toronto hotels where we would show up and do a one-hour show without any run-through or rehearsal, and then head home.

We had now lost two people, both at the same time, and had to make a new plan. Ted Roberts did not sing, and stood back as mainly our lead guitar player, so we moved him up front with me and Joe, and found Aileen Ahern, an accomplished singer from a musical Halifax family. Her brother was Brian Ahern. An arranger and guitar player on many Halifax TV shows, as well as an early arranger and accompanist for Anne Murray. When her career took off, Brian did not want to go on the road, and moved instead to Nashville where he became a record producer, and eventually married Emmy Lou Harris. They had one child and later divorced. Aileen had a sister who was also a singer. While Pam Fernie was the jingle lady, Aileen was the national anthem lady, often singing "O Canada" at many of the conventions we did. Then she would sing with the band that was hired for dancing. So, we lost two people, and really replaced them with one.

Aileen was a quick learner, never complained, and fit in well with what we were singing. She was fun to work with and laughed at all the stage humour we had developed over the years. So, it was a good fit. Even so, it took us many months to "regroup" and be prepared to do all the different types of songs that were now part of our repertoire.

The first gig of the year on May 8 was easy because it was in Toronto for a convention of the Steelworkers Union. Union performances were mainly boisterous sing-alongs interspersed with some of our Canadian regional songs. And then Aileen sang "Danny Boy" and "Farewell to Nova Scotia" so well that she brought the audience to tears. A good start and a good one under our belt, and more to come.

In July we travelled to Calgary for the Stampede to sing for three straight days. During the Calgary Stampede Parade, we sat in a convertible and drove through the Calgary streets. Then it was back to Toronto to appear at the Mariposa Folk Festival on July 22. That summer I began to appear as an occasional guest on *The Bruno Gerussi Show* on CBC radio. I would dig up a song about something that was part of the overnight news—either geographical or political. Doing that over the summer kept me in shape until we built up our network again.

On October 31, The Travellers became part of a Canadian concert record for doing three shows in one day at the same place. We were booked to do two children's concerts in Oakville, Ontario when the sponsors came to us saying that their adult evening concert performer had cancelled. They asked us to fill in that evening. We discussed the proposition. We asked for our fee as well as dinner at a restaurant, and then we did the show. That was three full performances in one day, including two high energy kids' shows! The following Canada Day, we again did three shows in one day: a morning one at Queen's Park, then we drove to Kitchener for a noon show, then late in the afternoon we did a third one at Toronto City Hall.

That year, we were doing two kids' concerts at Seneca College, our favourite place. The sponsoring group sold out the first two concerts, and then two nights before the show they asked if we could do a <u>third</u> concert that same afternoon. Being a stalwart group of performers, we agreed. Kids' shows are not easy to do, as they are participatory. We have to do all the motions we ask the kids to do, and we have to build each concert to a powerful participatory climax. Building three concerts to that type of ending in one afternoon takes a lot of energy, and we always finished our concerts with pre-planned high points. But as it had been only a few months since that season's shake-up, it took a lot of effort. I am always proud of the group, who were still learning the ropes about singing together, so I'll list them for you here now: Our drummer, Don Vickery who was always present; our front line of Jerry Gray, Joe Hampson and Ted Roberts, now singing up front. Our new singer, Aileen Ahern, doing three shows in one day after only singing with the group for a few months, was exemplary, and so deserving of mention. I might add here that this group would remain together for over thirty years, until the death of Joe Hampson in 2006! Hail to the champions.

The Travellers (1975-2006) Don Vickery, Joe Hampson, Jerry Gray,
Ted Roberts, Aileen Ahern, 1979

1976

The following year in 1976, we decide to slow down a bit and
spend some time rehearsing to rebuild our performances. We didn't do
much performing, but we decide to accept a bid to appear in Montreal
for three days in June, at the Canadian Paperworkers' convention
where we sang at breakfast before the morning session and then again

to start off the afternoon sessions. We had already been doing some union performances, and this was second nature for us. It was the first time we took the train from Toronto to Montreal and then back. We found it to be a nice way to travel as we didn't really need a car in Montreal, nor were we faced with the long drive home when we were done and the sound system was provided.

In addition, that year Ted and I did some radio work and personal gigs for the CBC, Aileen did a few gigs singing with some Toronto bands, Joe helped start his wife's group, Sharon Lois & Bram, and Don always had work teaching at Humber College and filling in as a drummer. 1977 was the target date for The Travellers to start performing on the circuit again.

1977

The bookings had come in for the year with the first date on May 10. That day we appeared at a national convention at Toronto's Prince Hotel, and it was like old times again. On June 15, we were back singing at another convention at the Royal York Hotel. In June we appeared inside at the Scarborough Civic Centre to do a concert for the Metro Parks Department, and we ended up doing this for about five straight years. On July 1, Canada Day, we were asked to fly out to Portage La Prairie, Manitoba where we came through for the Federal Government's promise, and gave them a headliner for their Canada Day celebrations. That was another of the many days that I missed at home, for on July 1, I try to spend our anniversary together if possible.

On August 10, I appeared at a Muskoka summer camp in a children's program geared for kids. The next day, The Travellers assembled at the Royal Ontario Museum to do a show with singer and folk veteran, Klaus Van Graaf that went well. On August 18, we were back home at, drum roll...the Royal York Hotel! for the Toastmasters International meeting, and again the next day for a meeting of the Federation of Women Teachers of Ontario. After the Maple Leaf Gardens rally we had done for teachers in 1973, we were greeted with a standing ovation before we had even started singing, then again during and after our show. We were back in the saddle again! Guess what? On August 25, we were again at The Royal York, for another international convention in the large Canadian Room.

Fall was coming, and we were invited, to sing (for the third time) at Pierre Berton's Bindertwine Festival in Kleinburg, Ontario, the home town of Pierre Berton, author, journalist, and panelist on *Front Page Challenge* as we sang Canadian songs with Pierre and his friends and neighbours. Three days later, we were in Belleville, Ontario for another fall concert, and then on October 1 and 15, we were back at the Royal York Hotel for two international conventions. We had been signed up by the George King Agency, which was responsible for many of those international conventions in downtown Toronto hotels.

It was getting close to the end of the season, so, on October 30 we were back at the Royal York Hotel for a meeting of the North American Oral Surgeons Society. I was proud to represent both The Travellers and the dental community of Toronto in welcoming them to Toronto. (Whenever I do these dental conventions, they all seem to know that I'm a practicing dentist as well as a performer.) At the end of the month, my family and I headed north to our home in Collingwood where I did a single concert for the Craigleith Ski Club. A ski club member and fellow dentist, who had been two years ahead of me at U. of T., had worked on some of our *Dentantics* shows, and had seen me do a concert for my neighbouring Alpine Ski Club the previous year, so he hired me to do one for them! The year ended with our family skiing together in Collingwood—always a happy ending to the year. We didn't have too many gigs on the books, but we had plans to do another children's record, which may prompt some notice in the press. Let's wait and see.

1978

It was now 1978, and The Travellers had many kids' shows booked and some cross-country travel, and lots of repeats. It was always nice to be wanted.

The first gig of the New Year was on January 31. The Toronto Labour Council had invited us to add our support to protest the labour policies of J.P. Stevens Ltd. in the U.S. The protest was held at the St.

Lawrence Hall, with a large boisterous crowd ready to sing pro-labour songs in protest. Several days later, we were at Waterloo University, which was sponsoring two concerts for children of staff on the afternoon of February 4. It was a full house and typical fun for both concerts. On February 22, I was invited to do a solo benefit concert for the Baycrest Centre for Creative Living. After that, in early March with nothing booked, I decided to go on a ski trip to Alta, Utah with friends, while Greta and a few friends headed to New York City.

April 2, it was back to work doing two more kids' concerts day at Seneca College. Once again, we had a sell-out crowd and sold many records. *The Travellers Sing for Kids* was the best-selling of any record we had ever made. The next day, there was a snowstorm in Toronto, and I had a large suitcase full of cash in small bills from yesterday's record sales that I was attempting to deposit into our account at a local bank. Just outside the bank, I met a friend, Dr. Cy Marks, who told me he was trying to withdraw cash from the bank, but because of the weather, it was closed. This was long before banks had cash machines. When he asked if I had any cash that I might lend him, I opened my small suitcase filled with cash, and he almost fell down laughing as the small bills cascaded into the snow. I asked him how much he needed and we negotiated a loan, in small wet bills. To this day, he tells that story of Jerry and the cash.

Onward to June 5 we went to Halifax for a civic concert. It was a homecoming for Aileen Ahern, where she could finally be seen and heard singing with The Travellers in her home town! Aileen's parents were there, and we did a lot of songs that featured Aileen.

Festival Canada was the Ottawa Government Booking Agency that had booked our tours during 1967. That year we were contacted by a revitalized Festival Canada to do a five-day mini-tour all over the country. But it seemed that the folks from this 1978 Festival Canada did not plan this tour as well as our 1967 tours which, despite their complexity, had gone off like clockwork. This group simply did not realize how big Canada is, and you'll see what happens.

Back to the Arctic!

The tour began on June 26 with a return concert to Windsor, Ontario. We'd not been there since 1967, and we had a good house. But we had to drive back to Toronto right after the concert because Festival Canada had us booked the next morning to fly out west to sing at a school in Fort Nelson, B.C! That's a long trip after singing in Windsor, then driving back to Toronto to catch a few hours of sleep. I think perhaps the Festival Canada people had either been drinking or they had no knowledge of Canadian geography when they booked the next few dates.

On June 27, we caught an early flight to Edmonton, then a PWA flight to Fort Nelson to do two concerts—one for the kids after school in their auditorium, and one in the evening for the community. We arrived in the early afternoon and made our way to the school auditorium. There we discovered a play was taking place, and no one knew anything about any concerts that afternoon or evening. We left, saying we would be back at 7:30 for the evening concert, and someone should call us at our motel. Someone did call us all right. Apparently, the person who had booked these two concerts several months ago had left town without telling anyone at Festival Canada or in town what he'd booked. So, when fifteen people showed up for the evening concert, we did a half-hour show for them, left the stage and packed up for the next leg of our tour. We got paid by Festival Canada anyway for all the missed performances.

It took about four hours and two flights to get us from Fort Nelson to Whitehorse, in the Yukon. Luckily, we had a day off to rest in Whitehorse, and the next morning we awoke to do our outdoor afternoon concert on the main street. We set up our equipment and had a short rehearsal on the downtown street stage. I'd left my banjo case open on the stage as we went through some songs to warm up and do our sound check. As we rehearsed, a passerby, who saw my open banjo case, threw some coins in. He must have thought we were a travelling band of street buskers, and wasn't aware that in about an hour we'd be doing a full concert!

It was late June in the Arctic, with twenty-four hours of daylight and warm daytime weather. Most people knew there was an afternoon concert that day, and we had a good crowd for the free concert, as part of the tour sponsored by Festival Canada. However, they had not booked any more flights for us; so, we had no tickets to fly from Whitehorse to Frobisher Bay—about 4,000 miles from where we were, as the crow flies. But, at that time, there were no crows flying in the Arctic. There were also no cross-Arctic flights to connect these two communities, from Whitehorse in the west to Frobisher Bay in the eastern Arctic.

Whitehorse Airport, 1978

I phoned Ottawa, and they said we should book the flights ourselves. It turned out that the only way to get to Frobisher Bay was to catch a twice-a-week flight on Air Canada from Montreal, and that flight left at 8 A.M. the next morning out of Dorval Airport, so we booked that flight, and then had to figure out how to get to Montreal, fast. Here's what we did:

I booked a flight from Whitehorse to Yellowknife, in the western NWT. We then chartered a flight from Yellowknife to Moosonee on the western shore of James Bay, and then chartered another plane south to The Lakehead. The next leg was a flight to Toronto where we caught a connection that landed us at Dorval around 11:00 P.M. The next morning, after spending the night in an airport motel, we boarded the three hour, 8 A.M. flight to Frobisher Bay. You should now turn to your map of Canada, and see the distance we travelled in one day to get there. The travel day was now June 30, and we were booked to appear on CBC TV to kick off the Canada Day festivities from Ottawa on July 1. We were booked to sing several songs from the Arctic shores of Frobisher Bay!

Eastern Arctic Canada Day celebration, Iqualuit, 1978

That summer, Air Canada was offering a special flight to Frobisher Bay from Toronto, for "Canada Day in the Arctic", where one would leave Toronto late on June 30, have dinner on the flight, then land and tour Frobisher Bay for several hours before returning to the plane which would leave about midnight. On the return flight to Toronto, they would serve an Arctic char dinner with wine.

A friend of ours, Jack Gwartz, who at the time was chairman of Shoppers Drug Mart, and his wife, Judy,were on the flight, and they'd invited Greta to join them. This would allow her to see the Arctic, and us, to spend part of our anniversary together! The next morning, July 1, The Travellers set up on the shore. We then prepared ourselves for a CBC TV pick-up of our performance, as part of the Canada Day Special starting in the early morning in Frobisher Bay with us, and joining the full CBC Network show from Ottawa. We sang some songs and paired with the local Inuit "Throat Singers". Once our part in the TV special ended, we did a local show outdoors near the ice floes of Frobisher Bay. That night we checked our bags and instruments at the air terminal, and the next day we boarded the noon flight back to Montreal. We then caught a flight home to Toronto where we arrived on the evening of July 2 after thousands of miles of travel including the 4-hour time difference between Whitehorse and Frobisher Bay. Our name, The Travellers, was never more apt than during this experience!

I have a video of our performance in Frobisher Bay, part of the CBC coverage. Even if you didn't look at a map while reading this part, take a second now to follow our flight from Yellowknife to Frobisher Bay! It's probably a Canadian record for getting between gigs. I never found out who planned this schedule—and we never got a letter of apology either—but they paid us for every missed gig.

A small sub-plot occurred after we checked our gear in Frobisher Bay. Once home, we noticed that someone had been playing our instruments, probably in Frobisher Bay the same night we checked them in. Luckily, nothing was damaged. We filed a complaint, but no one seemed to know who did it. Another unsolved mystery of the Arctic North.

That summer, the Mariposa Folk Festival was being held someplace other than Orillia. But in early July, we'd been invited to do a kids' show in Orillia. The City of Orillia invited us to sing at two concerts as part of their "Folk and Funny Festival" on August 5 and 6 in the Legion Hall. We had good crowds with some of the nearby summer camps bringing campers to our concerts, where we did a lot of kids' songs.

A week later we did two kids' concerts in the lecture hall at the Royal Ontario Museum. Along with us was Sharon Hampson, wife of The Travellers' Joe Hampson, and our long-time friend, Klaus Van Graaf, who had appeared with us many times. One week later, The Travellers did two kids' concerts, again at Seneca College. The next day, August 17, we appeared at the Skyline Hotel in Toronto for the Toronto Women's Teachers Union, for whom we had sung last year, again with a raucous display of solidarity between the teachers and The Travellers.

It was now late August and what was on again? The CNE of course! From August 23 to September 1, we performed a show every day at the Bandshell, sponsored by our friends at Molson's, and shared the stage with people from The Boss Brass Jazz Orchestra. What a show! It was free, but it was worth at least fifty dollars to see a show like that! One week later, we were back in Kleinburg, at Pierre Berton's Bindertwine Festival, where we'd performed for the last few years. That evening, we returned to the CBC for a taping of their first late night show called *After Dark*. On September 20, we were at Toronto's Sheraton Hotel for the International Association of Assessors. On October 9, we returned for a second appearance at the Oakville Centre for the Arts to do two kids' shows again, and this time, no evening adult concert! On November 5 and 12, I did two solo appearances at the Toronto Jewish Book Fair. The last gig of the year was on November 13 at the Montreal Convention Centre for the Canadian Paper Workers Union Convention, doing two shows a day for two days. We did not need our sound equipment, so for the second time we took the train from Toronto to Montreal, stayed at a nearby hotel to do the convention, and on the last day we grabbed a cab back to the train station, and headed home in comfort. We had now sung for all three of their conventions.

This was an exciting year for us, with repeat performances for many organizations and a crazy cross-Canada flying chase to fulfill our contract with Festival Canada. We were also amazed at how many kids' concerts we were doing again. We had created an event for children that was truly Canadian, and not being matched by anyone in either the U.S. or Canada. Let's continue on, as the decade nears the end.

1979

Well, here we are, another year. The first part was slow, but it picked up. Over the years, we'd done a lot of work for Air Canada, including making a recording for them in 1960 when they started their DC-8 service. Once again, they were starting a new service, from Toronto to Dallas and to Houston, Texas. In each city, they were presenting the new service to travel agents at a hotel and providing entertainment, for which they hired The Travellers. We left on February 26 and flew non-stop to Dallas on their new flight for our first show on February 27, and we sang at a lavish buffet. The next morning, we flew to Houston and did the same thing, to great success before we returned to Toronto the next day. I believe the reason we got these repeats is because we had a solid repertoire of good sounding music, peppered with amusing repartee and humour, and a big finish as we sang about, and acquainted the audience with Canada.

That year, Greta decided it was time for her to return to school to get her B.A. degree. Greta had graduated as a teacher in Quebec where she needed only one year of Teachers College. She had always wanted to get her BA to qualify for a higher salary, but she waited until our youngest, Michael, had started public school. Now the Gray family would learn how the house would run without the head chef and organizer around!

On March 15, we did a performance in Toronto for an international corporation, to explain about Canada. On March 25, we were back at Seneca College for two afternoon kids' concerts, with the usual results. (I wish I could do more of them, and we seem to have set a high standard for others who've tried.) Greta and I took some time off on March Break, and booked a short trip to New York City with our two eldest sons, James and Rob. We took in Rodney Dangerfield at his club, and saw *Sweeney Todd* on Broadway. It was nice to tour New York City with the kids.

Summer approached, and we were invited to sing at a picnic on Toronto Island for a group of adults and kids, celebrating The Year of The Child '79. On July 19, we did a performance for summer students at the University of Guelph. Our connection with university students through our songs was strong and entertaining, as we'd been doing them now for twenty years. In mid-July, I did a Yiddish program at Toronto's Baycrest Seniors Centre, one of the finest seniors' facilities in Canada.

Summer's end was approaching, so, what else was new? Not the CNE? Yes, it was. We were asked to do three shows a day for two weeks at the Bandshell, our summer place away from home. And, since I was in Toronto, I was in my dental office in the morning, and then at the CNE each afternoon until the end of the day. The day shows' audiences started the same way every day. The people came by, sat down for a couple of minutes, and then stayed for most of the hour. We'd done a lot of appearances at various places around the CNE for many years now.

Fall began, and we got another call to appear on September 8 at the Bindertwine Festival in Kleinburg, just north of Toronto. This was our fourth year in a row, and it was always a well-attended event. It's amazing how many "repeats" we do. Here's another; the Toronto Parks Department invited us back for the third year to do a concert at the Scarborough Civic Centre City Hall. Then, we were back at the Royal York Hotel on September 10, to sing for another international convention group. To finish off a busy month, on September 14 we were back at the Ontario Place Forum with comedian Dave Broadfoot for three nights on the revolving stage.

The leaves began to change, and we drove around Lake Ontario to St. Catharines to do two children's shows on October 14. New place, new audience, same results! Fun for all. Two days later, we did a public promotion at Toronto's Eaton Centre as they welcomed a new tenant. On October 25, we appeared live on *The Bob McLean* TV Show. We'd done that show many times over the years, updating audiences on what we were up to, and singing some newer songs we'd been working on, and it met our, and the producer's tastes. Lots more coming this fall.

On November 4, we were back at Seneca College for two kids' shows, sponsored by the Montessori Schools, at one of our favourite concert halls. The beauty of that hall is that it's a very vertical amphitheatre bowl, so we're never too far from the kids as we ask them to do some silly songs, and scare them with the story of the giant Abeeyoyo. Then I got busy.

On November 12, I was back singing at the Baycrest Centre's senior home. On November 17, I was asked to appear in Galt at a small synagogue, as a fundraiser for fixing up this very old synagogue. On December 2, I sang at The Terraces, the assisted living centre part of the Baycrest Centre. On December 6, we were invited to do a public concert in Chatham, Ontario as part of a community fundraiser. The next day, we were in Kitchener for another public concert.

When the UJPO had broken apart in 1955, some members, including my parents, had formed an organization called the New Fraternal Jewish Organization and, on December 15, they had a Chanukah party. How could I say no? I did the show, and still do many Chanukah and Christmas events, right up to the time of this writing. The next day, I did a one-person kids' show at the Toronto Jewish Community Centre. That evening, the Travellers did their last show of the year, a repeat Christmas party for the employees of Imperial Optical Company. With the fall having been so busy, Greta and I planned a ski trip in the new year.

In summarizing the year, it was amazing how many kids' concerts we were still doing and kept getting requests for. We took consummate pride in doing those shows—still having the ability to cajole the kids into doing the crazy things we asked them to do, watched them react to the Giant Abeeyoyo, taught them new songs, and had them repeat them with ease. It was still a learning thing both for the kids and for us. Even with the many changes we'd undergone, we put out a supreme effort at every event where we sang, and thus we succeeded. This was the end of another calendar decade that seemed to keep on, keeping on. Let's try to end the 1970s on a high note.

1980

The previous decade of the '70s had been uneven, and we were starting to think about whether we should continue. However, late in the decade, things turned around and we decided to try and make it to our fortieth anniversary in 1983. This became a very busy year for me, for I took on the job of writing and directing a two-hour variety show for Alpha Omega, the Jewish Dental Fraternity I still belong to. It was to be done during Christmas week at the end of 1980. In between all the work with The Travellers as well as my dental practice, I started rehearsals and writing the show with a friend, Dr. Sid Golden, a Toronto periodontist, who could easily have been in showbiz, as a writer and composer I'll update you along the way as this year progresses.

Early in January, we recorded the final episodes of *Let's Sing Out*, Oscar Brand's TV show. On the last taping, The Travellers did a regular show with Oscar; then he and I taped a half-hour kids' show with the Beers family. That's another show I've never seen and, as I said earlier, it would be an interesting project to find all those lost and never-seen TV shows. Over the past four years, we had recorded about twelve of Oscar's folk shows, done originally on CTV and then later on the CBC. I had a long relationship with Oscar, and we often did lecture sessions at Mariposa. Sadly, Oscar died in 2016 in New York City at the advanced age of ninety-six.

In January, the group went into a recording studio to record our second kids' album, *The Travellers Merry-go-round*, this time for Elephant Records, the company owned by Sharon, Lois & Bram as they began the same type of staged concert format used by The Travellers in the children's song market. Then, the dental friends and I went to Lake Tahoe to ski for a week and returned refreshed and uninjured.

The Owen Sound Folk Festival ran a series of winter concerts called The Winterfest Folk- Festival and, on March 12, The Travellers appeared there for the first time. In April, I accepted a new challenge when I was asked by the Northern Branch of the YMHA to teach a five-week course on Yiddish music. Called "From Shtetl to Statehood tsu Amerika", it would be illustrated by playing recorded music by

Theodore Bikel and others. If I lacked a suitable recording, I would perform the songs myself. The course drew about twenty people, and I enjoyed doing it for the interested and enthusiastic students. I didn't think anyone had ever done such a course in Toronto before, and I marked that down in my mind, perhaps, as a later project.

On May 26, the group appeared again on the Bob McLain show on CBC for an interview, and to sing a few numbers, including "This Land". On June 21, we were invited to sing at a "sweet picnic", on the grounds of the Neilson Chocolate factory, two blocks south of College and Dovercourt. When I was a kid, I used to bike past that place frequently, and liked to stop and smell the chocolate wafting sweetly from the plant. This would be my first time inside the grounds to see up close what was causing those sweet smells. When we played at the Savarin and other bars, we'd come home reeking of cigarette smoke and beer that would be hard to get rid of. But singing on the grounds of Neilson Chocolate was a dream come true! And we got paid for it!

That same week, Elephant records released The Travellers' new recording of children's songs, *The Travellers Merry Go Round*. I was not too happy with it at first, and didn't think it was as good as our first one. I decided to wait and see, and perhaps it would grow on me. As time passed, I began to really like some of the new techniques we used, while also including our story songs and audience participation songs. I actually perform one of the original songs from the *Merry Go Round* album in 2018, thirty years later in Florida, at a large and significant event. Stick around and I'll tell you about it.

Juno-nominated children's LP "Merry Go Round", 1980

On May 28, the group would mark its approximately twenty-fifth anniversary with a concert in the Brigantine Room in the York Quay Centre at Harbourfront. The *Globe and Mail* learned about it, and sent feature writer, Paul McGrath, to do a story prior to the concert about our twenty-five years. Paul wrote a half-page story that covered many of the highlights of our career, always asking what the future looked like. As a result, I invited former Travellers to this event to help mark the occasion. Those who were able to come would be invited to join us on stage, and sing along with a few songs. My sister Helen said she would come, along with Simone Taylor, Sid Dolgay, and Martin

Meslin. Oscar Ross couldn't come, and Jerry Goodis responded that he was "expecting a previous engagement" which told me that he wouldn't be coming at all. Pam Fernie was out of the country, as was Ray Woodley.

It was a well-attended event, co-sponsored by Harbourfront, and was an important milestone for any folk act in Canada. If you recall, The Travellers were actually the first act that played at Harbourfront on their opening weekend. All the former members in attendance took the stage, and sang a few songs with us.

My sister Helen and I used to do an Indonesian lullaby called "Suliram". Many in the audience remembered us singing it, and some of them shouted out that we should do it "one more time". So, with no rehearsal we did it, and there was not a dry eye in the place. We could not have known it, but this was the last time we would sing that song together. Several months later, Helen was diagnosed with lung cancer, and passed away within months. I have such great memories of growing up in Toronto, and singing together with my sister. As I often do, I had hired a videographer to take movies of that reunion, and I gave copies to all her four kids.

On June 24, Toronto's first Yiddish Concert took place at Earl Bales Park, near Bathurst and Sheppard. I was the headliner accompanied by my son, James. The show was sponsored by the Yiddish Committee of Toronto and organized by Beth Silburt. I grew up with Beth at Camp Naivelt, and she commented that "the apple does not fall far from the tree", in reference to my interpretation of Yiddish songs based on my Yiddish heritage. That concert still runs to this day. Son James and I repeated the concert the following year, and several more times after that. That program continues to the present, but as we approach its fortieth anniversary, I don't think there are many people who remember that Jerry and James Gray began this important part of the Yiddish music calendar in Toronto. But I do, and now you're in on it, too. Hopefully, there are some people who remember those opening nights in 1980 and 1981.

July 1 is Canada Day, and The Travellers got an opportunity to sing the new words to "O Canada" on Parliament Hill. Before we sang, we were presented to Canada's governor general, Edward Schreyer, at his residence, and I gave him a copy of our new children's record, *The Travellers Merry Go Round*. As we were talking, a figure literally hopped into the gathering, surrounded by the press. It was Terry Fox, one of Canada's greatest heroes, on his soon-to-be-legendary, cross-country run for cancer. He had achieved his well-publicized goal of making it to Ottawa for Canada Day, and we were fortunate enough to see him in person!

This was now the third or fourth time The Travellers had sung on the Hill on Canada Day, and we got thousands of people to sing "This Land" along with us, as the song had been around now for some twenty-five years, and everyone knew it. You, my reader, may remember when The Travellers went to Ottawa in 1962 to be the first Canadian entertainers to perform on stage for the CBC's cross-country TV show, on Canada Day. And we were back again!

On July 29, I was invited to take part in another Yiddish concert in Earl Bales Park. Later in August, The Travellers were invited to do two concerts at the Ontario Place Forum. I've actually lost track of how many times we've appeared there. But I have such great memories of performing on that revolving stage as it made a complete circle, in exactly one hour, before an audience stretched out in the carousel and on the grass. I think they made an error in destroying that innovative stage when they went for the big noise of rock bands on the new stage.

On August 22, we were invited to sing at another Ontario Federation of Labour rally at Queen's Park against some injustice, usually for a good cause, and we always lent our support. A quiet September was followed by a first-time invitation from Georgian College in Barrie, Ontario to do two kids' concerts for the children of the staff on October 22. Even in Barrie they'd heard of our prowess at singing for kids! Four days later, we did the exact same thing for Seneca College at their Minkler Auditorium. A few days later, we headed to Sudbury to do two kids' shows for the Mine Mill and Smelter Workers Union that I first sang for in 1952! The next day, we did a single concert for the Union members, thirty years after I first sang for them!

Remember last year we did a Christmas concert at the Royal York for the employees of the Imperial Optical firm? Well, by popular demand, they called us to repeat that performance this year on December 20. We loved getting all those repeat invitations! We were still in demand, and still doing those two-a-day kids' concerts, and the kids still left with the same memories of the riotous fun they had singing along with us.

When I finish this book, I'll have time to look up and count all the kids' concerts we did, along with all the union concerts and appearances. It's tough enough trying to remember, and I try to write down as many as I can recall.

I mentioned earlier that that year I would be writing, directing, and appearing in a two-hour variety show at the Harbour Castle Hotel for 500 delegates of the International Alpha Omega Dental Fraternity convention. We had a cast of fifty people in the show, mostly people I had worked with over thirty years ago on those *Dentantics* shows at Hart House during the 1950s. They were simply tremendous again, and everyone had a wonderful time. I really had to thank them all—especially my wife, Greta, who played in many of the skits and helped write some of them. We did only one performance and I had the foresight to have it videotaped so we could enjoy it forever. The evening was a huge success, and left us all with a great feeling of accomplishment.

Alpha Omega Dental Convention, Toronto, 1980

Another decade had gone by and the group was still busy. There was a marvellous feeling of camaraderie between the new members of The Travellers, who wrote new songs, which we tried out in performance. We still answered the many requests to appear again all across the country. Wow, what a ride it has been! We were starting the

'80s, and I was still excited to continue, looking forward to the '90s and into the new century.

CHAPTER 6:
TRAVELLED WITH THE RICH AND TRAVELLED WITH THE POOR

1981 AND BEYOND

It is now 1981, and I've given you a chronological list of all the performance dates that both I and The Travellers have done. It's time to take a rest from that format, because it might be overwhelming to keep hearing about them. You'll have to agree it was a huge amount of dates both across Canada, and around the world.

Now I'd like to do a bit of a summary of where we've sung in this first twenty-seven or so, years of performances. I've been involved with about 1,000 full concerts for adults and children, in a huge number of venues which included; on an ice floe on Baffin Island, an outdoor street festival in the Arctic at 8:00 A.M. because of the 24-hour days of sunshine there, a Roman amphitheatre on Cyprus, on the Canadian government stages, at two world fairs in Canada and Japan, as well as at the London Palladium.

Long before The Travellers began, I was doing children's programs. In 1961, I was the first Canadian to do a kids' program live on TV when we did a show at the CNE for CBC TV. That same year when we opened the first Mariposa Folk Festival, I did the first concert of folk songs for children at Mariposa 1, 2, 3 and 4, and then eight times more over the years. In 1965, I recorded a children's TV special with Oscar Brand, as well as a TV special for the United Church of Canada as we sang and discussed the politics of the civil rights movement with high school and university undergrads. I sang at many summer camps in Ontario, Quebec, and even in New York and Pennsylvania, as well as at many Chanuka and Christmas kids' concerts. The Travellers did the first folk song concert for kids in coffee houses in Toronto at the Gate of Cleve Club, The Seven of Clubs, and several other folk clubs that followed. *The Travellers' Sing for Kids* album was Canada's first children's album, and sold over

50,000 copies. In the year 2000, I personally reissued it as a CD and went on to sell about 4,000 more copies. Before the record was first released in 1971, The Travellers had done about twenty-five concerts for kids in public halls. Then, during the 1970s and '80s, we often did two or three performances in one day at venues across Ontario and New York State at least fifty times. I had also done live TV kids' performances with people like Sharon Hampson, Klaus Van Graaf, and Oscar Brand. During the 1990s, I'd also appeared with Toronto public school principal Lorne Brown at his Kensington Public School, on several occasions.

I first began singing for labour unions in 1950 with the UJPO Youth Singers—on picket lines in Windsor, Oshawa, Sudbury and Toronto. Over the years, The Travellers sang at many union conventions across the country, and continued on past 1981—the events about which you'll hear soon. In 1962, I was the principal singer at the founding convention of the Ontario Federation of Labour. You might recall that date in December 1973 when we inspired 22,000 teachers in singing "Solidarity Forever", as they marched from Maple Leaf Gardens to the Ontario Legislature Buildings at Queen's Park. You'll hear more about our work in the labour movement, right up to this time of writing, as we proceed.

The Travellers sang for all three major political parties at venues from picnics in parks to major rallies at Maple Leaf Gardens and other big Canadian arenas. The irony was, even though many people knew The Travellers were politically left of centre, all three national and provincial parties hired us because we were never really delivering a political message; instead, we were delivering a program that put "Canada First," as we sang about the love of this country.

You may have noticed how many times we sang at conventions across the country, often at the biggest convention hotel auditoriums, and most often at The Royal York Hotel—for groups with agendas from the left, the right, and the centre. It seemed we sang most often at the Royal York, so much so that they should have given us access to the guest rooms for free! All the booking agents in the convention trade knew that, when they hired The Travellers for a post-dinner musicale, they were getting a proven "class act" that would end with everyone present singing feel-good Canadian songs. The program always included "This Land is Your Land", even though many of the people were from foreign countries from all over the world. We were also a self-contained musical group that required no help from the band hired for dancing and other items in the program, while The Travellers provided the entertainment. You'll also note that many of the conventions were repeats for the second or third time, and even more.

The 1950s and '60s were the glory years of CBC TV variety musical shows. Toronto had a huge number of top musicians, many of whom played with the Toronto Symphony, at Toronto jazz clubs, and did commercials. After watching shows on CBC TV during 1953–1954, we thought we would do well in that medium, so we auditioned for a summer replacement series and got good reviews for the show we did. For the next eight years, we did at least three TV appearances per year. In the early '60s, when CFTO helped form the CTV network and bound together stations from across the country to form the new network they hired The Travellers to be an integral part of the opening network show. The idea was that there would be people in Halifax, Calgary, Toronto, Montreal, and Vancouver—each singing a verse of Oscar Brand's song "Something to Sing About". The Travellers would do the first verse, and then bring in Catherine McKinnon from Halifax, the Raftsmen from Montreal, someone from Vancouver, and then lead all the cities in the final chorus of the song. The event went pretty well, but there were inevitable glitches while bringing in each city for the first time as a network. CTV never did well in saving these important shows for history and, after trying to find a copy, I came up empty-handed. We also did a kids' show in Vancouver in the '70s, and I had no success getting a copy of that from their archives either. It seemed that the CTV network was bound together coaxially by fear, everyone thinking that CFTO was trying to take over the network for themselves—which it turns out they actually were, and finally did.

The Travellers made four appearances on CBC's *Front Page Challenge* with Pierre Berton, Betty Kennedy, Gordon Sinclair, and Fred Davis as moderator. These appearances had something to do with an announcement in the papers that the group was on its way out of the country for an event. We did several tours with Fred Davis across

Canada with CBC jazz musicians, as well as comedian Rich Little. There came a time when we'd been on most of the Toronto-produced TV shows, and they stopped returning phone calls from our manager Marty Bockner, so a new tactic was needed.

I used to play squash close to my office during lunch hour, and when I finished, I still had time. I'd go to manager Marty Bockner's office, and from there I would call the TV producers at CBC and tell them it was Dr. Gray calling (not a lie). The return call would come within two minutes, when it normally took at least a week to get a response to this kind of call. When I used this ruse, I'd hand the phone to Marty, and then they'd say they were just about to call us about doing a show, and a contract would be made for a future TV appearance. And that's one of the reasons we were on so many shows.

But that's only part of the reason. The real reason was that The Travellers did quite well on television, and I have many of the reviews in the daily papers that often commented on how well we looked on TV. In 1954, the first year we were together, I was still in college and working at the CNE before starting my next year at U. of T. On September 7, Jerry Goodis and I took time off and went to the waterfront to meet and greet Marilyn Bell as she came in just after 8 p.m. from her historic swim across Lake Ontario. At age sixteen, Marilyn became Canada's sweetheart and a Canadian heroine by completing her swim in just under twenty hours. (Florence Chadwick, the American marathon swimmer, had actually been challenged by the CNE to swim the lake, became sick after only two hours, and had to be pulled from the water. Jerry Goodis kept in touch with Marilyn for several years, and The Travellers wrote a song about her swim. But at the time there was no recording industry in Canada, and therefore no way to play it on the air. Nevertheless, we performed the song in our concert appearances.

If you read about all the performances in our early years, you'll recall how often The Travellers played in Charlottetown, even before they built the new theatre. After opening that theatre with the command performance in 1964, The Travellers returned to PEI five more times. In the summer of 1971, we were there for a week, playing nightly at the bar in Charlottetown but finishing the week with a two-hour concert which was recorded by CBC Radio, and then broadcast several times over the network. Of all the shows we did over the years, that was probably our best performance because we were breaking away from our folkie origins and presenting more cosmopolitan programming for all tastes. We played songs of the Mamas and Papas, Gordon Lightfoot, Jimmy Webb, and James Taylor along with others. That was the change we made in our repertoire, so the type of performances we did all through the 1970's allowed us to reach all audiences. That's the reason we consistently had such a great response to our songs at the many conventions we sang at.

Individually I was asked to help out on some two-hour variety shows. Throughout my university years, I sang at the annual undergrad show *Dentantics* for four years, and helped with the productions. The reviews called our show the best one on campus, and I got a lot of positive reviews in *The Varsity,* the university newspaper. The 100th anniversary of licencing dentistry in Canada was 1975. That year, the school of dentistry staged a special anniversary show called *Dentantics100,* for which I was one the directors as well as appearing in many parts of the show. I was a member of the Alpha Omega Jewish Dental Fraternity, and appeared at their international conventions in different cities, where the host city would produce an original show. In 1964 and again in 1980, this convention was held in Toronto. I was the producer of both shows, and also found time to take part as an actor and singer. The people who performed in all these shows were my friends and colleagues from the early dental shows, and whenever a show was planned, one call brought together our original cast.

Up in Collingwood, my family belonged to the Alpine Ski Club and, whenever there was an event at the club such as Ladies' Day or Men's Day or any significant Club anniversary, we put on a show like Mickey Rooney used to do. My wife Greta was always a willing member of the casts for all these post-grad events, and had as much fun and success as I did. Fellow dentist Dr. Sid Golden was often my co-producer, and could write lyrics like a pro. He was great to work with and, later in his retirement years, he used his artistic talents in other fields.

Family Matters

This is only part of my life so far, and I've still got a "lot of livin' to do" and more to tell. Although I was on tour during the earlier decades, once I was home, Greta would go on an island vacation or a cruise with a girlfriend for a week, and I'd look after the kids. But now, with not as much time on the road, I could plan a skiing vacation with my friends and sometimes with the family or alone with Greta. In October, I'd go to the Toronto Ski Show to get in the mood for skiing. Then, in 1981 I got a call after the Ski Show ended, asking if I had attended this year's show. I thought I might have bumped someone's car in the parking lot, but it wasn't that. While at the show, we'd fill out a card at each booth, in hopes of having our card selected for a prize. This call was to inform me that I had won the Grand Prize! This consisted of: four pairs of skis and poles, four pairs of boots, four down outfits—and a trip for four to Whistler, BC, from Air Canada, which included the rental of a van and a week of skiing and accommodations in the Village, along with ski lessons from Olympic skiing great, Nancy Greene! Wow!

There were six in my family, so I got kids' fares for my two youngest, and split the prizes up among my kids as best as I could. My sister Helen had only recently passed away, so I took one of her daughters, my niece Brenda, along with us as well. So, during the first week of January 1982, my entire family flew to British Columbia, and had a great week skiing at Whistler! While we were there, we ended up meeting Pierre Trudeau on the mountain top where he was skiing with an RCMP officer. After our ski lessons, we also visited with Nancy Greene and her kids at her chalet.

I loved skiing, so in '82 I went to St. Moritz, and in '83 we went to Val D'Isere. In '85 we drove with another couple to a friend's place in Vermont and skied in Stowe for a weekend. In 1985, Greta and I took a driving trip down the California coast road to visit relatives and to attend a wedding in San Francisco. Two months later in 1986, some male friends and I went to Courcheval in France for another week of skiing. The following winter, we went to a time-share in Pompano Beach, Florida, with our friends, the Feldmans. In January of 1988, we took the whole family to Aspen, Colorado with four other families—

part of our Collingwood "six-pack"— and the following winter of 1989, Greta and I went to Harrah's in Lake Tahoe for another week of skiing. We also skied virtually every weekend from December to March in Collingwood. That was our winter pleasure. I had a family of four boys, so my choice of not being part of the hockey team culture, but instead to create a recreational skiing family, with other similar-minded families, created a perfectly clean and wonderful winter experience for all of us. I continued skiing until I was over seventy years old.

As I mentioned above, in early 1982, Greta and I, along with our two youngest boys, Kevin and Michael joined the Feldmans and their two boys, David and Larry (who were the same age as our two youngest) in Pompano Beach. We had a great time, but there was one event that left us with lifelong memories. Near our hotel was the mooring port for the Goodyear Blimp. We had heard that, if you called in, you could get a free trip on the blimp. One morning we called the "Blimp line" for over an hour but could not get through, so we packed up and were prepared to do something else. I forgot something and went back upstairs to get it, and dialled the Blimp Line one more time. To my amazement, someone answered! They said they could accommodate six of us in about half an hour. We were only about ten minutes from the Blimp Port, so we headed over, and boarded the Blimp for a supposed one-hour round trip up to West Palm Beach and back.

But once we were aloft, the pilot announced that due to wind conditions, we would not be back for two hours. Irv Feldman and his sons, and I and my two boys had a trip we would always remember. Not long after that, two movies came out about bad guys hijacking a blimp to try and bomb the Super Bowl Game. As a result, all passenger travel on blimps was banned. No one can now duplicate that trip by being a passenger on a blimp. It was a first for us, never to be duplicated by anyone telling such a tall tale – but ours is true and I have pictures to prove it!

As I mentioned before, besides the skiing that I did with friends, we belonged to the Alpine Ski Club in Collingwood that had events during the ski season. Like Mickey Rooney, we were asked if we would put on a show for members at the club's twenty-fifth anniversary. I asked my old *Dentantics* crew, and they were happy to help. By now, my oldest son James was a music major at U. of T., and a gifted musician. We also had the gift of James as accompanist for the show. The next year, the ski club asked Greta if she would help put on a show for Ladies Ski Day in February, when the ladies took over the club. Once again, James was the accompanist for a musical show. It was such a success that another show was called for the following year, with the same cast, accompanist and arranger (James) —both with similar results. One show was called *The Adventures of Parallella*, and the other was a variety show. As the writer and producer of both shows, Greta received well-earned acclaim. Greta had a knack for writing lyrics which I did not have, and she was very successful in writing material for all the shows, and starring in them as well.

When our youngest son Michael was about eight, Greta, who had obtained her teaching certificate in Montreal without a university degree, decided to go back to school at York University and get her degree. She graduated in 1982 with an honour English degree, and a scholarship offer from the University of Michigan in Ann Arbour to do a post-grad degree there. While at York, she took a course with Professor Elaine Newton who won best teacher award at York. After Greta graduated, they formed a partnership: Elaine gave book reviews outside of the university, and Greta was the administrator for the course.

Meanwhile James was at U. of T. and majoring in composition and theory of music, he went to several summer camps as part of their stage events of putting on plays and musicals. In 1982, son Michael turned thirteen, and the Gray Family Singers put on a musical show with all six members of the family as part of his bar mitzvah celebration. As each son had a bar mitzvah, the Gray Family Singers would re-emerge to entertain the guests.

In 1982, an opportunity arose for The Travellers to do a national tour for a large American company that had a Canadian subsidiary,

The Canadian Amway Corporation. This company had pyramid type sales and, every year, they had large rallies for those who had achieved high sales for the company. These rallies were held in major cities across the country. The company asked The Travellers to do our Canadian program in five cities at a fairly high fee, with all expenses paid. The first one was held in Hamilton and the show went well, but the company did not like what we were wearing on stage. They said we needed new clothes for our performances and suggested new suits for the men and a gown for the woman in the group. They would pay for all of these clothes. We went to clothier friend, Harry Rosen, and we ordered five light beige suits, ties, and shirts. Harry had been a long-time friend of The Travellers and had a good laugh at how we looked now but also appreciated the business.

Cross Canada Tour for Amway Corporation, 1982

The tour went well with the addition of a new outfit to wear at prestigious gigs. Later, we were told that the Amway group was an extreme right-wing conservative company, and they must have known what they were getting in hiring our left-wing group. We also found out that the company was started by Jay Van Andel and Richard Devos, who had supplied enormous funds for the Trump campaign. In looking back to that time and realizing what their new parameters are, I don't think they really knew about us and we didn't know what their ultimate political ideals were.

1983 was an eventful year. During the summer, all my friends regularly rode their bikes. On July 1st they had an annual biking day where they would ride through the trails in Toronto's park system, and then return for a BBQ. But every July 1st since 1960, I was singing somewhere else in the world on my anniversary. This was the first year I was not booked anywhere, so I was excited to join them. We started in the park right behind Sunnybrook Hospital, and I was sailing along when I hit a small speed-bump on the trail. My front wheel collapsed, and I flew over the handlebars and landed about ten feet ahead. No one wore helmets in those days, and when I awoke (after the police car drove me up the hill to the hospital), I had received about seventy-five micro-stitches as they removed the gravel from my face.

I later attempted to sue the manufacturer of the bike, but to no avail. This was the second time my face had been subjected to surgery. I had played about seven years of football and never had a broken bone, but I had my nose slightly bent, once in a high school all-star game. Greta kept suggesting I needed to get it straightened by an ENT plastic surgeon. In 1960, the Hitchcock movie *Psycho* opened in Toronto at a theatre near Yonge and Eglinton. That same week, I had the surgery on my nose, and emerged with all kinds of bandages on my face. After being home all week, we decided to go see that movie, and entered the theatre in the dark just after it started so no one would recognize me. With all those bandages, my mother couldn't even recognize me!

We sat near the front, so when the movie ended, we could slip out through the exit beside the screen. Part way through the movie, there is the famous shower-stabbing scene where the slashing takes place. Greta was suddenly frightened, and reacted by lashing out with her left arm, in the process hitting my still tender, bandaged-up nose. I ran into the aisle to escape her. Now you had a grisly murder on the screen, and a man with bandages on his face, who hadn't shaved in two weeks, was running up and down the aisle in deep pain from the post-surgical arm assault on his nose by his wife, all accompanied by screaming violin crescendos on the screen. I finally got seated again, but stayed away from my wife's arm. She was chuckling but I was definitely not. The nose was later checked, and the surgery was successful, with no damage to my beak from the armed assault.

1983 was also my fiftieth birthday year. In keeping with what we usually did, we decided to have a large party that Greta organized. And, in keeping with our tradition, she organized the different groups of our friends to be part of a salute to me on my fiftieth. Accordingly, she invited about one hundred people to our home, set up a stage in front of the fireplace, and fitted it with The Travellers' sound equipment. We had invited our once-a-month club, the Collingwood six-pack, The Travellers, and friends from other groups and individuals—all to take part in *The Jerry Gray Show*, which of course we videotaped. My kids also organized a sound-alike group of The Travellers, and they sang some of the songs we had made famous. As usual, we closed the evening with all singing, "United We Stand" and "This Land". My mother was there and, at about age eighty-three, she embraced the moment and took part in the singing.

That year 1983 was also the year Greta received her Bachelor of Arts degree from York University. She decided not to accept the offer to go to Ann Arbour, and the five males in the house were all very glad to have her back at home.

In 1985 my son James, graduated from U. of T. with a music degree in composition and theory, and began looking for work in the field. That summer, James and I performed at Camp Naivelt's fiftieth anniversary celebration. By that time, my only relatives had all left Detroit, mainly for the west coast of the U. S. There was a marriage coming up in San Francisco, so Greta and I flew to San Diego, rented a car, and started driving up the California coast, stopping to visit relatives at various spots along the way, and ending up in San Francisco for the wedding. It turned out that there was also a dental convention there, so I registered for it and that allowed me to write off the entire trip for tax purposes!

Later in the '80s, it was Greta's fiftieth birthday party, so we organized an evening of friends to come to our home. The event took place on our tennis court, with people watching from the Jerry Gray Memorial Deck (still standing, and so am I) that I had built overlooking the court. Luckily, Greta's birthday is in July, so it was a perfect spot. Greta used to be a folk dancer and had appeared on TV during the '60s. We had some friends who were also in folk dance groups, and they performed some Israeli and other dances, to much applause. During the event, she made a speech to the large crowd on the tennis court. Here is part of her speech:

> "I look upon this birthday as an opportunity for reflection. I realize that my life has been full of adventure and excitement, a few disappointments, some achievements, fascinating trips, and certainly a great deal of joy. I am surrounded by a loving family and my friends, who make up the people who count in my world".

I told you she was a great writer. She has been a primary school teacher, a French immersion teacher, running *Gifts from Greta,* a home gift-service business, a lyric writer, and now an organizer of book reviews. She has been a loyal and loving wife for thirty years, putting up with all my travels and being a part of many of them.

Beginning in the late 1980s, my son, James became part of the award-winning Canadian band, Blue Rodeo, leaving after fourteen years with them. In 1988, son Rob got married to a girl we were not too happy with, and they separated after about seven years. The whole family, including Rob, celebrated this parting of ways. Luckily for both parties, there were no children. Kevin went to McGill University in Montreal, and then went to the University of Windsor Law School where he met his wife, Claudia. The two of them did a year at the London School of Economics, each getting their masters' degrees. Last-born son, Michael, took his time and waited until the new century to get married.

At this time of writing in 2018, I have just received news of the death of Dr. Sam Green, a dentist several years behind me at U. of T.

I knew Sam from dental school, and from our Alpha Omega Dental fraternity. He also worked at my dental office in the 1960s, filling in occasionally when I was on one of my out-of-country experiences. Sam became an employee of the City of Toronto and Peel County as the Dental Officer in charge of Public Health Dentistry. If you recall from chapter five, it was Sam Green who, back in 1972, asked me and the Travellers to help out with the singing commercial for dental health, using a stylized singing molar tooth on skates called Murphy the Molar! I did the voice for Murphy, who would tell watchers that they should wear a helmet while playing hockey and brush their teeth often.

The announcement about Sam Green's death said that he was recognized in the dental world and in the public health world as the creator of Murphy the Molar. I wrote a note of condolence to his family, agreeing that Sam was the creator and the heart of the commercial, and I was the voice serving with pleasure for all these years. Another part of Canadian history that The Travellers and I played a part in, that a lot of people never knew about, so get out there and brush often and wear a helmet for all sports! You can still catch the commercial on You Tube.

As the memories of the '80s pass, I must update you with more history about The Travellers. My relationship with labour unions began in the 1950s when I sang and gave lectures for the United Auto Workers (UAW), an American union with Canadian locals. Now, this international union made decisions that did not always serve the members of the Canadian union.

For the next thirty-five years or so, the Canadian union locals began expanding. They wanted more input into the policies of the parent union. As the Canadian auto plants began expanding, Bob White, the Canadian president of the Canadian branch of the UAW, began a move to secede from the UAW. They formed the Canadian Auto Workers (CAW), and in 1985 held their first convention in Toronto at the Royal York Hotel. Guess who they called to sing at the first convention of the "new" Canadian union? If you guessed The Travellers, you would be right! Bob White won the Order of Canada for leading the CAW to becoming a truly self-governing Canadian union. The Canadian Auto Workers Union held conventions across the country every three years, and The Travellers sang at <u>every</u> national convention, including the last one when the CAW merged with our friends The Paperworkers Union (CPA) to form UNIFOR in the second decade of the new century. I'll tell you more about our continuing relationship with CAW and Bob White, right to the present as I write this.

During the 1980s, The Travellers were still singing at conventions as we'd done over the previous ten years. In 1983, we were invited to ride the train to Ottawa dressed in railroad overalls and sing our way to the Conservative Party National Convention. Once there, we would then entertain the throng with our Canadian songs. We were also still in demand to sing for union conventions and at kids' concerts.

During that decade, The Travellers began doing an annual concert at the Scarborough City Hall. Every year, we packed the place doing our national concert music. Noticing the large number of kids in the audience, we interspersed the program with our kids' songs that were sung also by the adults in the audience, just as we had done that throughout the '70s. Then, in 1985, we were asked by the Ladies Auxiliary of Baycrest Hospital to appear again—not for the patients, but for the staff! That day, we received a special plaque from Baycrest for all the years we sang there for the patients, the residents, and now for the staff of Baycrest. Then, in the late '80s, I was invited again, alone to sing for the seniors at the Baycrest Centre. My program of Yiddish songs always went over well.

In 1989, we sang at one event that takes on a lot more meaning now than on the date it happened. There was an Ontario provincial election slated for that year, and the pundits had trouble calling the result in advance. On the Sunday evening before the Monday election day, the NDP held a rally at the Italian Hall at Dufferin and Lawrence. The Travellers had been invited to sing, as it was a last-day pep rally for Bob Rae, leader of the NDP.

When we finished our part of the program, I hung around and overheard the brain trust members of the party discussing their chances at winning. I overheard some concern about who might be in the cabinet if they won, and the consensus was that they would wait to see who won and solve these problems later. Well, they did win and quickly discovered the financial condition of the province had been misstated by the previous government. A recession was just setting in. The inexperienced NDP cabinet ministers were unable to stem the flow, called for "Rae Days", and were ridiculed for not solving the problems right up to the 2018 federal election almost thirty years later when Bob Rae was running for the Liberal Party of Canada. We were witness to an historic event. Who knew it would turn out to be such a significant date? I enjoyed my experiences of speaking often with Bob Rae in his Bi-Party life—both when he was an NDP member and later as a Liberal. A chance meeting with Bob Rae in Stratford in 2015 led to an award for me. Hope you stick around to read about it.

In December of 1985, I was asked by the *Toronto Star* if they could write a continuing story of The Travellers by interviewing me at my home. Of course, I agreed, so *Star* reporter Phil Johnson came and interviewed me about our past and future. He then wrote a half-page story which appeared in *The Star* on December 26, 1985. With such a long career, people wanted to read about our past, and what our future looked like.

In these last pages, I have told you about my family, as well as my life and travels. And while The Travellers were still performing, although not as much, life was going to change in this next decade and beyond. Before we end the '80s, I have to tell you about son, James Gray. After his graduation from the U. of T. in 1985 with a music degree, James played and sat in with many Toronto bands, creating a name for himself in Toronto's rock scene. The Toronto-based band, Blue Rodeo, had formed in 1984. In the early summer of 1987, their original keyboard player, Bob Wiseman, was leaving and they were interviewing people to replace him. On the weekend before their Ontario Place gig, they asked James if he could play an accordion. James figured that, having a keyboard like a piano, all you have to do is squeeze it as you play it, so he said sure! He then spent the weekend listening to the three Blue Rodeo LPs, and learning what Bob was playing behind the singers. James had a phenomenal ability to fit in with every group he played with, and seamlessly slide right in. That first 1987 gig at Ontario Place was a success, and they invited him to join the band. James then played as a member of Blue Rodeo for the next fourteen years. I'll tell you more about his long career with Blue Rodeo a bit later on.

When I looked back at all The Travellers' singing engagements over this past twenty years or so, I noticed we rarely had a performance in the month of January. At first, I thought that there just weren't too many gigs available right after Christmas. But then I looked at Greta's historic picture albums, and noted that I often went on a ski trip with my friends and sometimes with Greta and other couples, and noted that most of them were in January! Perhaps there were gigs available, but at times skiing took precedence. We all loved to ski, and to ski together, and the dental appointment books were a little empty in January anyway, so it was always a good time to get together and ski. I have no regrets about that, and we still have about thirty exciting years to go—and go! In the coming '90s some exciting events happened as the group began to get recognized for the things we had pioneered. It's worth reading about, so hang on.

Jerry and Greta Gray, Canadian Rockies, 1985

The 1990s

Yes, we were approaching a new century, and I had been singing, playing, and performing for over thirty-five years now. I didn't know how much longer The Travellers would be performing, so I began taking stock of all my memoirs, posters, and write-ups with an eye to donating them to the federal Archives in Ottawa. I was told that they would be interested in my archival collection, and that the materials would be adjudicated by someone familiar with the genre. They would then send me a figure of value that I could use as an income tax deduction for my donation, so I began to put my collection into some sort of order for adjudication. It took a while, and this project would be with me for about three years.

In late November of 1990, my mother, Mary Gray, died at the age of eighty-nine. When my father passed away in 1969, the eulogy has been given by J.B. Salsberg, the noted left-wing Jewish MPP and firebrand. Salsberg had abandoned the Stalinist Communist ideology in 1955 when Khrushchev revealed Stalin's misdeeds at the twenty-fifth anniversary of the Communist Party of the Soviet Union. Many people in the UJPO also left, including my father, and formed a new left-of-centre Jewish organization called the New Fraternal Jewish Association. J.B. Salsberg was on the executive of this new group for many years. My father had been active in both organizations and, when he passed away, Salsberg was asked to deliver a fitting eulogy for him in Yiddish. It was truly thrilling for me, and for the several hundred people who attended his funeral, to hear a eulogy delivered in the "King's Yiddish." Those who were present remember the profound silence as J.B. Salsberg delivered his oration.

When it was time for someone to give a eulogy for my mother, the NFJA asked Mania Lifschitz, to also deliver the words in Yiddish. As an author, Mania had written several historical books in Yiddish, and had been a *Yiddishe lehrer,* a teacher of Yiddish, for fifty years. She had been everyone's Yiddish teacher. Again, many of my friends were impressed by not only what she said but also how she said it. They still speak of it almost thirty years later. My mother was not politically involved much, but she was a wonderful caring mother, not only to Helen and me, but to her eight grandchildren to whom she was known affectionately as "the Bobbe" a term of extreme endearment. We had a non-religious *shiva* for one week that was attended by friends, both Jewish and non. My kids were very upset and sad when their grandmother died. Whenever Greta and I would be away for a week or so, Bobbe was always there for them, to help solve arguments and look after them, and this was the one time in their lives when she would not be there.

Jerry Gray with his beloved mom, Mary Gray

I was getting closer to donating my artifacts from The Travellers to Archives Canada. As to the rest of The Travellers at the time, Joe had been with us since 1965, Ted Roberts since1968, Aileen since 1975, and Don Vickery since 1970. They had been around for much of the glory years of the group, but I was the only one with a first-hand grasp about what triggered five people in 1953 to form a group that would sing songs of protest, standing behind the teachings of Woody Guthrie and Pete Seeger, and tell Canadians about their treasure trove of Canadian songs.

The departure of these many items from The Travellers' history from my home was okay with me, for I knew they'd now be available for public viewing forever. I never learned the name of the person who evaluated all my articles that were sent to Ottawa. But I received an evaluation of about $18,000 for my donation, which I used as a tax receipt in 1994. In the year 2000, I finally learned who it was that had appraised my collection and I'll reveal the secret as that year gets closer. As I approached age sixty-five, the patients in my practice had started to either move away or depart from life, so there were fewer patients for me to work on as my possible retirement came closer. (This happens to many dental practitioners as they near retirement age.)

In the winter of 1991, three of my close and long-time friends, Marvin, Irving and Cal and I decided to take a four-day trip to Pompano Beach in Florida to play golf. On the second-last day, we went out to a steak house for dinner. After we had finished the meal, it was still early, so we drove down Federal Highway to a night club and disco bar. None of us had ever gone to a place like that without our wives, but we dropped in to have a drink, and sat near a table with about four people. One was a thirtyish young woman, and Marvin struck up a conversation with her. Soon she asked him if he'd like to dance. After thinking for a moment, Marvin said sure. Then she asked if he would like to dance with her mother, who was seated beside her! Without hesitation Marvin said sure again, and they danced one dance. Then we left, and when we were back in the car, we burst out laughing for fifteen minutes. Marvin was the dentist who had said yes, when I asked if he would like to come with me to the Kingston Penitentiary to watch The Travellers do a Christmas CBC Radio Show for the inmates. Marvin was who he was, and rarely turned down an invitation that might bring him a new experience.

One time while skiing with Marvin in Vail, I skied over a hidden bare spot and fell, dislocating my pointing finger. Marvin took me aside and relocated my finger by pulling it back in place, and then told me to bury it in the snow to prevent swelling. We stayed there for about fifteen minutes, and little swelling ensued. However, I did have problems with that finger for many years. About ten years later, Marvin developed breast cancer. He wrote a series in our *Toronto Dental* magazine about being the only male in the waiting room of a well-known mammary oncologist. He wrote of his problems in treatment, and many people who were not dentists asked for copies of his humorous stories. Sadly, Marvin's cancer had metastasized and he passed away. Marvin is the only one of our close skiing and golfing friends who passed away early. Just about all the others are like me, in their mid-eighties, still around and living out their retirement years in various ways.

Early in 1993, I went skiing in Jackson Hole, Wyoming with Irving Petroff and two of his sons, Jay and Howie. There, we went to the "other side of the mountain" to ski the untracked hills using a "snow cat" to carry us up the mountain. It's like heli-skiing without the need of a plane, and much cheaper. Irv's son Jay had a movie camera, so we have video proof of skiing uncharted snow out west. As the winter progressed, I took my sons Kevin and Michael on a weekend excursion to Stowe in Vermont for skiing, and for eating ice cream at Ben and Jerry's Vermont factory!

Jackson Hole, Wyoming, 1990's

At this point, son James was flourishing playing with Blue Rodeo. His degree in music composition meant he surpassed both his father and the other members of Blue Rodeo in his knowledge of music. The group wanted to put out a *Best of Blue Rodeo* book with their music charts. But just like The Travellers, they made up their arrangements as they went along, and never wrote them out, so they had no musical charts. To solve this problem, they gave James their old recordings and, as they travelled on their tour bus, he listened on earphones, and tried to capture their musical arrangements note by note, and then write them down. It was a great task, and when it was completed and the book released, it was lauded by all at Blue Rodeo. Third son Kevin was hard at work at McGill University in Montreal. Michael was still unmarried.

February of 1993 was the one hundredth anniversary of my former high school, Harbord Collegiate, and many of us attended the reunion. Harbord's graduates included people like Johnny Wayne and Frank Shuster (the "Wayne and Shuster" comedy team), Sam Shopsowitz (SHOPSY the Hot Dog man), many musical conductors and composers, as well as many government officials among its recent graduates. Some also mentioned that I was a forty-year member of The Travellers.

We had a few convention gigs coming up, but with a new century approaching, people were also asking about future dates for the group. In November 1993, The Travellers took part in a salute to an old theatre on The Danforth, and performed at a fund-raising concert for the Toronto Lung Association. I knew some of the people on the planning committee and we couldn't say no. Along with The Travellers on the bill were Salome Bey and Dan Hill. The MC for the evening was Harvey Atkin, a well-known TV actor and comedian whom I had worked with many times doing Yiddish concerts, and who had appeared many times as a judge on the TV show *Law and Order* as well as many other shows. This event gained us a lot of respect in the community, as we closed the evening and raised a lot of money for a worthy charity.

In the summer of 1993, The Travellers appeared again at the Mariposa Folk Festival, this year held on one of the Toronto Islands. We headed the concert, I did a workshop with Oscar Brand on Yiddish music, and later he and I did another workshop on children's music. Guy and Candi Carawan were also there. Back in 1960, Guy had worked at a labour union music camp in Tennessee, and had inspired all the people in the 1960s to work for Dr. King. It was Guy Carawan and Pete Seeger who transformed a song by changing the wording from "We Will Overcome" to "We <u>Shall</u> Overcome", creating Dr. King's powerful 1960s anthem. As you may recall, Guy had also come to Camp Naivelt in 1954 when we debuted our new Canadian version of "This Land". He said it was great, and we would keep the song alive until the political system would change, as it did in the 1960s when the song came alive again. Guy Carawan helped me out some fifteen years later from now.

All through the years, I continued to play squash and, in 1993 when I turned sixty, I decided to enter the Ontario Championships held in Toronto in the sixty and over category. I got to the final and then, in a long five-set championship match against ladies' clothier Alan Cherry, I won 15–8 in the final set and won the match 3–2. It felt pretty good because all the friends I had grown up with had stopped playing singles squash and were only playing doubles. The following year, I again entered the "over-sixty" tournament, this time held in Guelph, Ontario, and once again won the Ontario Championship in my age category. As a prelude to that, in 1992 I played for the Mayfair West Veterans Championship defeating good friend Len Banks in the final. In speaking about squash, I must give credit to close friends, Marvin Kopel and Irv Petroff, who gave time to start me off in squash, and also thank Dr. Irv Feldman for playing squash with me at 12:40 p.m. at Mayfair West every Monday for about thirty years. He and his wife Marsha and their children still remain close long-time friends.

As I looked at the calendar earlier in the year of 1993, I noticed it was The Travellers' fortieth anniversary! So, let's have a show! The planning group we sang for in 1992 at a benefit concert wanted to be part of our fortieth, and tie in the funds to go to several Toronto charities. The MC of the concert was CBC Radio broadcaster Andy Barrie, a long-time friend and supporter of folk music and The Travellers, as well as liberal causes. The show was recorded by the Ryerson University Radio station CJRT, and letters of support were sent to the committee by several people. Toronto's Mayor Mel Lastman sent a greeting to The Travellers on their fortieth saying:

"They've been delighting audiences for four decades with their unique program of Canadian songs. And they're still going strong."

Oscar Brand, who I had worked with at Mariposa the previous summer, could not come but wrote: "It was wonderful performing with you last year. It reminded me of the exciting days when we worked together on CBC and CTV, and thank you for making my song "Something to Sing About" into a Canadian anthem."

Pete Seeger sent his personal congratulations, and a letter came from Alan Borovoy: "On many occasions my life has intersected with The Travellers in concert halls, at union conventions and at protest rallies. The sheer vivacity of their music lifts the spirits of everyone. To this day I play a tape of The Travellers to psyche myself up whenever I have a speech to make. For all that The Travellers have contributed to Canadian life, and for what I know they have contributed to mine, I salute them on this anniversary, and express the hope that they continue singing in this way for at least the next forty years."

Alan and I had begun working together in the 1950s while we were both at U. of T. His words about psyching himself up by playing our music just before delivering one of his fiery speeches were so uplifting for us. After receiving words like these, I decided we had to try to keep going. That same year, we were on the CBC Radio *Morningside Show* for an interview, and performed some songs as we talked about our last forty years.

I discovered, in the early days of the internet, that the Canadian Music Encyclopaedia had added a page to its website about The Travellers. It's been updated since then, and is a pretty accurate story of the group. See it yourself by Googling Canadian Music Encyclopaedia, and ask for The Travellers. It's an interesting and well-produced portrait of the achievements of the group.

1994

The year before, I had skied in Jackson Hole and had a great time (even at my age), so Dr. Irv Petroff, the original Doc Holiday (because he took more ski trips than I ever did), decided we should go out west again to ski untracked snow. Irv took three of his sons, Jay, Howie, and Stephen, and I took my son Michael, and we went out to Crested Butte in Colorado, the "Double-Black" capital of extreme skiing. Again, Jay Petroff brought his video camera and captured us all in our pratfalls and remarkable skiing, making parallel tracks through the unmarked snow. The kids had a truly great time, while for Irv and me it was a little harder. But we persisted and remained unscathed at the end.

The Petroffs had a ski cottage on Highway 26 in the Collingwood area, and the Grays had a place across the road from them. We had bought a ski cottage there in 1980, and I built a deck there under a large tree in the backyard. Time caught up with the tree, so I had to take it down and removed the stump to make a new deck. During the spring of 1994, I again created a new deck, even larger than its predecessor, and it stands solidly up to the present day, even though we sold our place in 2008 when we stopped skiing.

In June 1994, I lived up to the group's name, and Greta and I went travelling again—this time to Baltimore to attend a wedding. There I ran into Mel Green, a folksinger, originally from a folk trio in Johannesburg and Cape Town, South Africa called Mel, Mel and Julian. The group also recorded for Columbia Records. Mel Green and I still exchange emails and, for all you ex-South Africans, he is now living in Boston and still performing.

In 1980 when The Travellers stopped recording albums, I wrote to the Juno Awards people. I addressed the fact that they were giving out Founders' awards to many of the people who had started with us, and were on the Juneau Commission of the federal government looking into broadcasting in Canada. Every year during the 1960s, either our manager Martin Bockner or one of The Travellers had made a submission to the Commission.

We would write that The Travellers were the <u>first</u> group in Canada to make recordings in Canada, to have national recognition in the early years of recording 1956–1969, and that many of those early recordings had been done with <u>one</u> microphone in a living room in a house, as there were no recording studios in Toronto at that time. There were other groups like The Four Lads and The Diamonds who started after us, but they recorded their first songs in New York City and Cleveland, in studios that had more than one microphone. My letter to the Junos advocated that The Travellers should have some recognition, at least as a founder and participant of the recording industry before there even was an industry.

As I have reported earlier, my first three letters were totally ignored; I received no reply. I repeated this type of letter every two or three years. Sometime during the 1980s, I managed to get a "hearing" at a board meeting. I brought all seventeen of the recordings The Travellers had produced up to 1969 to show them what we had wrought on behalf of the Canadian recording industry—an industry now booming because of the decision by the Juneau Commission that radio stations in Canada had to have a minimum of Canadian-produced records to be included in the air-play. This led to the <u>Junos</u> being founded, but with absolutely no mention ever of the part our group had played in certainly being at least a "founder" of the now thriving Canadian recording industry. I even suggested that, on several anniversaries of the group like our fortieth in 1993, it afforded a great opportunity to award some honour to the group for its early participation in the industry. The board committee said they would put it to the Awards Committee, who simply voted "no" with no reasons ever given.

Up to this point, The Travellers had been a part of at least nineteen recordings for various companies. If you're fortunate to own many or any of them, there are some things you may not know about. Intentionally, from the very first recording we ever did, through the years up to and including all the recordings done up to the end of Canada's birthday year 1967 and the children's recording in 1970, each recording contained at least one French Canadian song! We always felt that, since we were Canadian, we had an obligation to include at least one in each recording. As we approached 1967, we also wrote a chorus for "This Land Is Your Land", in French. A little-known fact, but we did it because we thought it was right.

1995 and 1996

On April 22, 1995 there was a rally held in Nathan Phillips Square in front of the Toronto City Hall. It was called Earth Day '95, and sponsored by several groups of the "save the planet" persuasion. They were warning of the things that might happen in the future. Well, that future is now our present, and many of the things they were warning about are actually taking place—with climate change leading to the melting of the polar ice caps, the huge hurricanes and high waters we are now seeing, among other things. We had sung many times for these types of groups under their various names over the years, and we had the repertoire of songs that warned those who came to the rally to try and help keep us from the dangers. We had earlier recorded a parody song by Tom Lehrer called "Pollution", which I still perform.

In February of 1997, The Travellers were invited to perform a concert held at the Performing Arts Lodge (PAL) for retired performing artists on the Esplanade in Toronto. Our early member, Sid Dolgay, was living there, and was on the committee to bring us there. The concert was booked for February 14 of 1997. Later we discovered that a convention of The North American Folk Alliance was being held that same weekend at the Harbour Castle Hotel, just a few blocks away from the PAL. Well, The Travellers appeared on the Friday night at the convention and we were introduced by Peter Yarrow of Peter, Paul and Mary. In addition, I was delighted to find Pete Seeger in attendance. We asked him if he'd like to come and join us at the PAL concert the next night, and sing with The Travellers again. He agreed, and we arranged that I would pick him up. After The Travellers had done the first half of the Saturday concert, I drove over to the hotel and got him, and then headed back to the PAL event. To make it even more fun, I had invited my son James to play keyboard with us that night, and he was thrilled to also be backing up the legendary Pete Seeger.

Pete Seeger and Jerry Gray, Toronto, 1997

It was an amazing night that lasted an hour more than planned. A lot of money was raised and it was a surprise to have Pete at the PAL concert; quite an event happened with his surprise inclusion. After the show, I drove Pete back to the Harbour Castle Hotel. At this point in his career, Pete was not travelling as much as he used to, and hadn't been in Toronto for a long time. He told us he was very glad to sing with The Travellers again because of our long relationship which now was now over forty-five years. Then, in August of 1997, The Travellers were invited to return to Camp Naivelt to do a summertime concert in the place where it had all begun.

In 1985, the company that we signed with to record *The Travellers Sing For Kids*, went out of business. By default, over time I secured the future rights to that recording with plans to release it as a CD. In 1959, when The Travellers had originally signed with Columbia Records, the head of Columbia Canada was Charlie Camillari. I phoned Columbia and found that Mr. Camilleri's son was now the president. I approached him and asked to have Columbia take over producing *The Travellers Sing For Kids* as a CD. I learned then that

Sony Music would take over Columbia the following year. He wished us good luck and so I waited. Later I did some work and managed to re-release *The Travellers Sing for Kids* CD myself.

Previously, in the summer of '96, the group was again invited to Mariposa and we sang on the program with a group from the original Mariposa 1, The Sinners. The banjo player was one Eddie Sokoloff, whom I'd seen over the many years, and it was good to be with old friends and old memories again.

Kevin Gray, our third son, received an undergrad degree at McGill University in 1992, and was accepted into the Radio and Television Arts program at Ryerson University. He had taken a trip across the U.S. and Canada in an old van with a friend, and was actually in Vancouver staying with a long-time friend of the family when another letter came. As he was readying to return to Toronto, he received a letter from the University of Windsor accepting him into the first year of their law school. Now he had to make a choice. RTA at Ryerson? Or Law at Windsor. He made what we also thought was the best choice for him, and in 1992 began law school in Windsor. During his time there, he served one semester in his third year as a clerk with the NWT judicial system, following in his dad's footsteps by being in the Arctic. In 1996, he had graduated from law school. In his graduating class that year was a young woman named Claudia Santoro. As these stories go, they ended up getting married! Kevin and his bride, Claudia were married in 1997 at a Jewish-Italian wedding, which was the highlight of all our lives that year, even as it was overlaid with the sadness of Claudia learning that her father had an inoperable medical condition. He was able to attend the wedding, but sadly passed away not long after.

The Gray Brothers: Michael, James, Kevin, Rob

We ended up with two lawyers in the family. Kevin and Claudia have now been married for more than twenty years, and along the way they had two kids, Sebastian and Maya. They live in Ottawa, and both work as lawyers for the federal government. In 2018, as Canada was arguing with the U.S. President Trump about trade, Kevin was on Canada's negotiating team.

That same summer of 1997, I was off again, travelling with Irv Petroff to South Carolina for four days of playing golf. One day, we had an interesting experience. We were playing a "dog-leg hole" around a bend. When we got around the bend, we saw my ball lying close to the green—right near a ten-foot alligator! What to do? The first thing, of course, was to get out the camera and take a picture with the 'gator. Now how to get the ball? I have a twenty-foot ball retriever, so I extended it to its maximum length and gently prodded the 'gator, who quickly scurried into the water. I picked up the ball and wrote down the score, which I will not reveal, and then we drove to the next hole.

Retiring Back to My First Love for the Rest of My Life!

Around the same time, I made the decision to sell my dental practice to a nearby dentist. After the deal was complete, I worked for him for about a year. However, when it wasn't working well for either of us, I decided to retire from dentistry as I reached the age of sixty-five. The year was 1997, and I now had to choose what to do with the rest of my life. I had lots of ideas about how I could "retire" seamlessly into my parallel career of professional singing. Teaching had often been my other first love for forty-five years. Now I could do it for the rest of my life!

After having taped a TV show for the United Church of Canada in 1965, I was invited to do a week-long seminar at the University of Saskatchewan for the United Church in Regina. Since then, I have taught one-day seminars many times to different groups, about the history of Yiddish music or the history of North American Folk Music.

The Travellers' programs were always filled with a wide variety of subjects, and we all told stories about the songs we were singing. Andy Barrie was a war resister from Boston who left the U.S. and came to Canada before his induction into the army. He had a radio program on station CJAD in Montreal, and then moved to Toronto where he worked for CFRB and became friends with the folk music community. He then left CFRB to become the morning man at CBC radio. Over the years, we had shared stages together at folk events, and had travelled to New York City to see a concert that you'll hear more about later. His wife (get this) was Mary Barrie! How alliterative can one get? She was the head of "Later Studies" programs at the University of Toronto; so, on the day I retired from my dental practice,

I called and asked if she had room for an instructor in her faculty. When she asked if I was applying to teach about dentistry, I said no, about folk music. I had been doing a second parallel career beside dentistry for forty years, and I wanted to retire into my parallel career. She asked what the name of the course might be, and I answered, "I know about folk, protest, and labour music."

"An excellent name for the course," she replied. There was only one problem. The calendar listing programs for the next fall season was going to print the next day. I told her I would get a CV and course description written overnight, and send it to her by email. She agreed. I was slated to begin teaching an eight-week course in the fall of 1998. I find a lot of people when they retire, get bored because they have no plans on what to do. And a lot of other people don't retire when they can because they don't know what they can do. I was very fortunate to be able to retire into my parallel career of the past forty years and to begin teaching.

About fifteen students registered, who were paying about $350.00 each—a huge amount—and absolutely loving it. One of those students was Harry Rosen— yes, the clothier, who had once outfitted us when we did a tour for an American company. Harry was also a "closet banjo player", and used to be our number one fan. I taught the course by talking about the history of folk and labour songs from the Chicago strikes of 1885, through Joe Hill and the Wobblies, on to the strikes in the U.S. mills in New England, the coal strikes, and "Sixteen Tons", through the war in Spain, the auto strikes in the U.S., Dr. King and the songs of civil rights into the Viet Nam War, all the struggles in Central and South America, and in South Africa. I used the songs that had been recorded by Pete, Woody, Bikel, Belafonte, Judy Collins, The Travellers and many others. When in doubt, I would sing the song myself. This was the first time I had ever taught a course of that length. I learned a lot about teaching and about myself and my abilities as a communicator on a podium. The first course went well, and it was renewed for another fall semester in 1999.

In August of 1998, we were notified that Sony Music had purchased the catalogue of Columbia Records of Canada, and planned to release a CD of our music in honour of the upcoming New

Millennium in the year 2000. They would call this new CD, *The Best of The Travellers: This Land Is Your Land.* It would be comprised of at least two songs from each of the seven albums we had recorded for Columbia, plus several of the singles we had recorded along with the four tracks we had recorded in Nashville. They went to work re-mastering the tracks to bring them up to standards that had not been available in the 1960s when they had first been recorded. They asked Dr. Rob Bowman, head of the music department at York University, to select the tracks to be included, and we had no input. Rob has been mentioned previously in this book, and it turned out it was he who had evaluated the artifacts that I had given to Canada Archives in 1992. Rob had won a Grammy in the U.S. for the liner notes he had written several years earlier for Sony Music in Nashville. He was asked to interview Sid Dolgay and Jerry Gray for the history of The Travellers. After two sessions with Sid, Rob told me he found Sid totally filled with venom about The Travellers, and the fact that he hadn't been a member of the group for forty-four years still bothered him. So, I ended up being invited to Rob Bowman's house to replace Sid and talk about these recordings. During the many interviews with me, he got enough positive information to write the twenty pages of liner notes that were included with the new recording. Some of his liner notes appear on the first page of this book, and it's worth a look back to that page to see again what he wrote. The time I spent with Rob was a marvellous way for me to retell our story to someone who truly respected the history of the group, and the material we had chosen to record.

Sony Music Compilation: The Travellers – This Land Is Your Land
(1960-1966), 1999

Sam The Record Man, Toronto, 1999

Once the CD was released, we began selling them immediately at concerts and at other appearances. Then in 2015, Sony said they would stop the manufacture of that CD, so they gave me the copies of the record and all the remaining liner notes from Sony. I am still selling them as both I and the group still perform in live performances.

In 1998, Bob White, having now been head of the Canadian Labour Congress for about eight years, was retiring from his post. I asked him if The Travellers could appear at his closing appearance at the Congress the following year in 1999. We had sung at many CAW conventions and had not appeared for the CLC for a few years. Bob wrote back saying he would ask the planning committee and let me know.

Although I was no longer a dentist, I was personally still quite busy as my secondary life took over and became my primary life. At the end of '97, I was asked to appear and sing at a Christmas party for a social club in Collingwood. On May Day in 1998, I made arrangements to travel with Andy Barrie, as he and my wife Greta were going to the fiftieth anniversary of Folkways Records in New York City at Carnegie Hall. Andy's mother, who was about ninety years old, lived in New Jersey near the west end of the George Washington Bridge. Andy stayed with her overnight and, the next day, she picked us up at our nearby motel and transported us to Carnegie Hall in Manhattan. The last time I had been there was in 1955 for The Weaver's first reunion concert to fight the McCarthy blacklist. That concert had been memorable, and this one would also be.

It was raining hard as we entered New York City, but Mrs. Barrie got us to the Hall in good time. On the bill that night was Theodore Bikel, Pete Seeger, Arlo Guthrie, Ani Franco and a few other folk song veterans. Pete's voice was fading more, but the additional singers added to a memorable concert. After the concert, I met some of the people from Pete Seeger's life: Pete's wife Toshi, his manager Harold Leventhal, the publisher of Woody's songs, and Woody's daughter. It was one of those events where I felt so fortunate to be there, and with good friends.

In September, Joe Hampson couldn't make a Travellers' gig in Whitby, so son James filled in playing bass and keyboards. Also, that month, son Kevin, the lawyer, now was bound for Sweden for six months as part of an international advocacy group. In December, Aileen and Ted were away visiting family at Christmas, so Joe, James, and I did a Chanukah concert in Toronto.

It was now 1998 and, as I reached my sixty-fifth birthday, a sign at the Mayfair Lakeshore Tennis and Squash Club announced that the Canadian Squash Championships would be held at our club, so I entered. Eight people were registered for play in the 65- and-over category. I won my first match and awaited the second, which was a semi-final—there being only four of us left. I was playing against the #1 seed from Vancouver and I lost, which placed me at either #3 or #4 in Canada for people over sixty-five. I choose #4, and there I was— still standing and having the time of my life. Once again, all those people I had grown up with who were eligible did not enter because most of them were now playing only doubles, or not at all. Having a tennis court in my yard for the twenty-eight years I lived there made it possible to play tennis often, and at age eighty-five at this time of writing, I still play doubles a few times a week while in Florida for the winter.

1999

The end of the century was getting closer and the new one lay in wait. I'd been getting calls from groups about commemorative programs being planned to mark the new century the following year, so the next decade was looking good for both The Travellers and for me.

In early January, a few of us (those still skiing) decided to go skiing in Colorado. We'd gotten into the habit of skiing early in January during our dental years. It was less crowded on the hills then, and accommodations were cheaper. In May, the Canadian Labour Congress invited The Travellers to appear in Toronto at their convention, as Bob White retired from the presidency but remained on the board of the Canadian Auto Workers. The CAW conventions were held every three years, so I saw him every three years as we sang at all of them.

That summer, the Sony CD, *The Best of The Travellers*: *This Land Is Your Land* was due to be released, and promised to be a very exciting event. In addition, I had made copies of *The Travellers Sing for Kids* on a CD, and it sold well wherever we went (as well as by mail) as people had worn out their vinyl copies and wanted to replace them. But that was only the beginning of the year, and a lot of things were coming to fruition.

Early in the year, I get a call from ex-Traveller Jerry Goodis about a project he wanted to interest me in. Over the past twenty years, Goodis had had several bankruptcies, and been without a steady job in advertising for many years. It was not lost on me that, during all his time in advertising, he had never approached us for any jobs in that field, even though we'd done some positive advertising campaigns for others. Goodis now approached me as a spokesman for his partner, one Sid Dolgay, yes that Sid, the one who had been democratically removed from The Travellers in 1965. Its now35 years later and Sid seems to have a new ally on his side.

Goodis and Dolgay had come up with a plan to use The Travellers' name and history to approach the federal government to fund a series of books, videos, and recordings for the upcoming year 2000. Their plan was for me to give them complete access to the name of The Travellers, and to create a new partnership of the three of us going forward. Dolgay did not offer much, but Goodis claimed he had access to the federal government through his "friend", Sheila Copps. I did not agree to giving the two ex-Travellers an inroad back in to control the group's upcoming events, but I said, let's try and see what happens. I left it to Goodis to initiate contact with Sheila Copps for her views on our proposal.

I then called a close friend, Morris Langer, who was an accountant and aware of mergers, and told him of our attempts to contact Ms. Copps. He advised me to do as I was doing, but not to sign anything they submitted. Several months passed with no response from Ms Copps; so, Goodis wanted to make a proposal to her by mail, telling me it had to be sent on pink stationery which apparently was" her favourite colour". I went along with this ridiculous story, bought the pink stationery, and sent the proposal to her. Twenty years later, I am still waiting to hear back from her. Two years later, I met her in Ottawa and, when I queried her about getting correspondence from a Mr. Goodis, she said simply, "Who?"

When Sony Music released the new recording of songs from our previous LPs, which we had done with Columbia, the local press and media were very interested, and I did a great many interviews. When Michael Enright from CBC's radio network called with an invitation, Goodis and I appeared on his Sunday morning CBC radio show, and then other invitations began rolling in. Sid was very put out at not being invited to appear on Michael Enright's show, and I heard he thought it had been my fault. But the CBC said Goodis and Gray were all they would need. When I got home from the interview, there was a message from Cohen Siblings Inc., a TV company wanting to produce a documentary about The Travellers' up to the present, in partnership with the National Film Board. By now, I had been the sole owner of the name, "The Travellers," and all it entailed for many years, so neither Goodis nor Dolgay were invited to be a part of negotiations as we began several months of talks. The press got wind of this possible tie-in, and several newspapers called me for statements and interviews. As all this was going on, more invitations began coming in! Here I was, now retired from dentistry with a lot more time on my hands to oversee these new developments, but also with more time to promote The Travellers' interests.

In February, I got a note from Leah Stevenson, who was head of the Strike Committee of CUPE, the Canadian Union of Public Employees representing Toronto's education workers. Her father, Bill Stevenson, was the former president of the Mine Mill and Smelter Workers in Sudbury. I had first met him in 1951 when I went there to sing on their picket line; again, a year later at the end of my cross-Canada tour with the Fagel Gartner Jewish Singers; and once again, the following year in 1953 when I sang for them with the Youth Singers of the UJPO. The Travellers appeared for them several times during the following years. I found that Bill Stevenson was as staunch a union man as ever was, and I guess my relationship with him and his daughter now covered almost fifty years! Leah's note invited The

Travellers to sing at the next CUPE convention to lead off the first meeting with our patented opening. Of course, we agreed.

One month earlier, I had sung for the Toronto Yiddish Music Club for Marvin and Eda Schiff. In my earlier formative years, Marvin had been a columnist for *The Globe and Mail,* and then served a term at the Canadian Civil Rights office in Halifax. While at the *Globe*, he had written some good reviews of The Travellers' early concerts at Massey Hall. He invited me to sing again for the Friends of Yiddish group in Toronto.

Bob White, retiring president of the Canadian Labour Congress, made good on his promise of getting The Travellers to appear at his retirement at the CLC Convention '99 held in Toronto from May 3–7. These national union conventions were good money makers for the group, as during a five-day convention we would appear about nine separate times—each time singing union songs that would inspire and build their enthusiasm, and most often end with the whole room standing and singing "Solidarity Forever". For such a convention, we would be paid for the nine separate performances. There were no other groups in Canada at that time with a repertoire of union and socially significant songs, and an ability to inspire the audience and get them to sing along. Even today as I write this book, there appears to be no one trying to emulate what we were doing or had done, as we continued to sing out for labour causes. More recognition even internationally will follow in the next decade.

On June 5, 1999, *Toronto Star* music columnist Sid Adilman did an interview with me, resulting in a three-quarter page article in *The Star*. It was called "Folk Greats, The Travellers on Canadian Road Again, Social Conscience of the '60's return with a new CD and TV special". He quoted the first page of the new Travellers' CD liner notes written by Rob Bowman that you read on the first page of this book. He added, "… and as a fan too, I say The Travellers deserve to be heard again, and also to get an Order of Canada as well."

On June 10, Bill Gladstone of the *Canadian Jewish News* wrote in his column, "If you love folk music, you'll enjoy hearing The Travellers' new CD, available in record stores everywhere".

On September 19, 1999 we did a concert in support of the Oakville Community Centre for Peace, Ecology, and Human Rights that we'd sung for before. I received a letter from President Stephen Dankowich who wrote: "I appreciated very much your musical contributions from the stage in promotion of our theme of a world without war. Many remarked how much they enjoyed your performance." I still have a copy of the program we sang that day, which included one of the first three songs we ever sang, "Last Night I Had the Strangest Dream" by Wade Hemsworth. The words still ring true.

In mid-July of 1999, the new Sony CD, *The Best of The Travellers: This Land Is Your Land* was released and Sam Sniderman (Sam The Record Man) displayed it in his Yonge Street window, as did some of the Indigo book stores, as promised by Heather Reisman when I wrote to her about it. Indigo also featured the CD in its summer catalogue, saying, "This is the first comprehensive collection of music from The Travellers, Canada's pioneering folk group, whose political consciousness and distinctive Canadian identity imbued their songs with social significance." That's quite an endorsement from the largest book and record store in Canada.

On July 1, *The Bayview Post* magazine did another story. The cover was a picture of Jerry Gray and his banjo. Lisa Van De Ven interviewed me for several hours, and then wrote a two-page story that included these lines: "The history of The Travellers is almost the history of the Canadian music industry itself, as they forged an industry out of nothing until the early 1970's when the federal government stepped in to bring in Canadian content rules. The Travellers worked and lived through the monumental steps to bring in this legislation, but never received any recognition from the Juno Board, despite hearing from Jerry at least every two years."

In July, I received a copy of letters between the National Film Board and Cohen Siblings regarding the documentary film about The Travellers, as they were going into development. On August 9, I wrote a letter to Jerry Goodis in response to some points he had raised, and asking about information from Sheila Copps, the citizenship minister. I added to this letter, "In summary, we have known each other all our lives, and our common purpose in this venture is to have the project about The Travellers succeed. I would like our relationship to continue to be amicable so that our common goals can be obtained." Sadly, several days later, I got this response from him: "The idea for this project is 'mine,' and I asked Sid Dolgay whether he wanted to be a part of it." His last paragraph was as follows: "Please be aware that I will not let anyone snatch this project away from me re marketing its content and its fund-raising. Heritage Canada and Ms. Copps will give us the money. All I need from you is the fact that you have given permission to Sid and myself to be one-third owners of The Travellers, and let the bank know."

Now I understood clearly what Jerry Goodis and Sid Dolgay had wanted all along. I said, "Unless I get a commitment of funding from Ms. Copps, I will go no further with this plan. I am not going to make you both partners without some sort of reply from the government." Three months later on October 20, in response to my queries, I received a reply from Ms. Copps that her office had no record of any correspondence between her and Mr. Goodis. She then referred us to the Canada Council of the Arts to seek funding from them. But the funding from the federal government for year 2000 projects had now dried up. I never heard back from the Goodis-Dolgay group about this issue again. Jerry Goodis and his third wife moved to the interior of B.C. where he fell ill, and died several years later.

I'll never forget a statement Jerry made when the CBC interviewed him after he left the group, and asked about our being the first folk group in Canada. He then added on the tape "and we were the worst folk group in Canada". He probably meant it to be humorous, but I think he really meant it thinking that without him any group would not be successful.

In early December, the Faculty of Dentistry's monthly magazine featured a story about the CD release, the coming film by the NFB, and a picture of the group. Sid Adilman then wrote another article in the *Toronto Star* about the rerelease of our kids' album. He included the highlights of the CD so that people would know why to buy it:

The Travellers Sing for Kids:
- "Tons of holiday toons and tunes"
- "The first CD of the original recording"

- "Fresh as only the 1960's folk boom can be"
- "The performances are jaunty and most of the songs are classics"
- "Who can ever tire of hearing "Abiyoyo" or "Bingo""
- "Certainly not every generation of youngsters.

Late in 1999, I received a letter from Heather Reisman, president of Indigo Books, saying "we support any Travellers project to make Canadians aware of their heritage." The last letter of the year I received was a request for The Travellers to appear at Camp Naivelt the following summer for the purpose of filming a concert to be included in The Travellers' NFB documentary. With anticipation, I agreed to the present group performing there. We'll see what happens after the New Year, and the new century begins. Just a note about the remaining 19 years of the book. It contains awards, select memberships, great stories, a mystery, world class events, more "firsts" and some tragedies as well. Sit down and listen, and have a drink to the new century.

CHAPTER 7:
ONE OF THESE DAYS, I'M GONNA STOP ALL MY TRAVELLING

2000 - A New Century

Well, it's here. The New Century. I was now sixty-seven years old and, with all I'd done, I sometimes felt like I'd been at it for 100 years. By having had two parallel careers—perhaps a hundred years' worth of work—it was reasonable to feel like that. The new century brought a new interest in The Travellers, with calls for interviews and plans for the future.

The first story of the century about the Travellers was published by a Toronto News Magazine, *The Bayview Post* which, the previous year, had done a huge cover story on The Travellers. Now, to start the new millennium, its lead story was called "They Are Back". The article talked about "the glory years of several decades ago when we would do a kids' concert in the afternoon and an adult concert that same evening. With the release last year of *The Travellers Sing for Kids* CD and the *This Land* CD for Sony Music, a whole new generation could now enjoy what The Travellers have stood for, for all their forty-seven years". This was a nice beginning to what would be a tumultuous year.

Early in the year, I got a call from Barna-Alper Productions, a film company that had signed an agreement with the Canadian Labour Congress to produce an interactive CD-ROM called *The Story of Canadian Labour 1900–2000*.They wanted to use three tracks from our 1967 LP about the Canadian Labour movement, a ground-breaking LP that stands up to scrutiny to this day. Because of our active role in the labour movement, they asked if we would allow them to use the three tracks "gratis". The Travellers officially said "yes" on February 11, and appeared at the National Convention of the Canadian Union of Public Employees (CUPE). Afterwards, I asked for a video copy of our appearance there. Morna Ballentyne, managing director of CUPE wrote back, "I'm happy to enclose a copy of your Thursday morning performance at our CUPE National Convention. I hope you enjoy it as much as we did."

My relationship with this union goes back some thirty-five years when Gil Levine, an early friend at Camp Naivelt, who was a graduate student at U. of T., became the education director for CUPE in Ottawa, a post he held for at least thirty-five years. When Gil died in 2009 a group was set up in Ottawa in his memory to host a concert on May 1, often called "May Day". In view of the fact that I had been invited by both his family and the union to sing at his retirement and for his union many times, it would seem appropriate to have me and/or The Travellers appear at his remembrances. I still wonder why.

In February of 2000, we signed a letter to have us appear in Montreal at a convention for the Communications Energy and Paperworkers' Union of Canada (CEP) in September. We had sung for them more often than for the CAW because they hold their conventions every two years, unlike the three-year gap of the CAW. We also got an invitation from Owen Public School in Toronto for The Travellers to appear at a gathering for all the students because all four of my kids had attended that school in North York, and I was glad to agree.

We appeared at the national public service union (OPSEU) at the Sheraton Hotel in Toronto on April 6. That performance went well, for we had them singing all the labour songs, and ended with everyone singing "Solidarity Forever", the union anthem. These union conventions are always uplifting for both performers and audience members alike. It seems that the unions we have sung for all these many years have not forgotten us as we moved into a new century. The unions and the songs go on, and so do we.

On April 28, The Travellers fulfilled their commitment to appear at Owen Public School. We did many of our kids' songs, and some more adult ones for the senior grades. The Toronto Performing Arts Lodge for seniors had also invited us to sing at their outdoor courtyard on June 24. We would be performing with Nancy White, Rick Fielding, and Paul Mills. *The Canadian Jewish News* announced this concert with an article about The Travellers entitled "The Travellers:

Almost 50 years of Folk Tunes". This was the third time we had performed for PAL. The article also mentioned that The Travellers had just won a prestigious award. But I was off to Britain first.

Canada Day in London England!

In late June, my wife and I travelled to London to visit our son Kevin, who was getting his masters' degree in law at the London School of Economics. The residence where he was staying was home to many students from around the world. They asked me to bring my banjo to London and do a concert with Kevin for them on June 30. After we arrived, I called Canada House, the Canadian Embassy in London, and told them I was in town, and asked if they could use any help for their Embassy's Canada Day celebrations on July 1. They told me that their guest speaker, was to be Donald Sutherland, who was in London doing a play in the West End, and the theatre had added a matinee on July 1. That meant he could only attend for a few minutes at 12:00 noon when the festivities began.

Canada Day celebration, Canadian Embassy, London, 2001

They asked if I could do an approximately one-hour concert performance and, of course, I agreed. I met Sutherland for the first time and quickly realized he was not aware much of The Travellers since he spent very little time in Canada. He made a short speech and then, after reluctantly taking a picture with me, he turned over the afternoon to me and was off to the theatre. I did the show and then, following protocol, marched with everyone present about a mile to a local pub that specializes in Canadian beer and poutine, and ran hockey films on the TV all day. It was a grand afternoon of "Canadianism", and I was glad to help out. After we were back home in Canada, I received a letter from Debra Davis of The Canada House Embassy saying, "Thank you for agreeing to participate in our Canada Day celebrations. It was a generous offer especially after you arrived only two days earlier, and did a full concert the day after you arrived. The 500 visitors to Canada House certainly enjoyed your concert."

Just before I had left Canada for London, we were notified by the Toronto Musicians Association that, starting in 2001, they'd be initiating a Lifetime Achievement Award for a Toronto musician. The award would only be for living musicians and not be given posthumously—except for the first one, which would be given to the late Morris "Moe" Koffman, who was a jazz saxophonist and flautist, as well as a composer and arranger. Moe Koffman, a legend in the Toronto music scene, was tied to The Travellers because his record-setting recording of "Swingin' Shepherd Blues" had been popular at the same time as The Travellers' first recording of "This Land" had also been a record-setter.

The second Award for Lifetime Achievement was given to The Travellers for their forty-seven consecutive years of performing as members of the TMA. I had already been given a 25-Year pin and a 35-Year pin from the TMA, and it was indeed an honour to be so acknowledged and acclaimed by one's peers. The inauguration was to be held at a general meeting later in the year, so, I'll share the details then.

In early July, I had to return from London to appear with The Travellers at the Mariposa Folk Festival—this year being held back in

Orillia. (Greta stayed behind and toured London with her sister, Lucy.) The Travellers would appear in concert on the Friday night, and Jerry Gray would do a one-hour children's concert on Saturday afternoon. I had invited Sid Dolgay to appear with us as part of Mariposa 40 and all went well, although there had been grumbling in the group about his presence. There had been little time for rehearsal, and he lacked knowledge of our current repertoire some thirty-five years since he had left us in 1965. This was the fortieth anniversary of the Mariposa Folk Festival, and the Travellers had been invited to perform at all the "special" anniversaries of Mariposa. No one else can make that statement.

Sunday August 6 was the 75th anniversary of Camp Naivelt, where, as you recall, The Travellers had been invited to do a concert that would be filmed by the National Film Board, a concert that would be included in a documentary about the Travellers. It was an exciting Saturday afternoon under a big-top tent, with a lot of tears from the audience, many of whom were seeing and reliving their own history on stage again. During its hey-day years, Camp Naivelt used to have big hootenanny campfires every Friday and Saturday night. At this concert, the film people wanted me to sing with Jerry Goodis, Sid Dolgay, and Simone Johnston at what I later called "The Bonfire of the Inadequacies". The four of us rehearsed a couple of songs, for a few minutes and then closed the evening and bonfire with "This Land". The song ended the evening, as well as the film. By now, I was really perturbed by these events because there had still been no interviews with any of the current Travellers, nor with me, but they had already interviewed the three other early members of the group

Before the concert, I had received a letter from the other original member, Oscar Ross. Oscar was also perturbed by the fact that he wasn't interviewed by the Cohen siblings or the NFB, for he had been an original member of the group and best friend of Jerry Goodis. It seemed to me there were some strange things going on behind the scenes of this documentary, even though it was I who had supplied ninety per cent of the documents and films that were being used. To me, singing songs with people who hadn't sung anything for at least thirty-five years was not good music or good TV, and it all could have been much better if someone had asked me about it beforehand. There will obviously be more questions. As you read on, try and hold back the tears. I have to.

Later in the summer, August 18, 19, and 20, The Travellers were invited to take part in the Owen Sound Folk Festival as they celebrated their 25th anniversary. I sent a letter to the festival about two weeks before and they replied, facetiously, that it was our fault that there had been a record presale of tickets, so they were quite happy! We had done about four concerts in Owen Sound in the years before they had a folk festival. Also, because I had a cottage in nearby Collingwood, about ten years earlier, I had done a neighbourly fund-raising concert at the small synagogue in town, a concert which had been well attended and very successful. Don Bird, Festival Director, sent us a long letter thanking us for being so cooperative and, "for the wonderful reception we got because of our wonderful programming".

Earlier in the year, as I mentioned earlier, we had been signed by the Communication Energy and Paper Workers Union (CEP) for four performances in two days at their convention in Montreal on September 10–14. After having done about ten of their conventions, it was now like singing at a reunion.

Several days after the convention in Montreal, I started my second year teaching a course called "Folk, Protest and Labour Music" at the University of Toronto. I had more students than the previous year, and I thought that, unless the fee was subsidized by a labour union or some such group, the fee for the course was pretty high for an interest course that didn't lead to a degree.

I begin looking at other places to teach my course. Greta's brother and sister-in-law (that's always interesting because their actual surname is LAW) had helped start a series of Later Life Learning courses at Ryerson University, at a much lower tuition fee than at U. of T., so I made arrangements to teach my course at Ryerson for the next fall.

In the fall, I discovered that CUPE, the Union of Public Employees, had used our Union record to produce a record for CUPE's anniversary the previous year. They had made 2,000 copies, and had not notified The Travellers at all. That was certainly a non-union thing to do to a lifetime pro-union group. I did not want to penalize the union for its actions, but I was certainly not going to give up compensation, since the deed had been done surreptitiously. I figured out what the CD would have cost them had they purchased them from us and re-labelled them. We worked out a fee which they agreed with, and the matter was closed on September 20, 2000.

Early in the year, the Saskatchewan Arts Council called and invited us to do two concerts on September 29 and 30: one in Yorkton in the eastern part of the province, and the other in the west in Swift Current. The Travellers had not toured through Saskatchewan for many years, so this was a relatively new audience for us, and both concerts went well as usual.

My wife Greta had been born in Swift Current, and actually lived thirty miles away in a hamlet called Niedpath on the CNR line. I told the group that, since I was driving, I was going to drive through Niedpath for the first time, as it wasn't much out of the way. We turned south off the TransCanada Highway before we reached Swift Current, and drove for about twenty miles on a one lane road. The only thing we could see was miles and miles of wheat fields, and no farmhouses in sight. Finally, we saw a big combine coming down the hill against us. The combine moved over to the shoulder, and the blade of the combine rose way up in the air—and we drove under it! We all breathed a sigh of relief, and then said, "Wow, that was exciting!"

The farmer with the combine probably went home and said to his wife "You know, I saw a car on the road today. That's pretty rare!" A few miles more and we came to a sign that said, NIEDPATH. But we saw only one house and a post office building as big as my kitchen, and three empty grain elevators with their doors clacking in the wind. When my wife had lived there, Niedpath had been a community boasting two hotels and two grocery stores, one owned by Greta's mother, and was on the main CNR line. We could see that the tracks had been removed, and now the grain elevators were just standing there. There was no one home at the one house still there, so I guessed the town was abandoned. On the side of the hill, we saw about fifteen combines rusting away, and nothing else. It was all very sad.

We took some pictures for Greta and continued on to Swift Current. A week before leaving Toronto, I had done an interview on Swift Current radio and, during the interview, I had mentioned that my wife came from Niedpath. So, when we arrived in Swift Current, there was a committee from Niedpath waiting for me. It seemed that the remaining members of the town had all moved to Swift Current, wanted to speak to me and tell me what had happened to the town and to the houses and the residents.

By 1981, the CPR discontinued service and stopped picking up grain in Niedpath. The town had to close. All the houses were moved elsewhere as they had no basements, and no longer any reason to be there. This was my first visit to rural Saskatchewan and I realized what had happened to the rural part of the province. I am sure there are many stories like that, but it was a first for me. They remembered my wife as the youngest of four children, and her widowed mother who ran a grocery store.

On my return to Toronto, there was an announcement in the *Canadian Jewish News* describing my second set of lectures in the fall at the U. of T. that would include some early songs of Jewish settlers in rural areas of the country. On November 14, The Travellers were asked to sing at the Constellation Hotel near the Toronto Airport. That's a hotel I had never sung at before. We were there to sing at an NDP pep rally, paid for by the Canadian Labour Congress. This is what we did, and do.

At the end of the year, I received a copy of the *Owen Sound Sun Times*, stemming from our August performance at the Owen Sound Summerfolk Festival. It was a well-written history of the group, lauding what we had accomplished in our forty-seven-year career. On October 22, we returned to the Oakville Community Centre to sing for Peace Ecology and Human Rights, having sung for them the previous year. It was our part in doing something for the planet.

The year 2000 was a long one. Near the end, we did a Seasonal Concert on December 10 at the Tranzac Club at Bloor and Brunswick. During the year, I'd been negotiating with the Canadian Labour

Congress about their co-sponsoring a second recording about the Canadian Labour movement. They finally agree, but all the co-sponsorship between Jerry Goodis and the federal government had dried up, so the idea was shelved. Happy Holiday to all, and we look forward to the next year 2001 – but I still have worries about the documentary.

2001

Last year, we had signed an agreement with Robert Missen Artist Management to be the agent for The Travellers and, in 2000, he produced our tour to Saskatchewan and this year, one concert in Port Hope, Ontario on February 3. They have a theatre there that is very active with plays and concerts for the general community, and our concert was very successful. Leo Powell was a long-time friend who had grown up with me at Camp Naivelt. Leo ran a pub right behind the back door of the Port Hope Theatre, and after our rehearsal, rather than going out for dinner, Leo offered to provide us with a liquid dinner along with some pub food. That might be the reason why the concert was so successful! Sadly, several years later, Leo developed early onset Alzheimer's, and died before I was able to see him again.

Several weeks after our Port Hope concert, son James and I appeared at Temple Har Zion in Thornhill to do a concert of folk and Yiddish music. Several days later, I received a very heartfelt letter from the chair of the Har Zion music committee, thanking us for an outstanding evening.

The coming year did not have a lot of dates on the books, but in April, the NFB documentary about The Travellers would be the opening film at the Canadian Jewish Film Festival. I received word that the producers would finally film an interview with me to be included in the film. As I said before, the directors had not filmed any interviews with former original member, Oscar Ross, nor with any of the four newer Travellers, who had all joined the group between 1965 and 1972, and had been the face of this group for thirty consecutive years. As for why. I would soon find out.

NFB Documentary: The Travellers – This Land Is Your Land, 2001

The interview was done in my home by the male Cohen Sibling. On camera, I was first asked questions about the supposed ouster of Sid Dolgay and Simone Johnston in the 60s, and I answered with the known truth, that Sid Dolgay had been voted out of the group in 1965 by a 3–1 vote of the company made up of the four Travellers of the time, with no dissensions. In the film, Simone claimed she did not remember voting Sid out. But the vote was witnessed by our lawyer, and recorded in our company records. And in 1969, it was Simone Johnston who told The Travellers that she would be leaving after we got news that our bid for a CBC TV series called *Movin' On* had been turned down. Sid Adilman of the *Toronto Star* wrote an article saying the decision to cancel the bid was traitorous as, after viewing the pilot, the CBC thought the series would be approved, but later changed its mind. Simone announced to us that she was leaving, but on the film, she claimed she was voted out of the group against her knowledge.

The interviewer told me that the two dissident Travellers, Dolgay and Simone, said different things on the film. I asked, "Have you interviewed former Traveller Ray Woodley who was in the group when these events took place, or our manager at the time, Martin Bockner?" The answer was no, so it seemed I was on my own. It became clear the film company had listened to Sid and Simone's stories, and had taken their side. Apparently, they were not interested in hearing the other side, of how they had left the group in a proper, legal way.

I then asked, "Why?", since the film was supposed to be an accurate study of the forty-seven years of the group to the present, and not just centered on a petty, unsubstantiated charge by certain members. It left out entirely the thirty years after Simone and Sid had left. On camera, I asked about their leaving out interviews with Ray, Ted, Joe, Aileen, and Pam completely. In the film seen later, they spliced in a segment of the new Travellers appearing in the Arctic on Canada Day in 1979, with no comment by the narrator, but only mentioned by me in my interview. In addition, I was the one who supplied them with many of the pieces of film they used. In the film, Simone claimed that after she left in 1969, The Travellers never did any union appearances. But if you've read these pages up to now, you can count the number of union appearances that either the group or I have done for every union in the country, and they number in the hundreds. If you watch the film, you'll see me trying to defend myself against these false charges, and the facts speak for themselves, so this is a good spot to tell the truth.

When The Travellers had returned from Britain in February 1965, we had lost money. At that time, Sid was fighting a bankruptcy. Sid and his wife Ida managed our bank account, and they were the only signatories on our account, and of our cheques. Some of the group's money was removed from our account to pay off one of his creditors because of a writ served against the group's account by Sid's bankruptcy defaulters.

I'd had a problem with Sid in the Soviet Union when the Soviets wanted to stop us from singing Yiddish material on the tour, but I won out and the songs were included. When I visited my mother's sister in Vilna, Sid came along and when my aunt told us in Yiddish of the problems that Jews had in Lithuania, Sid told my aunt "Not to worry because the Soviets would live up to their promises." That's when my aunt pointed to a ceiling fan in my hotel room, warning us to be careful of what we said because the Soviets had been known to bug the rooms. Sid dismissed her words, saying they would never do that. My aunt, who had survived the Holocaust with only her son-in-law and a granddaughter left after the war, discounted Sid's pro-Soviet advice. After I returned to Canada, I got a letter from my aunt reporting that her son-in law, who drove a cab after the war because of his war injuries, told her a man had entered his cab and accused him of dealing with the enemy of the Soviet Union. So much for Sid's support of the Soviets! A year later, my aunt and her family got permission to immigrate to Israel.

These events, although disquieting to me, never entered into my decision to vote Sid out. The true reason was he was a bad manager, had used the group's funds for his own use, and musically was not serving to better the group. My comment on the film was that Sid was a Neanderthal hoping to live in the past. He was refusing to recognize that the folk music world was changing, and he wanted no part of a new definition for the group. In time, I was proven to be absolutely right.

With regard to Simone, she was fairly close to the Communist party line. When she was interviewed on the film about my aunt in

Russia (who had nothing but a meagre Russian pension) Simone claimed that my aunt and her friends had a dacha on the sea, and had nothing to say about Jews being discriminated against in Russia. In the film, her true feelings were displayed. It's worth a look to see that part of the film. One event that must be told is this: In 1967, when The Travellers were in Montreal singing at Expo 67, the Israeli/Egypt Six-Day War was at its height. I had a habit of reading the paper in the towns where we sang, and if I noticed a headline, I would refer to it in some of the song introductions. One morning, a Montreal paper said "Nasser in Trouble", so I fired off a line in a song where we sang about "Nasser and his misery". Following that show, Simone's husband at the time (an American anarchist from L.A.) approached me and warned me to never use a line like that again! My relationship with him ended then. I never said anything to Simone about it, but it certainly stayed in my mind as a singular event, but not forgotten.

So, there you have it. The National Film Board co-producers saw an opening, and the documentary changed from being an honest, fact-based laudatory story of the group's history and accomplishments to one of personality conflicts and unsubstantiated charges, and not facts. When Sid had been voted out from the group, I wrote to him and told him I felt he would never be a good fit with us but, in the spirit of friendship, I would include him whenever The Travellers sang at an event of significance. In keeping my word, I included him in seven Mariposa events, and about four anniversary events of The Travellers. I never got a thank you, only a grunt and goodbye.

In this year of 2001, I once again invited Sid to join us at Mariposa 40. Mariposa would not pay him, so I paid him out of my own personal fee. This is the true story of how these events unfolded. When I saw the preview of the film, I was shocked with what had been done and what had been omitted, and I tried to stop the showing. But I needed at least $20,000 in legal fees to do that, and was not able to. I thought the film would hang itself. I'll give you later reviews of the film by noted Canadian critics, and what Simone and Sid had done to the idea of the memory of the group by destroying it. When Jerry Goodis and Sid Dolgay had approached me several years ago, they did it claiming they wanted to perpetuate the good name of the group. As it turned out, Goodis really wanted to take over the group to his advantage, and Sid was looking for an opportunity to have revenge for the supposed wrongs done to him thirty-seven years earlier.

Jerry Goodis still did not give up. In February 2001, he sent me a letter threatening a lawsuit from his industry lawyer, Michael Levine. He accused me of having the liner notes to the new Sony CD written by Dr. Rob Bowman, and that I had altered the text by omitting any part played by his former partner, Sam Goldberg, and also not mentioning him in the film. I told him that Rob Bowman had been employed by Sony Music and did all the writing of the liner notes, and that I had had absolutely no input other than answering Rob's questions. In fact, I never saw the finished product until the CD came out. Manager Sam Goldberg was also not in the film because he had died many years earlier, and they had no footage of him.

Goodis also accused me of stealing the rights to a train whistle sound on the recording of "The Rock Island Line". In writing, I told him that the rights to those recordings were owned by Sony Records, and I, as the sole heir to The Travellers Productions, was given the royalties for that song. I told him that, in two years, the rights produced by that song amounted to $7.42 Canadian. Rather than share his claim with all the members of the historical group of Travellers in 1959, I suggested that he get a life, and if he wanted a share of that amount, he should get his lawyer, Michael Levine, to search the case law and get back to me.

The NFB film came out in late April and was shown three times at the Toronto Jewish Film Festival. It's interesting that they decided to use this film of The Travellers as their opening, because the first twenty minutes is all about The Travellers growing up in a Jewish environment, and all the original members of the group were indeed Jewish.

When Ray Woodley left the group in 1975. I was really disappointed, for I thought Ray was ready to be a star in our group. He had begun writing very humorous songs and doing solos well, but I think he was urged by his new wife to leave. After leaving, he did a TV show on his own that was just fair, and as a solo performer he received little acclaim. He and his wife went to Los Angeles as she was working as a set designer on her brother, David Cronenberg's films. Ray found work as a linotype operator and, after two children, they broke up and his wife returned to Toronto with their two kids. Ray and I kept in touch by mail, and I would get updates on his life. He was no longer singing, and had sold his guitar and moved to Phoenix for a linotype job, as there were no positions in L.A.

In late 2000, I got a note saying that he had throat cancer problems and was also fighting prostate cancer. He was turning sixty-five, and returning to Toronto for medical care. When he called me early in 2001, I invited some of the Travelers and ex-Travellers to dinner at my place to catch up and talk about old times. Along with Ray, there was Don Vickery and his wife Fay Olson, Ted Roberts, Joe Hampson, and my wife Greta, and we talked about getting together soon and maybe finding a guitar for Ray. He was staying with one of his first batch of kids, and said he would get back to me soon. After a month, when I did not hear from him, I called his kids. They told me he was back in hospital. He died shortly after on April 11, 2002. Later in the summer, we again showed up to do a musical tribute in Ray's memory with his first family at Hugh's Room, and the Cronenberg family made a video of his life and the event.

There was an obituary for Ray Woodley in the *Globe and Mail* on June 19, 2002, with some information I was aware of. In an earlier interview about his early folk years in the 60s, he told how people like Gordon Lightfoot and Ian and Sylvia and the odd Traveller would come to his place after their evening gigs, and Lightfoot would often sleep over on a couch. He also told a story of his wife, Joan, who evicted Phil Ochs from the house when he tried to light up a joint. He often told the story of our recording Oscar Brand's song "Something to Sing About", and how Oscar had written an account of the record saying, "The Travellers owe their success to quality musicianship, dedicated craftsmanship, unlimited good taste and unbridled enthusiasm." Ray was a Canadian enthusiast and a valuable teammate in the years he travelled with the Travellers. Long gone, but not ever forgotten by me, or Ted Roberts or Joe Hampson.

During that summer, announcements went out about Jerry Gray's eight-lecture course at the University of Toronto, and how a good crowd had registered for the fall of 2001. After all the tumult about the NFB documentary about The Travellers, it was nice to get back to actually singing.

Ruth Rubin was a New York City collector of Jewish songs, as well as the author of several books that were my source of historical information about songs I had learned from, or sought knowledge from. Fagel Gartner, my first mentor of Yiddish songs, had learned many of her songs from the Ruth Rubin collections and passed them on to me.

This concert of September 29 was sponsored by many of the Jewish music centres in Toronto. Ruth had appeared at Camp Naivelt to do a program of Yiddish songs. She was not a great singer, but her knowledge of European Jewish songs was incomparable. She died on June 11, 2000 in New York City. Her sister lived in Toronto and, Ben Steinberg, the head of Temple Sinai Synagogue's music department, held a memorial concert to which I was invited to sing on June 12 to a good crowd.

I had been going to Collingwood since 1969 and my family had had a ski chalet since that time. A group of Jewish skiers, mainly from Toronto, formed an organization called the B'nai Harim, the Brotherhood of the Hills. Greta and I joined and, at the first meeting on Saturday September 29, I was asked to do a program as they celebrated their inaugural gathering. That organization exists to the present day under the two co-chairs, Marsha Feldman and Merle Gottleib, who remain my close personal friends.

Near the end of the year, I learned about an article in *The Globe and Mail*. It seems that columnist Brent Hagerman wrote an article claiming it was Ian Tyson who wrote the Canadian words to "This Land". Peter Gzowski at the CBC claimed it was Oscar Brand. I had to send a letter to *The Globe* in order to enlighten them all that it had been The Travellers who wrote it. We also pointed out to Mr. Gzowski that he had incorrectly said the second line of the chorus was "from Buena Vista to the Vancouver Island." Shame on all of you. Buena Vista was in California, but we chose Bonavista, one of the most easterly ports in Newfoundland, Canada.

On Friday December 29, the NFB documentary on The Travellers opened at the New York City Jewish Film Festival. It had previously made the rounds at Montreal and Vancouver's festivals as well. When Oscar Brand saw the film in New York, he was appalled by what Sid and Simone had done to destroy a great beginning of the film. He asked me, rhetorically, "How could Sid still accept the fact that what the Soviets had done to Russian Jews, and not taken a stand, as many others had done?"

During the spring of 2001, The Travellers were presented with the first Toronto Musicians Lifetime Achievement Award. It is very good to be given a Lifetime Achievement Award while you are still alive. I've since made it known that all awards given to me would best be done that way, as I would not accept posthumous awards. At the presentation, I gave a review of my joining the union in 1954. As this award was for the Travellers, I accepted it on behalf of all those who had been part of the group over the years, and listed the names of everyone through to the present, and others who had worked closely with us like our managers Sam Goldberg, and Marty Bockner. I even mentioned my late sister Helen with reverence. The main thing I said was that receiving an award from one's peers was the greatest honour that one could get. And it truly is.

Lifetime Achievement Award, Toronto Musicians' Union, 2001

That year of 2001 was probably the toughest of my life, because of the release of NFB documentary film about The Travellers. The entire production had been hijacked by the two ex-Travellers, Sid and Simone, who bared their personal feelings and even their political feelings harboured deep in their psyche, and liberated them to some uninformed people from the Cohen Siblings to the National Film Board. All the people involved, including Sid and Simone, had vowed to create a laudatory film about something bigger than them— The Travellers. Each said they would not fail to keep their vow, and they both failed, and completely broke that vow. It's best to see the film yourself; you can call it up on You Tube and see what happened.

Gary Cristall saw the film when it came to Vancouver, and wrote a review. Gary, originally from Toronto, worked for six years in Ottawa at the Canada Council for the Arts during the 1967 Canadian centennial year. He then went to Vancouver where he was a founder and artistic director of the Vancouver Folk Music Festival for fifteen years. He was in the later stages of writing a book on the history of folk music in Canada when he saw Travellers' film. He writes how he looked forward to what he thought would be a "great" documentary. His review covers the film's pluses and failures, and you should read his professional review that follows:

"This is a film that betrays its own promise," he writes. "The first thirty minutes are outstanding, showing The Travellers emerging from their ghetto beginnings and rising to heights never thought possible. Then it is hijacked and flies off-course listening to two now retired individuals both with grudges. Jerry Gray was absolutely right in realizing that the 'Black Flies' and 'Solidarity' could not be sung forever, and 'The Times They Were a-Changing'. All the things the group had done were on behalf of Canadians learning about their country. Jerry Gray is wrongly painted by them as the group's Stalin, betraying the values of the group for his own twisted ends. Simone accuses Jerry of this, and says that the group had stopped singing for unions when, unknown to her, they sang for every major union in Canada following her leaving the group. Jerry became the only Canadian ever nominated to win the Joe Hill Award given to labour educators, and nominated by former winners Guy Carawan and Pete Seeger and every major union in Canada."

The producers of the film fell victim to the personal sobbing of Dolgay as he showed how right the group was in exiling him. His selfish, self-serving actions proved us to have been absolutely right.

I am glad now to return to the positivity of doing what we were proven to have been doing right all along— the education of Canadians about the background of most of the songs and the part they played in the history of events throughout our, and my, careers.

2002

I was glad the "Year of the Film" about The Travellers was over. It left a bad taste in my mouth because of the former Travellers' hijacking the film for their own personal interests. The situation about the film was compounded in 2002, as the rights to the film were sold by the NFB to several Canadian TV stations and appeared about four times during the year. I personally edited the film and made my own version by omitting Sid's tearful outbursts and Simone's anti-Semitic views of Soviet Jews; by eliminating these venomous bits from the "terrible two", the film is actually good. Then, early in 2002, I get word that Jerry Goodis, who had moved to Kamloops in 2001, was now in a Vancouver Cancer Hospital and not expected to survive.

Putting this disagreeable episode behind us, The Travellers were looking forward to marking their 50th consecutive year of performance and, as we always did, we wanted to mark the occasion with a special event. Once the date was set for May 1, May Day, at Hugh's Room, I sent out a mailing to announce this milestone. Various news outlets, some government agencies, and a few other organizations sent us tributes and congratulations of this ground-breaking event.

Another change occurring that year is that I would not be returning to the U. of T. for a third season; instead, starting in the fall, I would be lecturing at the Life Institute at Ryerson University.

In the March 7 issue of the *Canadian Jewish News*, columnist Bill Gladstone announced that The Travellers would be having a Hootenanny, a concert sing-along on May 1 at Hugh's Room.

Oh yes. There was also an announcement about that year's Juno Awards show. So, once again, I wrote to CARAS about the chance of The Travellers being honoured for their early work in starting the Junos. That was about the nth letter I had written to CARAS, and I expected another negative reply. I got an early reply that my letter would be added to my file, and it would be reviewed again. I informed them that last year, the group had received the first Lifetime Achievement Award ever given out by the Toronto Musicians' Association. I also told them that the group would be marking fifty consecutive years in our performance calendar, and we were expecting mentions as many civic, provincial and federal government agencies would be marking the occasion by sending greetings. I also told them we would be appearing at the national conventions of the CLC, the CAW, and the Communications Union (CEP) during the coming year. The *Toronto Star* made mention when The Travellers' Lifetime Award was presented, saying this was the second Lifetime award by a union given to The Travellers, for the group had also been honoured with Lifetime Awards by the Communications Union and the Ontario Federation of Labour.

Early in the year, Greta and I visited her brother and sister-in-law at their Boca Raton home in Florida. I spied a calendar from the local Florida Atlantic University (FAU) announcing its Later Life Learning Programs. Just like those at Ryerson University in Toronto, they are not degree-granting courses—just for learning and enjoyment. A good look told me there was no one teaching a folk music course. Upon my return to Toronto, I sent a letter to the registrar of the University asking if I might be allowed to teach a course the following winter. It usually takes a week for mail to travel from Toronto to Florida. On the seventh day, I got a phone call from Ely Myerson, course mentor at Florida Atlantic University. He said, "Will you be able to teach an eight-week course starting in January of 2003?".

I found this request strange, because I had never performed in Florida, and I'd only provided the FAU people with several recordings and a video of a concert we'd done in Toronto. As I mentioned earlier in this book, the merry-go-round offered a brass ring, and if you reached for it—it might be worthwhile. I accepted the FAU invitation, partly because my wife had reached her 65th birthday and was told she could not teach anymore. Because Greta wanted to keep teaching, the Teachers' union was going to try and make a test case of her forced retirement. Ultimately, Greta decided it might be time for a change and also grab that brass ring. We decided it might be an idea to go to Florida. Greta and I had both skied for many years in Collingwood, but as the years progressed, Greta felt it was not as easy as before to live the whole winter in Canada. We both decided we would at least try out the offer of my teaching in a Later Life Learning situation that was rated the best in Florida.

Now it was time to find a place to rent in Florida. It needed to be close to the I-95 Highway as FAU had two campuses, and both were near I-95. We had heard that a development called Century Village in Deerfield Beach was perfect because they had an extensive tennis program, an on-site bus service, and a bridge club where Greta could play while I was teaching. We rented an apartment there, and I was ready to start another new venture in the winter of 2003.

In the spring of 2002, I was interviewed by Lorne Brown, editor of the *Canadian Folk Music Bulletin*. It was probably the best interview I had ever done. Lorne was also a folkie and banjo player, and stood about six foot two. I always joked that he and I were born as identical twins but separated at birth. I always figured that I had the greatest collection of Pete Seeger memorabilia and records, anywhere, but when we began exchanging artifacts, I had to admit that he had more than I. Since that interview, he and I became muses to each other, and remain friends to the present. When he had been principal at Kensington Public School in Toronto, I had performed children's songs with him there on several occasions.

On May Day, May 1, The Travellers celebrated our 50th anniversary at Hugh's Room, to a full house and approval of our song program—so different from the first one five decades ago—but with the same power and musicality we'd nurtured during those fifty years.

Several days later, we sang for the Canadian Auto Workers at the Sheraton Hotel in Toronto, doing six performances in five days. You might be interested in how these events were done: The main executive of the Union was seated on a stage in the center of a ballroom. The Travellers had their own stage, a little lower right beside the main stage. We had five microphones to broadcast our sound, and a couple of video cameras out front so we could be seen on several large screens throughout the hall. Each session would start at the hour designated, and we would end each show with everyone singing "Solidarity Forever" with us. The gavel would then be banged, and the session would begin with everyone on a high from singing the labour union anthem. This was why our group was so popular at labour conventions. Our ability to bring out the best from our audience was well known.

Several days after the convention, I had been invited to take part in a Canadian Native Peoples' meeting at the U. of T.'s Convocation Hall to protest the death of Dudley George. I was the only non-native on the program, and I sang Buffy Ste. Marie's song, "Now That the Buffalo's Gone". Buffy St. Marie was on the organizing committee, and I had sung with her at the previous Canada Day show on July 1.

She had vouched for me to be a part of the protest; everyone there appreciated my appearance, support, and music.

Wayne Samuelson, president of the Ontario Federation of Labour, heard about our May 1 concert in celebration of our 50th and sent these words:

"The Travellers have always used their talents to address the needs for social justice in this province, this country, and this world, while never losing the ability to entertain their audiences. The history of The Travellers is intertwined with the history of our country. Their legacy lives through their songs and performances captured on radio, television, film, recordings and in the memories of their audiences. In Japan there is a special honour often given to an artist who embodies the best of Japanese philosophy and tradition. They are given the designation of "Living Treasure." Certainly, The Travellers have earned this title".

We next received a letter from the CLC congratulating us on our fiftieth. Ken V. Georgetti, president of the CLC wrote:

"It is hard to imagine what has not been written about The Travellers and their extraordinary contribution to Canadian Folk Music, and to Social Justice. Generations of working women and men have listened to your music. Union Halls from 'Bonavista to the Vancouver Island' have been filled with the voices of working people as they sang 'This Land' or 'Solidarity Forever' with The Travellers singing and leading the way. You are truly "pioneers". Congratulations to sisters and brothers and Travellers past and present. The road to social justice remains long and the journey difficult. Thanks to you that long road is not quite so lonely and the journey less daunting."

On June 2, 2002, I received a letter from Thomas Lee, president of the American Federation of Musicians: To Jerry Gray. "Congratulations on your many awards given in honour of your excellence. Congratulations to all members of your group, in their many achievements, and to you personally for your activities as a labour activist. Thank you for making me aware of what is clearly one of the AFM's outstanding groups."

We also received a letter from Sheila Copps, Minister of Canadian Heritage, thanking us for our "fifty consecutive years of enriching the lives of Canadians with our folk-singing performances about Canada." She made no mention of talks that were supposed to have taken place with Jerry Goodis, several years prior, and I no longer waited for word from her office about the year 2000. These laudatory letters from people who had seen us perform for thirty or forty years are why we continue to do what we have always done: to educate and to entertain.

After the protest on May 1, The Travellers gave a concert on May 2 concert at the University of Windsor, at Mackenzie Hall on the campus.

On July 1st, the group was invited to Ottawa to open the celebration of Canada Day #40 on Parliament Hill, followed by The Four Lads and Buffy Ste. Marie. It marked the 40th anniversary of The Travellers singing at the first Canada Day celebration back on July 1, 1962, a landmark event in our career. After our performance, Sheila Copps sent us another letter thanking us for our participation in the event.

Buffy Ste. Marie and Jerry Gray, Ottawa, 2002

Canada Day celebration, Ottawa, 2002

Back on April 11, 2000, our former guitar player Ray Woodley had passed away and on July 20 of that year, a memorial event was held at Hugh's Room by the Cronenberg family and by Ray's three children from his first marriage to Joan Woodley. The Cronenberg people made a video of the event—easy for them since they were all in the film business! It's a good retrospect of Ray. I have a clipping of Sid Adilman's column from the *Toronto Star* on Tuesday June 25, 2002 reviewing a film called *Rhinoceros Eyes* directed by David Cronenberg, the son of Ray Woodley and Denise Cronenberg. Too bad Ray didn't live long enough to see it.

During the week beginning September 29, the Communications, Energy, and Paperworkers Union held their national convention at the Toronto Convention Centre. That week, The Travellers showed up to do three consecutive early morning, pre-convention song fests for the members, the most times we had performed for this union. All went well, as expected, in front of many old friends from CEP.

In November, Jerry Goodis's first wife, Carol, notified me that on November 8, Jerry had passed away. Their kids asked me to sing at a memorial for Jerry, held in a reception area behind Sunnybrook Hospital. An eclectic mixture of people was present: a great number of people from the UJPO and from Camp Naivelt, and people who sang with us in the Youth Singers. That group was followed by a group of ad-men. All the advertising guys said that, if you wanted to be a success, you had to spend at least one year working for Goodis. I closed the afternoon of remembrance with some early Travellers' songs, and gave credit to Jerry for being an integral part of the early history of The Travellers. He later worked for several of Pierre Trudeau's campaigns, and was a speechwriter for him. They also had similar experiences to ours. Pierre was stopped at the U.S. border for his left leanings, and Jerry Goodis was stopped for similar reasons by U.S. Immigration. The Liberal party got dispensations for both of them.

In October, The Travellers had been invited by Ernie Eves, premier of Ontario, to sing at another command performance for the Queen and Prince Phillip at the National Trade Centre in Toronto. We did only one song as she passed by. The next day was the fiftieth anniversary of my graduation from Harbord Collegiate, Class of '52. I had the pleasure of entertaining my class members from many years ago, and closing the evening. Then on December 12, I was invited to sing for the B'nai B'rith League for Human Rights, which was holding a discussion on "Blacks and Jews in Dialogue". I sang songs of Christmas and Chanukah—easy for me as I've been doing events like this for many years.

That was the last time I would do a December event in Toronto, for in the winter of 2003, I would be in Florida teaching an eight-week course at Florida Atlantic University, and performing a concert there on January 8. That year of our 50th anniversary had been a year of repeats, singing again for major Canadian trade unions, and back again to Ottawa to sing on Canada Day. It was a financially successful year for The Travellers, with the receipt of many letters of congratulations for our 50th anniversary. Here now, I share with you, parts of a letter from Prime Minister Jean Chretien:

"It is with great pleasure that I extend my warmest greetings to the members of The Travellers, as you celebrate 50 years of music. Your special brand of folk music has served to inspire and delight Canadian and international audiences alike, for five decades. From Canada to the former Soviet Union, in concert halls, or at union rallies, before dignitaries or schoolchildren, The Travellers have made a lasting contribution to Canadian arts and culture, leaving their mark on Canada's musical history and helping to shape the multicultural character of our nation. Please accept my best wishes for an enjoyable and memorable celebration, as well as every success, in the years ahead."

I hope we can live up to these laudatory congratulations for as long as our future exists. Howard Hampton, leader of the Ontario NDP, notified us at the end of the year that he had nominated us for the Order of Ontario. We hoped we would get it for at least publicizing the song "The Black Flies" written by Wade Hemsworth, and "Give Us a Place to Stand", but awards people don't seem to be too knowledgeable about all the things the group has done. The first part of this book describes what The Travellers have accomplished. The congratulatory letters printed in this chapter encouraged us to continue what we do best: To inspire, educate, and to entertain.

2003
I Begin a New Career in Florida.

This year, I began a new career in a new country. In January, I started teaching at Florida Atlantic University. I first did a concert about my topic, "Folk, Protest, and Union Music", before starting the eight-week schedule of musically illustrated lectures and songs about the history and background of North American folk music. Later I did the same thing for their campus twenty-five miles north in Jupiter. The reception I got was marvellous, as this was the generation—now parents and grandparents who had been part of the '60s folk boom. They actually knew most of the songs, but not why they had been written. I had been teaching about this topic for five years now, but I had been singing these songs for over fifty years, and I knew a lot of "first person stories" about the writers and singers of this material, having worked with a great number of them.

Because I would be spending five months in Florida now, there was not much work for the group, so Aileen Ahern decided to go back to Halifax to take care of her aging parents. If a booking came up, I would come home, and the sponsor would pay for an air flight for her. We had been following this routine for the last few years. Too bad there weren't yet too many offers for airline points.

My lectures now were interspersed with video pieces recorded from TV, as well as with audio bits from all the early recordings I had purchased and listened to. And when all else failed, I would sing the songs myself—which was often. The theatres at FAU came with an engineer to look after the technical part of my lecture, and it made my life a lot easier. My first year at FAU, I had over 300 people in my class at Boca Raton, and about one hundred in a smaller lecture hall in Jupiter. The course began the second week of January and continued to the last week of February. I was paid in U.S. dollars, and a special reciprocal arrangement between the musician unions in Canada and the U.S provided me with a special status to work in the U.S. As the years went on, that relationship changed favouring U.S entrants, and I'll talk about that later.

That first year, I did the two campuses on the same day, going to Jupiter in the morning and Boca Raton in the afternoon on my way back home. But I was approaching the age of seventy, and found that two ninety-minute classes in two different communities started to become onerous, so after that first year, I asked to do them on separate days. Because payment was from the Florida state office, I had to get a U.S. Social Security Number so that taxes were not deducted, but I could not use my number to get benefits. In Toronto, I had been teaching a course, once per week, at the U. of T. for years, and now here I was at age seventy complaining about two in one day. While for the next five years, I was still doing two per day as I approached my 80th birthday. If you can, you do.

South-east Florida had a Public Radio Station called WLRN in Miami. It had a three-hour folk music program on Sunday afternoons where the host talked with, and about, performers who were touring through Florida. The DJ/host was Michael Stock, whose mother lived in Boca Raton and had attended my class at FAU. She told her son to book me on the show, as I had a long history of performing about and with people like Pete Seeger, Guy Carawan, and Theodore Bikel, and would be an interesting interviewee. Over the years since then, I have been on his show about twelve times including this past year of 2018. As a result, many people started to contact me about doing programs for various gated communities in the southeast Florida area.

The first booking was for Temple Beth Or, in Miami. So, on February 23, 2003 I did a performance for a group of Jewish Secular Humanists that someone video-taped. This was a place as close as I could get to my own brand of Judaism, and much like the UJPO of my early days. I sang there the following year as well.

I met other folkies who were attracted by me, the first person to ever do a folk music program at a university in this area. One was a retired dentist who had grown up in New York City, and went to a summer camp just north of there. He had stood up for Paul Robeson and Pete Seeger in a 1939 concert riot in Peekskill, N.Y.—about which I sang during one of my classes. Dr. Malvin Ring was a dental historian and text book author. He was much older than me, and sadly died the following year before I had an opportunity to quiz him about that seminal event in his American folk music history.

In Jupiter, I talked about some of the summer camps north of New York, and I had read of a workers' camp called WO-CHI-KA where many future folkies had gone. I remarked to the audience that it was terrific that, even in that time period, they named the camp after some Native Americans. That's when a man stood up and told me it was originally called The Workers' Children's Camp, and the name had been shortened to "Wo-Chi-Ka". Figure it out. Who knew? The next week, that same person brought me a book about the fiftieth anniversary of that camp. I gracefully apologized and, one week later when I read the book, I read a lot about familiar later-folksingers began in that camp, exactly like people who had grown up in Camp Naivelt outside of Toronto. It turned out that Ronnie Gilbert and Fred Hellerman of the Weavers and Mary Travers had cut their folk music teeth at Camp Wo-chi-ka.

I had rented a place in Century Village in Deerfield Beach, a gated community with many Americans, but also a huge number of Montrealers, because when the place was being built in the 1980s, the developers had pitched it to Montrealers. Greta had spent her high school years in Montreal and, to our amazement, discovered many people she'd gone to school with! She had an instant bond with her ex-classmates who were approximately the same age and also Jewish. She had an immediate rapport with this community, and we became friends with many like-minded people there and remain so to this day.

Unfortunately, at that time there were few Torontonians in Century Village, but more were coming in every year. We had only chosen to rent that place because of its proximity to the I-95, my important highway, but here we found people with similar values and histories, so we lucked in. We both joined tennis teams at Century Village, and played in house leagues and in local leagues as well. There was also bridge-playing available at the clubhouse four days a week, along with shows and movies throughout the week.

After my first season at FAU, I was notified that it had been successful, and they invited me to return for two months the following January. We ended up staying in Florida until early in April, and made arrangements to rent another place for the following season in 2004. While still there, I get another call from the Dora Teitelboim Center for Yiddish Culture in Miami inviting me to do a Yiddish program for them in March 2003, also to great success.

In April, we returned to Toronto, and I readied myself for a May 1 date for a law firm that works on behalf of many Canadian labour unions. Stephen Wahl was acting for the firm that I'd sung for several times on May Day. The event was in someone's house, and as I sang, everyone knew all the words. That was a fun evening for both the singer and the audience. At that time in Toronto, there was no one around who could do a labour or union-oriented program for people interested in social causes. It was nice to feel wanted and appreciated.

After some discussion, Greta and I made a decision to sell our long-time home in Toronto, and move to our vacation home in Collingwood. Our plan was to live there for seven months of the year, and spend the other five months in Florida. We joined a nearby golf course, belonged to a bridge club, and Greta and I took part in separate weekly tennis games, also nearby—all with no traffic to deal with. My brother-in- law had a place next door with a swimming pool which we could use whenever we wanted. Also, all our local skiing friends came up every weekend to do what we now did all week! So, socially we had the best of everything. The only problem was the frequent and necessary trips to Toronto. Once a month, Greta ran a program of book reviews there, as well as making several educational trips to the Stratford Festival. I still had commitments to Ryerson in their Life lecture series in the fall, so we were going to try it out.

In August, the Bravo network ran another repeat of The Travellers documentary, which reminded people about our achievements. In the fall, my eight-week folk music course at Ryerson on Friday mornings went well. At the end of the session, I learned that Ryerson had done a survey of students from my lectures. The results indicated that seventeen out of eighteen students liked my course, and the same number said they would attend if I did another course next season. It was gratifying to know that I was still on the right track, and I seemed to be the only person delivering a folk music course in this manner. I always announced in my classes and programs, "I am here to both entertain and educate!" Clearly it was working.

The *Canadian Jewish News* ran an article announcing that, since this was the fiftieth anniversary of The Travellers, who had written the new words to "This Land", it would be great to commemorate this occasion with a concert. Accordingly, the Mariposa Foundation joined with the North YMHA to stage a concert at the marvellous Leah Posluns Theatre, at the North Toronto YMHA's Koffler Centre. This was my favourite theatre in Toronto; shaped like a bowl, it seated about 500, and no one was too far from the stage. Set for October 30, the concert was billed as one about the life, times, and songs of Woody Guthrie—something I know at least a little about. The concert was a success financially and culturally. The Koffler Centre program was being run by Adrienne Cohen with whom I began a long association for future concerts.

On Sunday October 19, a column written by humanitarian Michelle Landsberg appeared in the *Toronto Star*. She wrote about missing folk music, and thanked The Travellers for creating a new medium by doing live folk song concerts for children. She also thanked us for creating a whole new industry of recordings for children, and acknowledged The Travellers for starting this Canadian industry nine years before either Raffi or Sharon Lois and Bram began doing what The Travellers had been doing for years.

Although it was not well known, Michelle Landsberg was married to Stephen Lewis, who served for many years as head of the Ontario NDP party, was the <u>Permanent Representative of Canada to the United Nations,</u> and the inaugural <u>United Nations Special Envoy for HIV/AIDS in Africa</u>. During the 1960s and '70s, Michelle and Stephen had come often to our early kids' concerts, and it was nice to know those concerts had been appreciated. She also didn't know it was an absolute pleasure for us to do them.

During the fall, I received a letter from the Venetian Isles Condo Group in Boca Raton, inviting me to do a concert in January. Apparently, someone had seen me at FAU and was enjoying the program! And the bookings continued to come.

In late November, Greta and I were preparing to leave for Florida. We had rented out our Collingwood residence for the ski season, so two days before leaving, I chopped about a cord of wood to ensure my renter had enough for the fireplace. I had no idea how to measure a cord of wood, but I know I chopped a lot! Around November 30, we packed our car and drove to Toronto where I played squash with two of my sons. The next morning, I had a doctor's appointment for my annual check up. We planned to get on the road to Florida as soon as I was done. But at the end of the check-up, my doctor announced that my cardiogram appeared to be different from all the other cardiograms—a take on a Passover question. He believed I might have some kind of heart issue, even though I'd just done what I usually do, chop wood and play squash and get ready to drive to Florida. He arranged a stress test, the result of which was non-committal, so I then saw a cardiologist who informed me that I had an obstruction in my heart arteries, and I needed a cardiac "bypass" operation. This was before the practice of putting in stents, which had not been perfected yet. They then put me down for a double bypass heart surgery.

This medical emergency came as a total surprise. It was a real shock, as I'd never had any problems of this nature before. I was sent to Sunnybrook Hospital from North York General, and told the surgery would be at Toronto General in about three days. A change of plans was needed quickly, so Greta and son Michael hopped into the loaded car and drove to Florida where they quickly unpacked and then flew back to Toronto in time for my surgery on December 5.

The double bypass surgery became a quad bypass event, where the "while we're at it syndrome" kicked in. They ended up repairing four external cardiac arteries in full open-chest surgery. I left the OR in good shape and, the next day, I was walking around unaided. The second full day following surgery, both the surgeon and the cardiologist agreed that I was able to go home. But they told me I must not drive. I had never received such a warning before, but I agreed. Our home in Collingwood had been rented for the winter, but my friend Marty Kane, who had already left for Florida, offered us his apartment at Bathurst and Sheppard—very handy as it was just one block away from my physician's office.

So, just two days after a quad bypass surgery, we were moving into a borrowed apartment. On the first day, I walked the halls of the building; for the next three days, I walked the streets. But it was December in Toronto and freezing out there! One week following my surgery, I took public transit back to Toronto General Hospital. Both the cardiologist and the surgeon agreed that everything was perfect, so I asked if I could do my post-surgical recovery work walking in Florida, rather than in the malls in Toronto, now filled with Christmas shoppers. They huddled and, after three days, agreed that I could fly to Florida, but I could not drive because my chest had been broken into, and driving behind a car steering wheel was banned. That was fine; my car was already in Florida!

But what about health insurance? As a retired teacher, Greta had an excellent insurance policy, and I learned that I was still covered by insurance as long as my doctor, the surgeon, and cardiologist all agreed it was okay. It was now right before Christmas, and we had to find a reasonable flight to Florida. With the help of the internet, I found a non-stop flight from Buffalo to Fort Lauderdale leaving in two days.

Son Rob drove us to the Buffalo airport where, with little checked luggage, we boarded a flight and flew to Fort Lauderdale where some new friends from Century Village met us at the airport and drove us to our winter home. Their names were Jack Lisogursky, Herb Isenberg, and Len Caplan, and our friendship has been renewed every year since then and continues.

A pamphlet I'd picked up in the hospital in Toronto claimed one could return to non-physical work within a month to six weeks following this type of surgery. Now, in the warm Florida sunshine, I began walking the perimeter of our complex. I had no physical problems other than the itching of the area around the many stitches running from my ankle to my chest, as they had used an area in my leg to extract the arteries needed to replace my cardiac arteries. Two weeks after surgery, I began driving, but a bit more carefully than usual. I was doing well and getting ready to resume my career in Florida in the "non-physically demanding" work of doing two concerts in two days, on January 6 and 7, exactly one month following quadruple heart bypass surgery!

2004

The year began with me now walking every day around the ring road of our condo complex in Deerfield Beach to prepare for my two concerts in early January at FAU in Boca Raton and Jupiter. Since my arrival several weeks ago, I'd been preparing for these two concerts, and my second year of teaching at FAU's Life Long Learning Facilities. I told no one at FAU about the surgery, and only my close friends in Century Village knew. I did both early concerts, one for each campus, to large acclaim, and no one questioned any loss of my ability to perform them alone. I'll admit that, after the second one, I was physically tired, as that kind of activity, thirty days post-surgery, does take a toll on one's energy.

That year luckily, I was only doing four sessions—one per week. It ended on February 4, which allowed me to return to Toronto for medical check-ups—first by the surgeon at Toronto General Hospital, and then the cardiologist at North York General and to my physician at the corner of Bathurst and Sheppard. All the doctors found me to be physically fine, and reported everything to be normal. I was allowed to play tennis beginning February 15, but only doubles. As it turned out, I was busy that winter preparing for various appearances, but my post-op appeared to go well and healing was well underway with no complications. Now some fourteen years later, my blood pressure is lower than it's ever been, and I'm off of most of my post-surgical medications.

Meanwhile, word continued to spread. Some folks from Brandeis University's Boca Raton Interest Group had seen me at FAU, and signed me to do some guest lectures at a Boca Raton Resort. So, on January 11, I presented *From Shtetl to Statehood,* a program on Yiddish music, and on February 15, I did one on the place of women in the folk and protest song movement of the first fifty years into the 2000s. Then, in early February, I did two more ninety-minute singing/lectures for the Brandeis grad group at Boca Pointe Clubhouse—one on the life of Pete Seeger, and one on the music of the turbulent '60s. We had great turnouts to (apparently) great acclaim, and I was asked to do more next year for Brandeis. On March 2, I was asked to sing at the unveiling of a new lecture hall being built at FAU's Jupiter Campus. It was an honour for such a relatively new member of FAU's faculty to be asked to appear at the ground-breaking event, so I sang some relevant songs.

On Sunday February 23, I was invited back to sing at Temple Beth Or, in Miami, same as last year on the subject of "Peace, Protest, and Jewish Culture". In March, I was invited to sing at Broward Greens in Boca, a closed community concert with a sing-along of labour songs, and the songs of Pete Seeger and Woody Guthrie. Before leaving Florida, I met with FAU program-director Eli Myerson, and asked him why he had hired me, virtually sight unseen, and unknown at FAU. He told me that, after he read my submission of "Folk, Protest and Union Music", he simply knew the program would be popular. In addition, his mother in New York City was on the executive of the International Ladies Garment Workers' Union! I didn't have to ask any more questions, and he invited me to return the following year. Also, before

I left for Toronto, I contacted Florida International University in North Miami Beach about doing one of my course subjects as part of their Lifelong Education programs.

When I returned to Toronto, I found a letter from George Brown College. I had written and asked if I could also deliver a course on the History of Folk Music there in their new program. I was told I would be doing such a program the following year 2005 in Toronto, but this fall of 2004 I'd be starting a ten-week course at the George Brown College downtown campus, near Toronto's landmark Casa Loma. Because the location was further from downtown, I had a different make-up of students. We had a good response and great interest.

In May of that year, I wrote to Harold Leventhal, who managed Pete Seeger, Judy Collins, and Arlo Guthrie. I told him how The Travellers had done a sold-out concert in Toronto last year on the life of Woody Guthrie, and this year we were planning a salute to The Weavers, a former group also managed by Leventhal. I told him how The Travellers were direct descendants of The Weavers when they were forced to disband, and asked him what he thought of the idea. He responded positively, saying he appreciated our approach to teaching audiences that music can change people's ideas and educate them.

On October 18, the Travellers performed again to a sold-out house at the Leah Posluns Theatre at the North Toronto YMHA's Koffler Centre, this time in honour of The Weavers. Once again with the help of Adrienne Cohen, it was a huge success. That summer in Toronto, an article was published by John Rogers of Associated Press about Pete Seeger, who would soon be turning 85. In the article, Pete said he knew his voice was now fading, but he kept on doing and egging people on to sing along with him. At the time of this writing in 2018, I have now reached eighty-five years of age. I seem to be singing as well as ever, and plan to follow Pete's record for as long as I can. Of course, I didn't have to sing "Wimoweh" almost every night for forty years.

That year on September 17, a new film by Jim Brown was released at the Toronto International Film Festival (TIFF) called *Isn't This a Time*! The film was dedicated to Harold Leventhal, and produced by

Jim Brown and Torontonian, Michael Cohl, an executive with the TIFF. Many of The Weavers who were still alive were in attendance and, after the film was shown, they performed a concert, augmented by Erik Weisberg of Deliverance fame and Eric Darling, a banjo player who played with The Weavers when Pete left in the 1960s. The concert included moments from a concert done the year before in New York City, augmented by Theodore Bikel and Leon Bibb. It was truly a time to enjoy folk music with the people who championed it, and still kept it alive. I met Lorne Brown, who I spoke about in the 2003 pages, and he was writing another five-page article about this event. He mentioned Jerry Gray and Sharon Hampson as being a part of the folk song community, melded together with their American counterparts. *Isn't This a Time!* is a film available to be rented, and revered.

In November, I received a thank you letter from the Queen's University archives. I had donated some artifacts about the life of J.B. Salsberg, the Canadian left-wing Jewish MPP and firebrand who I had known, and who had spoken at my father's funeral. The year ended with an invitation to sing in Florida when I returned at the end of the year, and I'll include it in my synopsis of 2005 along with some other events. I seemed to have created a niche in the folk music world of South Florida, and was invited to appear in January 2005 at the South Florida Folk Festival in Fort Lauderdale.

2005

This chapter begins by finishing off December of 2004. The Beth Am Synagogue in Boca Raton had invited me do another performance on December 11 at the FAU auditorium. Returning to sing a second time for a group is like singing for old friends, for I'd agreed to do another show one week later for the Venetian Isles Condo Group. I had also agreed to perform some lectures for the Brandeis University Study Groups, and the first class was at Boca Pointe on Sunday December 19—about two miles from my place. As usual, there was a great turnout. That year, I was teaching at both of FAU's campuses, and also trying something new by appearing for Florida International University (FIU) in North Miami Beach.

On Wednesday January 12, I did my usual Music Week opening concert at the Jupiter Campus of FAU, and the next day the same concert at FAU's main campus location in Boca Raton. That weekend was taken over by the South Florida Folk Festival and, on Saturday the 15th, I did a performance there for the first time to great success, doing a kids' show and a generally humorous show for adults.

Florida Folk Festival, 2005

I was not accepted too much by the regular southeast Florida Folkies. I think I was still considered to be an outsider, and not really a Florida regular, even though that was my fourth year in the area, staying for five months each time. Starting on January 19, I was doing a four-week Yiddish music study program at both locations of FAU. "From Shtetl Tsu Amerika" is about the music born in Eastern Europe, which then travels to "Amerika" to radio programs of the Lower East Side, and eventually to Broadway. I'd been teaching such a course in Toronto for many years, but that was the first time I'd done that program in the U.S.

On January 20, I taught my first class at FIU on the same theme of Yiddish music. The next four weeks were the same: On Wednesdays, I was at FAU Boca, and on Fridays I was at FAU Jupiter; in between, on Thursdays, I went to FIU in North Miami. This pattern continued for four straight weeks. In addition, on Saturday January 30 in the evening, I was doing a lecture for the Boca Brandeis group, and the following week again at Boca Pointe. On Friday February 11, I ended the cycle of classes at FAU and FIU but continued with the Brandeis classes. That last Friday morning at FAU, I had signed up to do a Friday evening class for the Brandeis Study Club of Delray Beach, not the Boca group I had worked with last year. This succession of events looks busy, and it was. Somehow, everyone at these locations was looking for me to provide an entertaining and educational class that was new and different.

On Saturday morning February 19, I appeared for the second time at Century Village's Deerfield Progressive Forum, a Left-leaning group that brings in speakers on social and progressive causes. I was there to talk and sing about the music of the American civil rights era. This lecture often ends with everyone singing along with the songs of their growing-up years, like "Blowin' in the Wind" and "If I Had a Hammer". What I always liked about this group was that after the Saturday morning meetings, many of them would go out and stand on the corner in Deerfield of Atlantic and Powerline Roads, carrying picket signs about anything they were unhappy with that had happened the previous week in Washington. Back in Canada, I always mentioned this group to whatever group I was singing for, and for what they did with popular protest. Pete Seeger would often do the same in the cold winter season in New York State, by standing outside in the snow on the main corners of his town of Beacon, New York.

In summary, after three years of being in Florida for the winter season, I had made quite an impact on the educational scene, talking and singing about the songs that helped educate the residents and about the impact that folk music had made in their lives.

On February 11, I did another class for Brandeis, and in mid-February I started a new four- week course for FIU with another final class for Brandeis of Delray in mid-March. This ended my programs in South Florida and, even working solo, I lived up to the name of my group, The Travellers. The execution of these twenty-six classes on various topics, each lasting at least ninety minutes, was a new Olympic performance record for me, not as I lived it but certainly as I total it up now. As there was not much happening with The Travellers in Toronto, I had begun a different life. Each year I appeared on the folk radio show on WLRN where host Michael Stock was amazed that I was still doing so much at my age. All this work was really cutting into my athletic and social life at Century Village, so I told Greta that next year I'd cut back on my Florida schedule.

With all the performances I'd given in Florida, I was now receiving email feedback, and I collected some thoughts that were sent to me. A guy who called himself "Banjo Jack" from Boynton Beach saw me at FAU and sent a review. He would go out dressed in a clown's costume complete with a cherry on his nose, and sing and play his banjo at local events. He wrote:

"You were fantastic at FAU. Your CD of Kids' songs is super, and I'll be using some of them in my show. My friend from Long Island and his wife will be here next week. It was they who clued me in on your fantastic classes on Pete Seeger at FAU. Your rendition of 'This Land', the 'Hammer Song' and 'Little Boxes' were all super. We came away from the FAU class ready to march for a free America. Thanks for the memories, from "Banjo Jack Williams."

In January2005, I received an email from Roberta Feinstein from Boca Raton who wrote; "Many years ago in another lifetime I saw The Travellers personally in Toronto, and I am still impressed so much so that I will be coming when you hopefully entertain next May for the Congress of Secular Jewish Organizations".

As I left my last class in Jupiter that year, I was given the following words to "Red River Valley" after my last class there:

From this classroom we all must be going.
We will miss your bright eyes and great smile.
And the songs full of protest you sang us.
Which have brightened our day for awhile.
But a message that will stay on with us,

Fight for truth, equal rights and fair trial.
These are days full of strife and injustice
Time to march for another long mile.

These are heartfelt words from a group of my students who really "got" what I'd been talking about.

Meanwhile, Back in Canada

I got back home to Collingwood, now my summer home, and assessed what dates I had coming up. These days they were mainly for me (as a solo act), unless we got some convention dates for the whole group of Travellers. Next year in 2006, we were planning a concert in Toronto about the songs and life of Pete Seeger, and maybe we'd have a few guests on stage to sing with us. A few service clubs in the Collingwood area had been asking me to sing for them, plus at some "significant age" birthday parties. During the past few years, I'd sung at two funerals—both for ex-Travellers: Jerry Goodis and Ray Woodley. I figured if I sang at all these funerals of people I worked with, "There ain't gonna be anyone around to talk about me at mine". So, I better keep going.

Merrick Jarrett was a folk singer in and around Toronto who used to sing songs for kids at libraries and museums. He made the odd album, but of course folk music wasn't as big a thing in the 1950s. In his later years, he moved to the Kitchener area, and died at the age of eighty-one while I was in Florida. A relatively new friend, writer/editor Lorne Brown, said he kept in touch with Merrick, and that fall, his friends were going to have a remembrance evening in Kitchener. He asked if I could come along and help out, and as you know by now, I rarely say no. He would tell me where and when as the date got closer.

Then bang, I got a call from Peter Kennedy from the Canadian Auto Workers Union. I knew their next convention was not until 2006 in Vancouver. But Peter told me the Union had a new contract coming up that needed discussion and ratification, and would The Travellers be available to give "spirit" to the discussions? It would be in late

August at the Sheraton Hotel, and of course we said yes. I'd have to call Aileen in Halifax and make travel arrangements for her, and inform Joe, Ted, and Don about the dates. As I was speaking with Lorne Brown, I mentioned our singing at union conventions to him. Lorne was the editor of the *Canadian Folk Song Bulletin*, and he had never seen a union convention, so he asked to be allowed to come along, and write an article in the *Canadian Folk Music Bulletin.*

The union agreed, and he got a pass from the union to walk around and see what we did, and interview some union people during our warm-up. As I've said before, The Travellers have a unique format to start off every session of any union convention. I could sell this information to anyone, but no one has ever asked! Many have wondered though, what we did at these conventions to warrant them paying us at all. Lorne's article ran about five large pages long. I'm going to give you the highlights here, including "The Secrets" to The Travellers being in demand for so many years:

The convention sessions started at exactly 9:00 a.m. and most of the delegates stayed in the hotel from the night before when registration took place. The large downstairs ballroom had long rows of tables, and there were two stages—one for the speakers and one for The Travellers. There was a TV camera setup to cover our singing and to project it onto large screens, so everyone could both see and hear us. We arrived about 7:45 a.m. to make sure the setup for the microphones and cameras were adequate, and our instruments were in tune. Usually, we had a rehearsal to go over the songs we might be doing. That morning, we would sing one song or so to get the microphone levels right, but it seemed the same sound guys worked there year after year, so they knew the levels and were consummate pros at what they did.

CAW Convention, Toronto, 2005

Lorne arrived at about that time and started talking to people who were there early, some with their kids. Before the convention actually began, he asked them what they liked about what The Travellers did. Many had been there before and one said, "They wake us up!" Others said we got their toes tapping and their ears open.

We usually started our program with Ted, Don, and Joe playing some soft jazz tunes, and then Aileen joined in and sang some familiar jazz songs. Then around 8:30, we started singing songs from across Canada, like "Farewell to Nova Scotia", or "I'se the B'y". Then we

287

did a medley of union songs everyone knew and, depending on how long they'd been up that morning, they sang or clapped along. We sang songs like "Hold the Fort", and "Down by the Riverside", and almost everyone joined in. We followed with "The Union Maid" saying, "Oh you can't scare me, I'm stickin' to the union", and, we followed with "This Land Is Your Land", "There is Power in the Union", and then we got to "United we Stand", which brought us close to 8:55 a.m.

I looked over to the main stage, and a series of finger signals from the chairman followed as he told me how many more minutes were needed. Within two minutes, the chairman called for everyone to stand to sing "Solidarity Forever", the anthem of the labour movement. There were 1,500 people in the hall, and everyone sang at least the choruses. In the last verse and chorus, they were on their feet and singing with us. The program ended with huge applause and the pounding of the chairman's gavel to announce the beginning of the meeting.

The timing of the songs was critical to the final success. With the whole crowd being able to both see and hear us on the many TV screens in the hall, we were a lot like cheerleaders, leading the throng of delegates to inspire them as they begin their discussions. As we finished, the chairman thanked us and we set about packing up our instruments. At some conventions, we also opened up the afternoon sessions in the same way, with different songs in the warm-up but always ending with "Solidarity". Lorne Brown wrote that the electricity of 1,500 people singing "Solidarity" together at the top of their lungs united them in their common purpose.

There is really no great secret to getting people on their feet if you have a solid program of great songs that build to an ending. We've always done that in concerts and performances, and it always leads to a standing ovation at the end. It's frequently been said that The Travellers sound better in concert than on in-studio recordings, and it's true because we know how to work with an audience. When we started singing for kids, we followed the same principle of urging them to stand up and sing, as we closed most of those shows with "This Land Is Your Land", and all of them sang as I shouted out the words for them. Now, don't tell anyone you know the secret of our success! You just have to be a part of it.

The Travellers sang at all CAW Triannual
conventions from 1985-2005

The Travellers have been singing at union gatherings from the time before there was a Travellers group. That's why, when unions gather in convention or on picket lines, the only people they get in touch with are The Travellers. Because of our years of success, they have faith that we will set the right tone for the occasion.

After the big CAW union contract meeting was done, I learned I'd be teaching an eight-week course at George Brown College's King Street Campus, starting at the end of September, and finishing just before I returned to Florida. This had been a very full year for me and, with some dates on the books for 2006, perhaps we'd have some more dates for people that we love to appear for.

Let's finish off the year 2005 first. When I returned to Florida in early November, I had a few gigs to finish off after Greta and I enjoyed a short Caribbean cruise. As soon as we were back, I appeared on Michael Stock's radio show to publicize an upcoming concert. A Boca resident had requested that I do another fund-raising event for them, to be held again at FAU. So, on December 17, I did a Christmas and Chanukah holiday season program for my old friends at Beth Am. The program at Brandeis University actually began again on December 18, so I showed up at the Horizon Club for my first class about the songs of the Spanish Civil War, the beginnings of folk music in New York City, and the formation of the Almanac Singers. (This group was one of the first organized folk song groups, and contained Pete, Woody, and anyone in New York City who was available.)

Back in the summer, I "heard" that I would not be renewed by FAU for the 2006 season. I had been doing this course now for five years, so of course I wondered why. But once in Florida, I learned that someone on the FAU board had suggested a local Floridian could do a similar course, feeling it might be better for the university if they signed an American who would be there all year rather than a Canadian on a part-time basis.

I'd heard rumours floating around about this issue last year, and that's why I'd signed up to do some classes at FIU, just in case those rumours were true. When I tried to contact the person responsible for hiring me five years ago, I learned he'd passed away over the summer, at a very young age. I was unable to change their minds, so this was the end of my career at FAU. I had a great time there, made a lot of friends, and entertained a lot of people who appreciated the time I spent in preparation and performance. I was a bit disappointed that I was never actually officially notified I should not return to work, nor was I given the reason. During my tenure at FAU, there was an article in a Los Angeles newspaper that said Jerry Gray was the only person doing that type of folk music course in the U.S. or in Canada.

2006

My gut feeling from before was right, but I had classes for the Brandeis people to start the year. My second class was on January 29 at the Horizon Club, a class I love to do: "The Story, Life and Songs of Woody Guthrie", a course which was well-attended. I did another set of two classes for Brandeis in February, also at the Horizon Club. They were called "Something about the Women", the story of Elizabeth Gurley Flynn in the early twentieth century, and later Joan Baez, Buffy Sainte Marie, Mary Travers (of Peter Paul and Mary), and Ronnie Gilbert of The Weavers.

That winter I also taught four classes for FIU weekly in January and February on various topics. I then received a wonderful email inviting The Travellers to appear in Vancouver for a week the following summer. Once again, they wanted us to do seven performances opening and closing the regular national convention meetings for the Canadian Auto Workers. I called all The Travellers, and they were excited to travel to Vancouver and sing in the summer for the longest-standing union organization we'd ever sung for. Joe and I planned to take our wives to B.C. with us and make it a working vacation.

The rest of the winter in Florida was relatively quiet for me, and Greta was happy I was not so busy. But I did one more show on March 14 for Na'amat, an Israeli charity, where I did an all-encompassing show of Israeli and Canadian Jewish songs, as well as American songs. That was a pretty diverse program, and it was so well received that the audience demanded I do two encores! There simply aren't many performers who can do that type of all-inclusive show.

When I returned to Canada in April, I received some alarming news. Joe Hampson, our long-time bass player and good friend since 1965, was not feeling well and had some tests done in May and June. I was upset after hearing about his condition. I had first scouted Joe, by accident, when The Travellers were performing in Niagara Falls in 1964. Joe was in another group, The Chanteclairs, playing a hotel bar several doors away. I made a note of this in my mind and, in 1965 when we parted company with Sid Dolgay, Joe was a perfect replacement, a professional, seasoned veteran.

But Joe had contracted pneumonia during the past winter, and couldn't seem to shake it. Then, just as we were packing for our trip to Vancouver, he was notified that he had lung cancer, but the doctors were not sure how serious it was. Joe was in no discomfort as he waited for word from the doctors about the next steps. He was told that, since his wife was accompanying him to Vancouver, it would make his trip a lot easier. My wife Greta would also come.The doctors told him he would be able to take part in the concerts with The Travellers in Vancouver.

The Travellers last concert appearance, CAW Convention, Vancouver, 2006

So off we went, and had a wonderful, productive trip to Vancouver. Both The Travellers and the union thought it was our best CAW performance ever. We had sung at every convention of the Canadian Auto Workers since Bob White started the union in 1985 by breaking away from the American UAW. When we returned to Toronto in early August, we were sad to learn Joe was given a verdict of stage IV lung cancer, and treatment would not help. Joe had been a two–three pack-a-day smoker for many years, and, even though he had quit about five years ago, the smoking had obviously caught up with him.

Coming up for The Travellers was another concert at the Leah Posluns Theatre in early October about the life of Pete Seeger. When I asked Joe's wife, Sharon, what she thought, she advised us to go ahead with planning, and we'd see how Joe was progressing. But by early September, Joe was confined to his bed. The concert plans had proceeded based on what Sharon had told us, rather than try and get a substitute bass player. But there was simply no way to replace what Joe did in our performances. We had already sold tickets and built up a relationship at the theatre, so I suggested finding a substitute group or individual to perform instead of The Travellers.

I tried several people including Pete, Arlo, and Theodore Bikel, but no one was available on October 3. Then I remembered that last year Mariposa had hired a group to do an off-season concert for them in Toronto as a fund-raiser. This was an unknown group that was just beginning, and they were having trouble selling tickets, so they hired my son James and I to share the stage with this group, The Work O' The Weavers, a sound-alike group doing the history and songs of The Weavers. They did a good job in 2005 for Mariposa, and it turned out they were available on October 3. Sharon said it was okay with her.

The concert went well, and I received a letter from Adrienne Cohen of the theatre saying, "I can't thank you enough for such a great evening. The concert was saved, and you all were received well, beyond the audience expectations. They did a fantastic show." I knew they would, I said. She added, "As always, you and James were terrific, and may we continue to work together for years to come". The Work O' the Weavers also wrote back, thanking us for giving them the work, which allowed them to be seen by such an appreciative audience. (I was planning to see them again in Florida in March 2007, as they would be performing nearby and, indeed, I did.) Then I was asked to appear on May 2, in Whitby, Ontario for a seniors' club, and they seemed to enjoy my performance.

Joe Hampson's condition continued to fail and he could not leave his second-floor bedroom. I saw him several times, but when I left for

Florida early in November, I knew it would be the last time we spoke. Joe passed away on November 30, and the family organized a memorial to his life for December 10 at 1:00 p.m. at the Cecil St. Community Centre. The Travellers, both collectively and individually, were asked to be a part of the remembrance, along with Sharon's band-mates Lois and Bram, and many long-time friends. I flew back from Florida to attend, although it turned out to be difficult. I had had a performance in Florida two days before, and on Friday morning caught a flight from Fort Lauderdale to Buffalo, where I rented a car and drove to Toronto. Then I slept over at one of my sons' place.

The afternoon memorial was attended by many. I did a ten-minute personal retrospective eulogy of Joe, and was followed by each of the individual Travellers who spoke about our forty years together. The afternoon closed with The Travellers performing, assisted by my son James on piano as we sang Joe's best-known song, "Talk About Peace", followed of course, by "This Land". I left shortly after the ceremony, and drove back to Buffalo to catch a 6:00 p.m. flight back to Fort Lauderdale. The problem was that the next day was Sunday, and around noon I was supposed to board a ship for a one-week cruise to the Caribbean. As befits my group's name, I made it with no difficulty. I was so glad all these precise arrangements were possible, allowing me to attend Joe's memorial, and also to catch the cruise on time, with time to ponder the previous hectic forty-eight hours. Friend Lorne Brown had been in attendance, and I could not stay after the ceremonies to talk and visit with him, so he wrote these words to me in an email: "I wanted to say that was an incredibly moving and powerful tribute to Joe. I really appreciated your contribution, and marvel that you were able to pull it off."

The End of The Travellers?

The repercussions following Joe's death set off serious problems of continuing The Travellers. I suggested we have a concert in Joe's honour with The Travellers leading the way. But each of The Travellers wrote back saying that, with Joe's death, they simply could not continue to be a part of the group any more. They had had almost forty years of experiences together that were remarkable, and they would continue their life of music in their own ways. They also knew I would continue in some capacity either as a solo act or with other people. In terms of a memorial concert for Joe, they each told me they had said all they needed to at the December service, and would do no more.

Several years prior to Joe's passing, my son James had left Blue Rodeo after fourteen years with them, so I asked him for help. He took some time and found me two people he'd worked with in several groups he now played with. I had nothing pending for a while for the group, although there had still been commitments in Toronto during Joe's illness. Myself, I taught a course on "Folk and Protest Music" for Toronto's George Brown College on King Street. My course filled the 250-person hall once a week for eight weeks. That was the biggest audience I ever had for a course I taught in Canada. The day after it ended, I received a letter from Ann Wigoda, who had attended the course. She wrote:

"I wanted to let you know how much I enjoyed your series of lectures. It was stupendous, and showed your dedication to the subject and to your students. I was familiar with some of the historical facts, but the series was truly an enlightenment to me. I hope you will continue to teach this wonderful and original course to many privileged students in the future".

Mildred Eisenberg PhD, wrote saying; "Thank you for a most unusual, interesting and nostalgic music series on Songs of Protest. We listened to your most-interesting commentary along with the audio and visual presentations. My husband and I both regret that the last class is tomorrow."

And then another sad event occurred. On October 14, long-time *Toronto Star* music columnist, Sid Adilman, passed away from a heart attack. I have at least fifteen clippings and stories from the *Toronto Star* that Sid wrote about the group, mostly complimentary, but if not, we probably deserved it. Sid also had a great time when he accompanied us on a trip to Cyprus to entertain Canadian service people. When The Travellers had been signed to appear at Expo '70 for three weeks in Japan, we selected a Japanese song we'd heard on a record by the New Christy Minstrels. Sid's wife, Toshiko, was from Japan and she got us the words to the eight-verse song, along with a translation, and taught us the right inflections for the Japanese words. We sang it every day in Osaka, to great applause, even to The Emperor.

When Sid died, his two sons asked me to sing at the remembrance service for their father. Of course, I would attend, along with my son James who knew Sid's two sons, who were also in the music biz. At the service were many showbiz people including Jack McAndrew, head of the Charlottetown Theatre we had opened in 1964. Over the years, we appeared there seven more times.

Back in Florida, in December I was doing another presentation in Century Village for the Progressive Forum of Florida. I also received a letter from the National Conference for Synagogue Youth (NCSY) and for Hillel for Greater Toronto commending me on my translation of the Yiddish partisan song, "Zog Nit Keynmol" that I had sung for them at a meeting. In singing at Yiddish concerts, I find that many younger people do not know the Yiddish words to that well-known Holocaust song, so I wrote three verses in English with Ruth Rubin, and do them every time I sing the song.

In addition, on June 17, I played at the evening of remembrance for Merrick Jarrett at the Victory Café in Toronto's Markham Village, along with Joanne Crabtree and Sharon Lois and Bram. I closed the evening with everyone singing "This Land". It was a pleasure to appear through the invitation of Lorne Brown, who had been a loyal friend to Merrick right up to his death.

In September of 2016, many newspapers noted the death of protest singer, Joe Glazer, who was known in the U.S. as "Labour's Troubadour." I sang with him in 1961 at the opening session of the Ontario Federation of Labour's first meeting. I noted that he was a winner of The Joe Hill Lifetime Achievement Award, given annually by the AFL/CIO and began looking it up. This sad year of my singing at two funerals ended with The Travellers having an uncertain future.

2007

This coming year would be a problem about booking ahead for The Travellers, as the death of Joe Hampson was a huge shock to the life of the group. When people have been together for so many years—on the road, in recording studios and on concert stages—there's a certain camaraderie and trust among all the participants. This latter stage was in contrast to the internal chemistry among the group members in the early days of the group, which had been a little troubled. As certain people departed, the new people coming in were mature and battle-seasoned musicians who'd been professionals for many years. We trusted one another, and I kept them all up to date as to what was happening and what might or might not happen. There was never an issue in our almost forty years together that triggered a discussion on repertoire or money, and that made life together so easy. There were periods of time when we didn't sing together for several months, like the time leading up to last year's appearances for the CAW.

Along the years, some people had said that ours was a bubble existence, but with Joe's death, the bubble burst. All the members said they felt that for the last couple of years we had been just waiting for something to happen. And then it finally did. Now was the official end of this group. But I'd had my seventy-four-year-old physical check-up the previous year, and with good results. So, I decided to keep going, and try to find a way to end our long career with more of a bang. I couldn't get the now ex-Travellers to do a *Last Waltz* kind of event with coverage by radio, print and TV. However, the theatre at the north YMHA had offered us a date in 2008 to do the concert about Pete Seeger that we had planned to do in 2006, so I set out to try and pull it off on Pete's birth date in 2008 when he turned ninety!

I started to plan, but first I had commitments to fulfill while I was in Florida. So here I was alone again—now the "Lonesome Traveller", with no group to plan for.

Concert sign, 2018

On January 6, I had committed to doing a program on "Folk Music of the World" at Century Village's Deerfield Progressive Club. Once again, this program came from my having done so much travelling, and having sung songs in many languages. The audience enjoyed my program.

At this point, I'd been living in Century Village for about seven years, and every year I went into the booking office and told them I'd like to teach a course at the Clubhouse, where they offer courses in the winter that run for four or six weeks. By this time, I'd been teaching for five years at two of Florida Atlantic's campuses. I had taught at FIU for three years, one year at Nova University, and three years for the Brandeis University groups. Certainly, I should be qualified to start a course at Century Village!

I finally began in 2007 to teach a four-week course on the "History of Folk, Protest, and Union Music". The group seemed to have been waiting for me for many years. I set the record that year with about fifty students in a very small music room. This appeared to be an audience who had grown up in the folk music era of the fifties and sixties, and were just waiting for someone to help them relive the happy periods of their lives.

The next morning was the second time I taught a class for Nova University. Then, at 1:30 p.m., I led a class on the subject of Woody Guthrie for a private group at the Sheraton Hotel. I didn't realize how many places I had booked that winter, so I'll reel them off. Fortunately, as each booking came in, I wrote it down, in chronological order, and I never said no. I ended up with a specific calendar order for the year, and for your perusal. But again I have to answer the question before you ask, quite simply, "I don't know how or why I did it."

At 1:00 p.m. on Monday January 21, I was at King's Point, a site similar to Century Village. Two days later at 2:00 p.m. I did my second class at Century Village. The next day, I did a second class at the Classic Hyatt on Sheridan. A week later, on Wednesday January 30, I gave my third lecture for Century Village, followed by the fourth on February 6. As this was my first year at Century, I had been told to do only a four-week course, and see how it went. It went well.

At 8:00 p.m. that evening, I did a third performance at the Hyatt Hotel, then on Saturday February 9, I did an evening Yiddish concert at a synagogue in Hollywood. On Tuesday February 12, I did a class for Nova U. in a Boca Assisted Living Centre. The next day, I did another class for Nova in Aventura, and on Thursday February 14, I did one for Nova University's main campus, and another on Tuesday February 19. On Wednesday March 5, I did a ninety-minute concert in Palm Beach for a private condo group. My last date of that season was on March 18 at the Nova University Main Campus. That totalled seventeen classes and concerts between January 16 and March 18. I think that was another new record for me. (It almost sounds like the many consecutive appearances we did across Canada in 1967 Centennial year.) I was a lot older now, but I still seemed to thrive on this type of scheduling.

In mid-March, I got a call from the *Toronto Star*, asking me to do a story about Peter Paul and Mary coming to Toronto for a concert, and Mary Travers was recuperating from surgery and on a new comeback tour. So, I wrote what turned out to be a two-page article, and told the history of the legendary trio. And I got a by-line for it. In earlier times, this story would have been written by Sid Adilman, but since Sid's death the year before, the *Star* said they had no one on staff who knew much about that era. After the article was published, I received a lot of mail about my story, even one from a Canadian in China.

The theme of that article was based on a song by activist, Anne Feeney, and recorded three years earlier by Peter Paul and Mary. The song was about what happened during the 1960s, and called "Have You Been to Jail for Justice, then You're a Friend of Mine". Anne Feeney had performed in Florida and had just won The Joe Hill Award for Lifetime Service to Labour causes the previous year. She sang at a church in Fort Lauderdale and asked me to come on stage with her as we sang her song together to close the concert.

On April 1, I escaped from busy southeast Florida to the relative quiet of southern Ontario. Or so I thought. But calls were waiting, and there were stages to be filled. On Wednesday April 9, I did a concert for a condo group in North York. The room was filled with people who had grown up with my music. On Tuesday May 6, I sang for a Lunch 'n Learn group at Beth Tikvah synagogue on Bayview Avenue. On Tuesday May 8, it was the inauguration of a new monument at Harbord Collegiate, honouring boys who had graduated from HCI and gone to fight in WW II, and had not returned. A classmate of mine, sculptor Morty Katz, had created the new monument and I was asked to sing at the dedication. On May 17, the Collingwood Probus Club asked me to sing for about 150 members at their luncheon. As before, these people were of an age who remembered and lived in the folk music era. They all stayed and sang along with me.

Jerry Gray and The New Travellers

I received an invitation for The Travellers to appear at the Canadian Labour Congress National Convention in Toronto on May 26–30. But there was no longer a Travellers group, so I considered the possibilities. My son James had handled my request to find a bass player, Greg Wyard, as well as an accomplished guitar player named Mike Daley, who had received his PhD in music while studying under

Rob Bowman at York University. Mike had been singing and playing in all kind of bands in Toronto, and had basically started a career doing what I did! Mike was happy to join me with Greg, and my son James, whom he also idolized.

We started rehearsing and, for the first time ever, The New Travellers worked without a female singer. But the group worked, and our way of doing labour rallies always met with standing ovations for what we did and how we did it. It was good warm-up for what followed, as the same group appeared at the national convention for guess who? The CAW! They reported there was no deterioration in the quality of what we did now with only four players, and we added another guitar player, Ken Whitely, while son James played the keyboards. It was truly gratifying to fulfill and continue the legacy of The Travellers.

New Travellers: James Gray, Jerry Gray, Greg Wyard, Mike Daley

When I finally returned to my chalet in Collingwood, I was really ready for some R & R. Then a local group called me to do a concert on Tuesday, September 16, a half-mile from my summer home. Easy to do and easy to drive to, and I got a great response to my program. During the summer I contacted Ryerson's Later Life Learning about returning in the fall to do another round of eight lectures. They agreed, and I began just after Labour Day. I was much better this time around because I now had video to illustrate my points. I was actually pretty good at recording shows from the TV to videotape, although I lacked the ability to do much editing. However, I could duplicate the film, and then use two parts of the same videotape.

Public Television always offered so many great shows that I could tape and use to illustrate my points. For example, I could talk for half an hour about the sheriff in a southern American town who urged dogs to attack children, and then tell his men to turn high intensity hoses on those children. But showing three minutes of that on film would tell the story better than I could ever do in words. Having these videos enhanced my lectures, and brought my audience into the picture and to the site of these historical events. The course was a success, and these eight weeks wrapped up in early November just before I left for Florida.

I had agreed to appear at Temple Sinai in Toronto to do an evening singing/lecture on the Jewish influence on folk music. It turned out to be the same day as one of my afternoon classes at Ryerson. It was a busy day. At the same time, I was working with Edward Aqua, Director of the Later Learning program at Nova University in Florida. We were setting up dates for me to begin that December of 2007, going through to mid-March. I also set up a date with Mel Reigler about returning to Palm Beach to do another musical lecture for the UJA on March 5. I also set up a January 19th date to appear for the Century Village Canadian Club, for President Sol Stober.

That fall of 2007, my friend Muni Basman and his wife Carol had written a book and made a recording of Yiddish songs by an old friend, Claire Klein, from Vancouver. Claire and I and my sister Helen had been part of the Fagel Gartner Singers, and we were all together on that historic 1952 cross-Canada tour, supported by the UJPO. On her first trip to Vancouver, Claire had met a Vancouver architect and, about a year later, they were married. She never returned to Toronto again except to appear as a concert singer.

Muni Basman's book was called *Zing un Lern Yiddish,* about how to learn and sing in Yiddish, and teach it to grandchildren and others who had no knowledge of Yiddish. I helped Muni sell the books in both Florida and Canada at my performances of Yiddish music. His father, Label Basman, had been the head of the children's camp at Camp Naivelt. He was also head of the children's school at the UJPO in the 1940s, and his son Muni had learned well from him, as did I.

Joe Hampson's death in 2006 resulted in the demise of The Travellers, the group that had been an entity for much of the forty years recounted in this book. At the beginning of 2007, the future was an unknown, but I had more musical lectures than any previous year. The new group filled in well, doing the same songs and programs we were famous for, as I've described in this book. Bob White, and other CAW presidents who followed him, always introduced the group as "Jerry Gray and The Travellers," so that naturally evolved to become the name of the new entity. At the end of this year, I was feeling optimistic for me and The New Travellers. The beat goes on.

2008

The beginning of the New Year always offers a good opportunity to assess what happened in the previous year, and to build on that going forward. I didn't think I was even going to try to be as productive in 2008 as in 2007, which had been an incomparable year of cultural success. I was now seventy-seven years old, and blessed with particularly good health, so I would continue to see what life had in store for me. I started off with some commitments negotiated the previous year for the beginning of 2008.

The Canadian Club at Century Village is almost as old as the village itself. When the Village had first been built in the late 1980s it was primarily for Americans from the New York City area, but the brochure had also been sent to many Montrealers. Consequently, many Montrealers moved to Century, many of whom were by now into their second and third generations. As a result, the Canadian Club was composed mainly of Montrealers, with more Torontonians appearing every year.

I had agreed with Canadian Club head, Sol Stober, to do a free Canadian music concert, even though I did get paid, at their opening meeting on January 10, 2008. A sold-out crowd enjoyed my program, attended by many Montrealers who had never seen me in concert before. The cultural distance between Montreal and Toronto was always far, but has changed because many of the Montrealers' children and grandchildren have moved to Toronto. I had also signed up to do a six-week lecture series at Century Village after a first-year success story last year. This series enjoyed an enthusiastic registration with many Canadians in attendance. I also had a series of eight lectures to do for Nova University at their Main Campus and some of their satellite locations beginning in January. On March 5, I had agreed to perform another concert/lecture in Palm Beach for Mel Reigler, after last year's first-time stop there for the UJA. On February 23, I was ready to sing another program called "Songs of Peace, Protest, and Jewish Culture", at Temple Beth Or in Miami. With a subject like that, I could do anything in my repertoire for that afternoon.

It was quiet for the rest of my winter season in Florida. I returned to Toronto in early April in time to sing for a condo group run by Rocky Meslin at his condo party room. Rocky Meslin was a cousin of our early Traveller, Marty Meslin, who'd been with us for a year in 1956, and his interest in folk music was a family affair. I had agreed to do a concert/lecture for Beth Tikvah Synagogue in Toronto on May 6, and I had a nice crowd as I knew a lot of people at Beth Tikvah. On June 15, I sang for a seniors' group in the Toronto suburb of Weston. I had never sung there before, but someone in their group had seen me do a show in Collingwood and had put the date together.

That summer, Greta and I made a decision to stop living in Collingwood. It had been lovely living there during the summer, but the "shoulder" months of April and November were a little wintry for us now. So, we made the decision to sell our chalet, and in the fall, we rented a condo in Thornhill. Before we left, I sang for the Collingwood Probus Club to many friends I had made there. One of these friends, Margie, was having a significant birthday party on September 20, so I had them all join in the songs to fete Margie. At a lot of these recent gigs, I was selling The Travellers' Sony CD, and *The Travellers Sing*

For Kids that I had reissued as a CD. (It's my hope that lots of people are still enjoying these recordings.)

So that's what was happening as we took leave of our long-time home in Collingwood. That year, we prepared to leave for Florida in November from our new location, our condo in north Toronto. With a new starting point, perhaps it would help initiate another successful season.

2009

When the New Year began on January 1, I'd already been in Florida for six weeks. I'd committed to two early December lectures for Nova University, and rather than list the whole schedule for the winter, I'll do it all at once: On January 5, 6, 13, 20 and 26, I had one class each day, and on January 27, I had both morning and afternoon classes. During February, I had one class each day on February 3, 10, 18, 26, and on March 17, I did my last class for Nova. This was a total of fourteen dates for Nova, two at their main campus, and the others at various other locations for their satellite campuses.

That's a lot so far, but they weren't the only dates I had. On February 15, I did a concert/lecture at Century Village for the National Council of Jewish Women, Montreal Section, billed as a community singsong—a hootenanny. On February 19, I sang for an hour at a mid-winter brunch held by one condo building at a golf course. On March 20, the director at Nova University invited me to sing at an *Oneg Shabbat* at her synagogue in Fort Lauderdale. Then, I managed to fit in a ski trip to Whistler, B.C. with two of my sons, Kevin and Michael.

On January 28, I flew to Vancouver and met my sons arriving from Ottawa and Toronto. We headed up to Whistler, and stayed at my old friend Leo Shimerl's chalet for free. This was to be my "last hurrah". I hadn't skied for about ten years; so, before leaving Florida, I'd tried to get in shape. But the best way to get in shape for skiing is to ski. Now at age seventy-five I did all right, but I could no longer ski until the lifts closed at 3:30 as I used to, so I knocked off at 2:30. I bought a season pass for myself for $150.00 because of my age, and we skied for four days, the bumps and the glacier, but I knew I wasn't coming back. On the fifth day, we flew back to our respective cities, and for me it was a goodbye to my ski life. I had actually stopped skiing when I started coming to Florida. My motto at all times was "nothing is forever," so I closed that chapter, unscathed and uninjured for all my years of skiing, but with a lot of pictures and videos to prove I'd been there, and so many unforgettable memories.

That winter in Florida, I was asked to captain one of our inter-condo tennis league teams, and my team won our division. The season went to early April and it kept me in shape all summer.

Back home in Toronto, I'd planned a Travellers' concert for May 3 on Pete Seeger's birthday, at the YMHA centre again. I arranged for CBC radio to record the evening for later radio broadcast, but unbeknownst to them, I also arranged for a friend in the video business, Mitch Belman, to videotape the concert using the sound feed from the CBC pickup.

Over the years, Mitch's father, Dr. Herb Belman, had filmed many of the Gray family's life events, as well as Alpha Omega and ski club shows. He was also a dentist with skill in videotaping the stories of our lives. His son Mitch is a videographer who then covered some later events for me. We had hoped Pete would be able to come, but he had another commitment in New York City. Then Pete did something rare. He sent us a three-minute video that we played at our concert. In it, he greeted and thanked The Travellers for doing what he, Pete, had done during his lifetime. He thanked The Travellers again, and all Canadians, for getting him work in Canada when he had been blacklisted in the mid '50s.

Pete Seeger Tribute Concert, Toronto, 2011

I had now known Pete Seeger since 1953, and it was a wonderful concert salute to him. Pete's neighbour in Beacon, N.Y., David Bernz, was a banjo player in the Work O' The Weavers from three years ago. He pursued Pete to record a message to be played at our Toronto tribute —and sent it to us. As it turns out, I was left with a radio sound recording of the concert and, even better, I also have a video of the concert that I use as a reference for what The Travellers do. It can be seen even now on YouTube. James and the people he had found to be the New Travellers were magnificent, and we hired Joanne Crabtree, Paul Mills, and Ken Whitely, three local folk mainstays, to do the concert with us.

I'd sung with Paul many times, and though I did not recall singing with Joanne, she did. She remembered singing on the televised show for kids we had done at the CNE on August 26, 1963. She told me it had been a long-remembered pleasure to be part of one of her first television shows, and working with me. I'm glad she remembered because it was such a very significant event for me.

It was a marvellously memorable concert which got great reviews in the Toronto papers, as The Travellers continued to do what they have always done.

That spring on April 28, I sang at Alan Borovoy's retirement party from his job as the first and only president of the Canadian Civil Liberties Union (CCLU). For many years, Alan had said he always wanted to sing with me on stage. So that night we did it, to great applause, before many of the country's labour presidents plus civic and provincial leaders. Alan Borovoy, my friend for so many years, had recently put out his own autobiography and one page caught my eye. He said he didn't want to get a job as an average lawyer. He wanted a job he could devote his life to, and not have to do it in his retirement years.

I said something similar when I left my dentistry practice and, within several days, had started to teach at the U. of T. in a continuation of what I'd been doing in my parallel career in music for forty years. I just rolled out of one part of my life into another. To me that is what retirees should do. Prepare for what you are going to do in your retirement, and as you leave one job, begin again with something significant. It sure has been that for me as I now marked ten years since I retired from dentistry.

On June 6, I did a concert with six-foot-two Lorne Brown at The Legless Stocking Club in Ed Mirvish's Village. In early November, I left for Florida, then flew back to Toronto at the end of the month. Once back, I was feted by the Ontario Federation of Labour with a Lifetime Ontario Award for "Labour Arts and Culture" and a lifetime (fifty-five years) of singing out for human rights. It was noted that I sang by myself at the very first OFL convention held in Niagara Falls in 1959. I was also notified that in 2010, I would be the next winner of the AFL/CIO's Joe Hill Award.

Before the end of 2009, I got a call from Michael Hill, stage director at the Mariposa Folk Festival, asking if I'd be available, along with The New Travellers, to appear in July 2010 at the fiftieth anniversary of Mariposa—the festival that The Travellers had helped start fifty years ago. They also wanted to present me with a new award for Lifetime Service. I was to call in April 2010 when I returned from

Florida, to set up the program and the dates for what promised to be a momentous event. Over the years, The Travellers had appeared many times at Mariposa, along with most of the anniversaries including Mariposa #40, now ten years past. The story of Mariposa will continue during the upcoming year, and beyond.

2010
The Joe Hill Award

The previous year, after I received the OFL's Lifetime Achievement Award, my son Michael started searching the internet and discovered an annual award dedicated to the life of Joe Hill, the great labour rebel from the early part of the twentieth century. Joe Hill had written many of the labour anthems we sing even to this day. The Joe Hill Award is awarded by The Labour Heritage Foundation, a group from the AFL/CIO of the United States. It begins with this credo:

"The Joe Hill Award honours leaders and artists who have contributed to the successful integration of arts and culture in the labour movement. Every year at the Great Labour Arts Exchange, the Labour Heritage Foundation gives the award to individuals based on their dedication, participation, and promotion of labour, labour arts, culture, organizing, and/or history".

The Joe Hill Award has been presented every year since 1989. Pete Seeger received it in 1992 and Guy Carawan in 1996, so Michael asked me for a list of all the labour executives I knew to see if they'd take the time to nominate me to receive the Joe Hill Award. I suggested he contact previous winners of this award, Pete Seeger and Guy Carawan, both of whom I'd been in touch with since 1953!

What happened next was nothing short of amazing. The nominations came in from every labour body we had ever sung for. One came from Guy Carawan, but the most expressive one came from Pete Seeger. Have you ever torn open an envelope and noticed how the remainder was now a series of angular pieces of paper? Pete wrote his nomination on October 28, 2008 on an old envelope with these words

"Dear Labor Heritage Folks: Jerry Gray should get the Joe Hill Award next year. Look at his record of a half century singing for unions, and I'm sure you'll agree. By himself, or with The Travellers, he's sung for many hundreds of thousands of working folks all across Canada. Tell Jerry to stay healthy, and keep on!
In Solidarity, (and signed)
Old Pete Seeger, in Beacon, N.Y."

Usually, the award ceremony is held in Washington, D.C. in late June, but that year it was being held in Detroit as a tribute to their labour unions' turnaround there. Greta and I drove to Detroit for the event, and I sang some Canadian labour songs as they presented me with the award. Here is what they said:

"2010 marks the first international awarding, as we honour one of Canada's leading troubadours, Jerry Gray. Jerry is a founding member of The Travellers, a Canadian Folk Group which began in Toronto in 1953, and is the last original member still with the group. Under banjo-player Jerry Gray's continuing leadership, the group would survive for almost sixty consecutive years through the changes of the movement, politics, and the evolution of folk music tradition."

The actual award had to be cast and was not yet ready on the Presentation Day. But one month later, I received a package containing the award with the following note from President Darryl Moch:

"Jerry, you are amazing! Thanks for your life and artistry, of giving to labour. You are a living legend."

It was quite an experience to be recognized with this award by so many people and showered with congratulatory words about what I had been doing. As I write this story, I may have shown you that "things just happened". People and organizations called for whatever talent I had, and to help them out in their time of need. I am still the only non-American to have received the award, for there aren't many in Canada following in Pete's or even my footsteps. So, I soldier on. My local paper, *The Thornhill Liberal*, headlined an article with "Folk

Legend Recognized with Achievement Award", written by Dave Gordon.

Michael and I sent letters of thanks to everyone who had sent in nominations on my behalf, and I received congratulatory messages from most of them. It was quite a time!

#

As usual, I actually began 2010 with something from 2009 as I arrived in Florida early and did a gig in December before really starting the calendar year. This time, it was a Chanukah and Christmas class on December 14, closing with Mary Travers singing with PPM, the song written by band-mate Peter Yarrow called "Light One Candle". This song worked well, and when called upon to do a class on holiday songs, I still use that program.

In January and February, I did about eleven classes for Nova University at their various locations and on various topics. On January 17, I also did a performance/lecture at Wynmoor, a community in Coconut Creek very much like my own Century Village, but with many Torontonians as new residents. I then planned a hootenanny in Century Village for March 8, which was well attended by many people who sang their hearts out. In mid-May, I did a performance/lecture for a B'nai B'rith Lodge in Boca Raton before heading home to Canada.

Back in Toronto, in late May I did a Yiddish music program at a condo party room. In late June, Greta and I drove to Detroit for the Joe Hill Award presentation, after which I kept receiving lots of mail, besides the congratulations from friends and associates. On October 7, I received an email from a man in Israel who had moved there many years ago from Toronto. He wanted a copy of *The Travellers Sing for Kids* as he had worn out his old LP, and wanted his own kids to learn real songs about growing up.

I also got an email from Shira, an Israeli who had also grown up with our kids' record. Back in Israel, her sister now had a family and Shira discovered the same CD was now available online in Toronto, and she could take it to Israel with her when visiting her sister. She also asked me to send a note to her mother "Honey", who years before had "done the right thing" in Toronto by bringing her kids many times to our kids' concerts. Of course, I did as she asked, and received a reply of many thanks.

The Fraynt Fun Yiddish, the Friends of Yiddish group I had helped start in 1982, asked me and son James to do a Sunday afternoon sing-along at Beth Tikvah Synagogue, of Yiddish songs. It was always such a pleasure to do a program with James, as he filled out the musical range with flawless accompaniment. As the season ended in Toronto, I received congratulatory emails from Bill Skolnick, vice president of the AFM Musicians Union International for Canada; Ken Georgetti, president of the CLC; Alan Borovoy; Sid Ryan, president of the OFL, and a postcard from Pete Seeger, also congratulating me for joining his august body after being given the Joe Hill Award. An early return to Florida found me doing a Chanukah concert at Valencia Lakes' gated community in Boca Raton.

Blacklisted and Banned

Back in October of 2009, I had received a phone call from Mike Hill, stage director at the Mariposa Folk Festival, inviting me and the New Travellers to appear in July 2010 at Mariposa's 50th Anniversary. He also advised me that I would be presented with a new Lifetime Achievement Award. I thanked him for the honour and told him I would be there with my new Traveller band-mates: James Gray, Mike Daley, and bass player Greg Wyard. Mike Hill told me then that he was off to Europe to visit his daughter, and I promised to get in touch with him in April 2010 when I returned from Florida.

Well, as agreed, I called Mike Hill in early April and left several messages. He finally called me back. He then told me, to my shock, that both I and The Travellers had been "disinvited". We would not be appearing at Mariposa #50, nor would I be receiving a Lifetime Award! When I asked for a reason, he replied that it was a ruling by the executive, and then he simply hung up!

The next day, I called again and asked for a reason for this "banishment". Mike Hill refused to provide any answer at all. If you've read this book so far, you can go back and count how many times I had appeared at Mariposa—at least fifteen, along with the times I had helped them out with concerts and by notifying people. I refreshed his memory with that information, and asked again what was going on. Still no explanation, but he offered to give me a one-day pass for one person to Mariposa, but I was not allowed to go backstage or to contact anyone! Stunned and hurt, I told him where he could shove the ticket (where the sun did not shine), and hung up.

Shortly after this conversation, I heard from my old friend Oscar Brand who asked if I would be at Mariposa with him that year. When I told him of my banishment, he could not believe it, saying it was impossible. He invited me to go as his accompanist. I told him it was a great idea but he'd better check to see if it was okay. Two days later, I got another call from Mike Hill, who told me I could not appear with Oscar Brand and, in fact, it might be better if I did not show up at all!

Jerry Gray and Oscar Brand, 2010

After all you've heard in this chapter about the Joe Hill Award, and the reverence and respect expressed by so many of my union peers, I wondered what on earth I had done to cause this rupture? I could not imagine what the reason was. I sent some emails to old friends in the folk community, and to other people I had worked with. But they had heard nothing about this, and in general, I was advised that they had me between a rock and a hard place and, if I pursued the matter further, someone might drag in some insignificant event to vilify me.

So, with great reluctance, I let the matter go and waited it out, but not happily. I decided to hang in until next year, and try again to discover the reason. But just before Mariposa began, I did write another letter to Mike Hill asking for some sort of explanation for their virtually banning and blacklisting me from a festival I'd had a hand in starting fifty years ago. I reminded him that when we began the festival, it was to be based on democratic and open principles that they clearly seemed to have forgotten. I asked them to lift this ban, and perhaps discuss it later. But I never received a reply.

I grew up during the blacklist time in the U.S. when good people were often fired with no reason ever given. Here I was back in the dark past, with no explanations available.

CHAPTER 8:
I'M GONNA KEEP RIGHT ON A-TRAVELLIN' DOWN THAT ROAD TO FREEDOM

2011

Back in Century Village, Florida, my January and February concert/lecture schedule for Nova University was much the same as it had been during previous years. I did fourteen events for Nova, and I'll list some of them soon. But as you might imagine, I was still not over what had happened with Mariposa, and I was truly puzzled. In March, I wrote Michael Hill another long email, asking again for their reason in banning me from any contact with Mariposa. The bad news is that he did not even acknowledge my letter, so I stopped even trying. In my mind, I wrote them off, and if anyone asked, I would not comment. The situation was left up in the air—both by them and by me.

As I write this book, I remember most of the events during those past fifty years; of starting and nurturing Mariposa; standing up for them and helping whenever they asked. All gone. But I must reassure you that there will be an ending to this story. I hope that, when the truth finally comes out, I'll still be around to write the musical coda—the ending about this mistreatment. I'm not trying to hide the truth of what actually happened, but it will be revealed the same way this book is being written chronologically.

The after-effects of this snub left me still wondering what had happened. I had a few suspicions, but no concrete information from anyone who had been a part of recent Mariposas. Luckily, as in all the stories about me and The Travellers, other things happened to buoy up my spirits. Woody Guthrie was born in 1912, and the coming year marked the 100th anniversary of his birth. I knew the Guthrie Foundation in New York City would plan some sort of event to mark this event. The YMHA concert hall in Toronto was no longer available, so I booked the Markham Theatre just north of Toronto, and planned a concert in honour of Woody's 100th anniversary of his birth.

In the summer, I was asked to appear with son James and do a retrospective concert of my Yiddish songs at Ashkenaz, the Toronto Jewish Festival of Yiddish. We had a sold-out crowd listening to my long history of singing Yiddish songs beginning at age four at Toronto's Strand Theatre. Janice Arnold of *The Canadian Jewish News* wrote an article with the headline, "Jerry Gray still trying to better the world." Bill Gladstone also wrote in *The Canadian Jewish News*, "Veteran Singer's Roots in Yiddish Music Run Deep," followed by a half-page article.

The winter in Florida passed with not too much performing, except for all the usual dates for Nova University, and preparing for a concert in Toronto in honour of Woody. I returned to Toronto with not too much on the books. My old friend, Sol Hermolin, was running a Yiddish program on the first Thursday of every month, at the Free Times Café on College Street near Spadina, where I had lived the first five years of my life. I had performed there a few times, and also about four times for what was called "The Yiddish Vinkl" (The Jewish Corner). This tradition really began in the 1940s, back in Camp Naivelt. There was an area by the river shaded by trees called the "Kultur Vinkl", the culture corner and here, Yiddish-speaking women, including my mother, would gather. Someone would read a book in Yiddish out loud. Sol Hermolin was about seven years younger than I, and he ran this club named after the Naivelt Korner. So, on July 7, I sang there for Sol and the audience, performing some of the Yiddish songs I had sung over the years. This was really going back to my original roots.

Jerry Gray Conducts the Mormon Tabernacle Choir

As we were preparing for the Woody concert, my phone rang. The call display said, "The Mormon Tabernacle Choir and the Mormon Church of Canada from Helen Warner". I thought it had to be a fundraiser for something, but it wasn't, and here's the great story:

Helen Warner was on the local historical committee in Brampton, and lived near a place called Camp Naivelt. She'd heard about its history, so for several years she'd been going there to learn about it. The people now in charge provided her with the long and rich cultural history of the camp. She had heard how The Travellers started there, and how they were responsible for the Canadianized words to "This Land". Subsequently, she and her committee had the camp designated as a Canadian Historical Site.

Helen Warner also worked for the Mormon Church, and when she learned that the Mormon Tabernacle Choir was ending their 2011 tour in Toronto, she had an idea. She knew the Choir always closed their concerts with two encores: "The Battle Hymn of the Republic" followed by Woody Guthrie's version of "This Land is Your Land". She talked them into readying the Canadian version of "This Land" to appropriately close their tour in Canada.

The purpose of her call that day was to invite me to conduct the Mormon Tabernacle Choir and orchestra at Roy Thompson Hall, as they sang my Travellers' Canadian words to "This Land Is Your Land". The way she asked me was to give <u>them</u> the honour of having <u>me</u> conduct the Choir. My jaw had dropped, but I managed to respond that it was really <u>you</u> giving <u>me</u> the honour of conducting your world-famous Choir!

Of course, I said <u>yes</u>! She told me the concert was happening in just a few days. She had heard I was still alive and singing, and thought my participation would lend some local authenticity to the concert. The day before the concert, I received the sheet music to their version, and I said, "Great". The only thing was that, being a self-taught musician, I really don't read music. I knew that when the black notes rose on the page the music rose, and when they went down, the music went down. I certainly knew the tune, and on the day before the concert, I attended their rehearsal where they sang it <u>once</u> and that was it!

Now I had to get ready! I needed to dress fairly formally, I thought, and I had a tuxedo I had last worn some fifteen years ago at the wedding of one of my sons. The problem, as most of you know, is when you put a suit or any garment in the closet for some years, you stay the same but the garment seems to shrink! Well, it happens to me also, but this time "The Tux" and I had somehow stayed the same. When I asked son Michael if he could come along and photograph me conducting the choir and orchestra, of course, he agreed.

Then, after watching the first half of the concert from the audience, Michael had an idea. When you are in the audience, and you take a picture of someone conducting, all you get is a picture of their *tush*. He said he had seen my *tush* and it wasn't that remarkable, so he had an idea. When I walked up onto the stage to conduct our song, Michael came along with me and sat at the back of the first violin section where he could look me right in the eye. He had a new camera that, when you pressed hard on the trigger, it would record the image as a video. That is why there is a video of me conducting the 350-voice Mormon Tabernacle Choir and the 150- person orchestra, with me smiling joyfully through the entire performance. It was truly one of the most exciting experiences I've ever had as a musician.

Helen Warner was ecstatic with the show, and I was given a standing ovation by the audience, the choir, and the orchestra and their regular conductor. Helen said I was in good company, as one of the last people of note who had conducted the choir was CBS newsman, Walter Cronkite. He said that conducting the choir was "one of the greatest experiences of my life, and perhaps the greatest emotional experience also."

I basically reiterated his words in an interview that went back to the Salt Lake City Church Headquarters, and was captured in some of the Salt Lake City newspapers. I also told the regular conductor the history of the song and how, in the early 1960s, it had been blacklisted by McCarthyism; The Travellers had resurrected the song with Canadian words to at least be sung in Canada until the blacklist was broken. This took some eight years to occur, but it was another fifteen years before Pete Seeger appeared again on network TV.

"How could such a great American patriotic song be banned?" asked the conductor, and this also appeared in the Salt Lake City's newspapers of that day. I had performed for queens and prime ministers, but I can honestly say that conducting that choir was one of the most memorable things I have ever done as a musician. You can see that video on YouTube, to this day, by entering: 'This Land' by Jerry Gray and the Mormon Tabernacle Choir. With credit to Michael Gray as the videographer.

https://www.youtube.com/watch?v=jatwPTk1jWM

Jerry Gray with Mormon Tabernacle Choir, Roy Thompson Hall, Toronto, 2011

After the concert, I received this letter from Helen Warner, Director of Public Affairs Council of the Church of Jesus Christ of Latter Day Saints:

June 28, 2011
Dear Jerry:
Words can't express my thanks for your part in the program last night. You were SENSATIONAL! Everyone I talked to after the performance was singing your praises. I hope you had the opportunity to hear some of the accolades. You made us proud. I'd like to hear what it was like for you to conduct the choir singing the words you wrote. It certainly was a thrill for us to watch you do it.
Thank you again, and best wishes in your continuing fabulous career.
Helen Warner.

Of course, I wrote back, and part of my reply was, "Thanks for taking the time to search me out. I hope it was worth the effort." After the Roy Thomson Hall concert with the Choir, the board of Roy Thomson Hall and Massey Hall asked me to do a retrospective article about my history in both those halls for their magazine. Of course, I said yes. In my story, I told how I had performed at Massey Hall in a concert with the Jewish Folk Choir in the 1940s, with guest singers Paul Robeson and Jan Peerce. When I was eleven years old in 1944, I was the only person from my school selected to appear in the Toronto Board of Education's Spring Concert, and perform for three nights at Massey Hall, and I did this for three consecutive years. Some ten years later, The Travellers invited Pete Seeger to perform with us at Massey Hall, and two years later, we hosted Judy Collins at Massey Hall. In the 1990s, we appeared with the Kingston Trio at Roy Thomson Hall, and finally I appeared with the Mormon Tabernacle Choir in 2011. Certainly, a unique historical relationship with these two halls.

Son Michael was responsible for the video of the concert. He had recently married and was now the father two children. The Woody Guthrie concert was set for October 2, 2011 at the Markham Theatre with some members of the Guthrie family coming to share stories of Woody. I used the same people as I had done at the Seeger concert two years prior, but some of our songs required a female voice, so I hired local singer Teresa Tova to sing with The Travellers for this one night. We did some twenty-four of Woody's songs including some of the Chanukah songs he'd written for his Jewish mother-in-law who lived across the road from him in Brooklyn. No longer singing, Woody spent his days talking to his mother-in-law about Jewish holiday themes. We had a good crowd again with great response, and I recorded the show on video and audiotape. The headline in *The Canadian Jewish News* read, "Jerry Gray Still Trying to Better the World". We invited Pete Seeger, of course, but he could not travel easily, and so he sent another video message for us to play for the audience. He said:

"This is Pete Seeger in the month of September 2013. Hello to Jerry Gray and all The Travellers, and all the people who sang songs with them and got the idea that if you wanted there to be a better world today, keep singing the songs. Some could be fun and some serious, and some so serious that you might have to explain to some people when they ask 'why are you singing that song?'"

Pete continued: "I met Woody in 1940. He taught me how to hitchhike and how to ride freight trains. I was with him when he wrote the song, 'Oh, You Can't scare me, I'm stickin' to the Union'. I also found a scrap of paper where he wrote down the words to 'This Land Is Your Land'."

"Now up in Canada, you added new words as part of the folk process. I hope that one hundred years from now we'll still be singing these songs, and we can thank the folk process for saving us. Thanks to all of you in Canada for honouring Woody's 100th birthday."

Earlier, Pete had sent us a postcard about the ninetieth Birthday Concert we had done for him. He wrote, "Jerry, get some kids to sing some of my songs on May 3, 2010. They'll be running the world when

I'm pushing up the daisies." Signed, "OLD PETE". Prophetic words from Pete.

So, a time of sadness about Mariposa this year grew to two wonderful events in Toronto. *The Canadian Jewish News* wrote a review with the title, "Jerry Gray Kvelling with the Mormon Tabernacle Choir (a video)". Another newspaper wrote the headline: "Folk Legend Jerry Gray Still Honouring Canada with Music". We also had a wonderful letter to The Travellers and all Canadians, from our best friend, Pete Seeger, for what we'd done, and continued to do.

2012

The year-end events of 2011 reverberated into the new year of 2012 and, as in the past, the publicity those events garnered gave ideas to some that The Travellers and Jerry Gray were still viable as an entity, and the phone began to ring. On October 26, just before I left Toronto, I did a singing/lecture for Temple Emanu-el as part of their fall series, as this synagogue often brings in speakers who lecture on fascinating topics. My class seemed to fit right in. The year began like previous years with a series of about ten places for me to sing for Nova University. We had two dates in December of 2011, and about ten more in January, February and March at the same places I'd sung at before. Each year, at these Assisted Living homes, I would ask about certain people I'd met before whose faces were missing. Sadly, they were now either incapacitated or deceased, some being younger than me. I guess we all wonder when our number might be called, and I did, too. I decided to give another course at Century Village, and this time over fifty-five people registered. It was quite gratifying to have my own condo-mates around, and to share with them what I do and how I do it.

I had time these days to look back and reflect on what made me tick. As a youth in sports, I had been short and slight, but I decided to try and lead by example, and that's why I was chosen to be captain of most teams I was on. I played the full game on the football teams I was on. I was captain, the offensive quarterback and the defensive safety, and in one year after playing the Junior game I was called to play quarterback for the Senior team in the second game.

I found the same thing happened when we started The Travellers. Of all the originals in the group, I was by far the youngest, but I was always given the toughest or most emotional songs to sing. Fagel Gartner, my left-wing Jewish muse, told me I had the power in my voice to sing the most powerful songs we did, like "The Klan", "The Strangest Dream", and "Zog Nit Keynmol" the song of the Jewish Partisans. Because most of the original members of the group had left, it was up to me to decide on the "batting order" of the songs. I enjoyed this task and, in many ways, it made the concerts sound better. Now in my solo appearances, I try to put the songs in a particular order to contrast with what the audience heard in the song before. In some of The Travellers' concerts, when I was not happy with how the program was going, I would change the order on stage through a series of whispers to the others.

Now I was a senior in the folk music world, respected by many, but obviously not respected by some others as had been made clear by Mariposa. There was no new word from Mariposa and that was fine, but I still wondered, as I was approaching eighty years old, how long could they keep this up, and when would I get an answer?

As more people saw the video of me conducting the Mormon Choir, I began receiving a volley of emails from long ago friends, and people I had sung for many years ago. I was mildly busy in Florida, and I created a six-week course at Century Village which was well attended and left most people happy. And the letters kept coming. Some were nostalgic of times long ago and how people had been affected by our performances. One person from the Huntington Disease Foundation, the disease that Woody Guthrie had, wrote to my wife saying, "Jerry must feel an incredible sense of satisfaction when he looks back on his career, and is aware of how many lives he has touched through his performances. We still remember the songs The Travellers sang for kids because we played the songs on every car trip we made when travelling the country with our children."

Another letter came from Anna Canoni, Woody's granddaughter, who wrote from her office at the Guthrie Foundation: "We are so appreciative of all the things you have done to keep Woody's name around. We are so appreciative for all the wonderful work you have done throughout your years of performance." Words like this truly make you want to keep on".

Soon, I got a call from Gary Cristall in Vancouver, the "Dean" of Canadian folk music writers. He invited me to appear in Edmonton, and be the main speaker at a panel of American authors discussing what Woody Guthrie had meant to Canada and Canadians. The University of Alberta in Edmonton had entered into a partnership with the Library of Congress in Washington, and were now co-owners of Folkways Records from the early days of folk music. Present were a phalanx of American writers responsible for most of the books about Woody and early American folk music. They had heard of me, but had never heard me sing or speak about Woody. Rob Bowman from York University introduced me in a twenty-minute resume of my qualifications, and why I could talk about Woody even though I had never met him. But I always felt I had, because I knew everything about him.

I spoke during the day and that evening, the Edmonton Folk Festival was beginning, and I was part of the opening night concert. I shared the stage with Arlo Guthrie and his daughter, as well as Emmy Lou Harris. What a night! Woody's daughter, Nora Guthrie (Arlo's sister) wrote to me about Woody and The Travellers saying, "Groups like The Travellers seem to have known and embraced our view of the planet. My brother Arlo said, "What if 'This Land Is Your Land' means going from California to New York the long way ... through Canada?"

Arlo Guthrie and Jerry Gray, Edmonton, 2013

Jerry Gray with members of the Guthrie family, A Celebration of
Woody's 100th Birthday, Edmonton Folk Festival, 2013

I returned to Toronto with the feeling of having done a good job, and being respected for my contribution to the meeting. It was also a pleasure for me to help open the Edmonton Folk Festival on stage with Arlo and his family, Emmy Lou Harris, and former Torontonian Amos Garrett, who had performed with us in Mariposa and on a recording in Nashville back in 1966.

I arrived home to a letter from the Canadian Auto Workers Union, apologizing for not having confirmed our appearance at the Toronto CAW convention in late summer. I called Aileen Ahern and asked her to fly in from Halifax to sing with The New Travellers, and she agreed. This was a big event, which meant so much because it was a re-forming of The Travellers. It was a short convention, as this union was in merger talks with another of our favourite unions, the Paperworkers Union, and together they would become the largest private sector union in the country. Old friends, some getting older (like several of the former presidents including Bob White) were there, with a strong handshake of solidarity because of our fifty years of sharing a stage together.

There was one more noteworthy event in this year of 2012. During the summer, I was in Stratford, and bumped into Bob Rae, acting head of the Liberal Party of Canada at the time. We talked a bit about our pasts—even back to the night before he was elected as premier of Ontario, when The Travellers sang at a pre-election night party. He asked if I had received this year's medal from the Queen on her Diamond Jubilee Celebration. I told him that no one had nominated me. He remembered that, back in 1964, I had once given a command performance for the Queen, and he felt I should get the Queen's Jubilee medal. One month later, I was invited by the Queen and Bob Rae to receive the medal, which Bob presented to me. I cherish this award for being included in a special group of those honoured for having done something for the Queen, and for Canada. God Save the Queen! And goodbye to 2012.

2013

The year 2013 began with me back at Nova University in Florida, and teaching another six-week course at Century Village. I had altered the makeup of these courses by doing a little more singing of the songs I do in concert situations. I was reflecting that I did a lot of songs from my early years with The Travellers, and found I was doing a lot of them in the same key as I had fifty years ago. This year I would turn eighty in October, and I wondered what the year would bring. I felt the same, and I was doing all the same things I'd done for years. Greta took me down a peg by adding, "But not quite as well." I really didn't reduce my work load, so the winter went on as usual. There was also the possibility of doing another CAW convention that coming August, so that motivated me to look for people to join me on the stage.

My son Michael and I had been working on an application to the Federal Government Awards Office, for me to be awarded the Order of Canada. It was a large application covering many of the events I had been a part of, which you have read about in these preceding pages. It takes time for these applications to filter their way through the process, but it was done, and now the decision was up to their committee.

After our return to Toronto in April, Greta and I had a round of doctors' appointments, not for anything specific, but it was necessary to prepare for our annual return to Florida. We'd both been lucky for a long time, but we followed this routine anyway. Work for me in Toronto had slowed down a bit, but I got the odd call to do some charity events. Then, in mid-summer, an earth-shattering event happened to our family.

The End of an Era

During the summer in Toronto, I play poker on Monday nights with a group of guys; most of them are in Century Village during the winter, so the game is with the same guys all year. One of the players lives across the street from me in Thornhill and his wife needs the car on Mondays, so I drive him to the game.

On one particular day in early August, he called and said his wife was staying in, so he'd drive us both this time. Around 9:30 p.m., I got a call at the game from Greta with some bad news. During the previous night, our eldest son James had been found lying on Queen Street West and police had been looking for an address as there were no personal ID items on him. He was taken to Toronto General Hospital in serious condition and treated for a heart attack—most likely caused by an undiagnosed diabetic condition that neither he nor we had knowledge of.

I needed to leave for the hospital immediately, but I had no car, so son Michael picked me up and drove me home. Greta had been in touch with the hospital who told her that James was in very serious condition. I got in my car to head downtown, but soon got a call on my cell phone advising me that my son James had passed away. To say this was a difficult moment would be an understatement. There was no reason to continue downtown, so I turned around and went home. I could speak to the attending physician the next morning.

Apparently, our son had had a serious diabetic problem, and was not in good health. He hadn't been to a doctor in years. His life as an itinerant musician living abnormal hours had caught up with him, and with us. As you can only imagine, we were shocked and devastated. He was only fifty-two years old.

Despite being in shock, we had to arrange a funeral of some type for our son. I wanted his passage to be marked with music, but Jewish funeral homes do not allow any music to be played at a funeral in their buildings. They suggested we try Kane's, a more liberal, non-denominational funeral home nearby that would comply with our wishes. James was cremated and afterward, we had a service where I and all his brothers spoke and sang about his talents and prowess as a musician, and as a person. The funeral home videotaped the entire event and gave us copies. In honour of my first-born son James, I include here these words that I spoke then:

James Gray, 1960-2013

Coda for James Gray:

"My name is Jerry Gray, the father of the late James Gray. I am awed by the presence of so many people from all walks of city of Toronto life. Can it be that a person in the music business, who has never had a solo album or concert on his own, is being honoured by so many people for his ability and prowess in so many musical ventures? I can think of no one in my sixty years of being in the biz that is being given the love and respect by the community of musicians, and is being lauded by so many publications across the country, for a too-shortened career.

As a child, James was an early talent, blessed with perfect pitch and an ability to absorb and reproduce music with ease. Born into a family of musical people who put on shows at the drop of a hat, be it for birthdays, a bar mitzvah, weddings, or helping his parents put on performances at ski clubs and dental conventions. We, the family, are happy that we captured his early talents on film at many of the events, and we will cherish his memory and share with others the pictures of his short lifetime.

Geniuses in the arts are often possessed by demons which drive them to perfection in their field at the expense of some social skills. Yet these faults are excused when faced with the brilliance of their works and minds. James was always strong-willed, and the only time we exercised parental veto was when, after completing Grade 13, he wanted to run away and join a rock band. We were able to convince him to continue with his musical studies at the U. of T. School of Music, majoring in Theory and Composition. This training served him well when he was asked to audition for the Blue Rodeo band.

In replacing Bobby Wiseman, the original keyboardist, he brought a whole new genre to an already successful band. I can remember him being asked to play a full concert at Ontario Place three days after joining them, and being asked if he could play an accordion for the show. He had never played an accordion, but learned to play well enough in two days to appear with them. When asked by Blue Rodeo to take the first three Rodeo albums and annotate the music being played on them, he took earphones on the tour bus and began recreating the unwritten arrangements of the pre-James years into three music books for Blue Rodeo.

The demons forced his departure from Blue Rodeo, but I am so proud to hear about their website lauding James' contribution to the band, plus the fact that so many of the band members and office staff are here today. He was always proud of being in such a socially conscious group that connected so easily with common folk. And I was proud in the same way.

James was a product of a Toronto-born family with many roots in the community, and present today are so many of mine and Greta's friends and also their children who grew up with James, and treated him like a brother. His true brothers, Rob, Kevin and Mike, were always awed by his talent and always supportive of his ventures. And you'll hear from them soon. I am happy that their children, my grandchildren, had the benefit of knowing their Uncle James, who played many of his instruments with and for them, and hopefully inspired a new generation of Gray Family Musicians.

James began helping out and filling in for my band, The Travellers, at the age of about twenty, when someone couldn't make a show or by augmenting our performance. In the Travellers' later years, he replaced a deceased member and took over some solo singing for us, which you will see in some videos that we will show you. He also helped me out by getting Mike Daley and Greg Wyard to perform, and together we formed The New Travellers, hoping to do our last gig in three weeks from now for the merging convention of the Canadian Auto Workers Union and the Communication and Newspaper Union to form the largest private sector union in the country, called UNIFOR.

He also toured the clubs by night, plying his trade and helping out others in many ways, always available, by playing his many instruments. To you young musicians out there, you have learned a great deal from him but the one thing you can now learn from James is that in a country blessed with a free medical plan, you must take advantage of it and maintain your own personal health. I always said that James' appearance on a bandstand enhanced the musicality of everyone he played with. He had an innate ability to find the little holes in the arrangements, and filled them in his special way. When James performed with The Travellers last year at a concert honouring Woody Guthrie's 100th Birthday, I gave him the opportunity of singing Woody's song himself, which is now the official Oklahoma State song, 'The Oklahoma Hills'.

So, we are here to honour his life and to help give some closure to many of us. I have asked a close family friend to help lead a prayer, and honour the life of James Allen Gray."

The rest of the service followed with prayers and songs and words by his brothers, and by others. To close the formal part of the service, I finished with these words:

"I, as a senior member of the Folk Song Community, have had the good fortune to survive the deaths of many folk song people and writers. As such I am asked to sing an appropriate farewell song. Tom Paxton had written a song to say goodbye, and I'll do a couple of choruses to ease James' travels to await us all."

I then sang the song, with this chorus:

And here's to you my ramblin' boy
May all your ramblin' bring you joy.

Here's to you my ramblin' boy
May all your ramblin' bring you joy.[13]
After that final song, we adjourned upstairs where we had a
reception to meet well-wishers. That evening, and for the next three
days, we received visitors at our building's party room in an informal
reception. Because of James' lifestyle, we had not been speaking with
him on a regular basis, but he kept in touch according to his schedule.
It was hard, and is still hard, not to have him around. His mother and
I and his brothers and their children were always in awe of his talent,
and still miss him.

In spite of our sorrow, we had a commitment to fulfill. That next
performance was coming up now in three weeks. We had agreed to
perform one last time for the CAW as they merged with the CPE Union
to become UNIFOR. They had one last meeting in Toronto the day
before the merger took place, and invited us to be a part of ending that
union. We did the gig, but had an empty chair on stage for James, with
his accordion resting on it.

Before we started to sing, I did a three-minute talk about how The
Travellers had been singing for the UAW and CAW since 1950, and
for the last few times those events had included my son James playing
with us, since he left the Blue Rodeo band eight years ago. I then
explained to the audience why we had an empty chair on the stage, and
they gave my son James a standing ovation goodbye. It was truly
moving, and definitely the end of an era for us, and most especially for
me personally. At the funeral, I had said that James made every band
he played with sound better, and the Blue Rodeo guys all agreed.

#

In late October, just before leaving for Florida, my wife had an
appointment with a dermatologist, Dr. Michael Davis, and I came
along. When she had finished with him, she asked him to look at my
nose which had had a brown mark on it for several years. My GP had
said we'd have a look at it when I returned in the spring. Dr. Davis
(who was also a folk music fan) froze my nose and took a biopsy. He

---

[13] *Ramblin Boy*, ©Tom Paxton, 1964

also took my email address, and promised to get back to me in Florida in a couple of weeks. In exactly that amount of time, I got an email giving me one week to get my *tush* back to the Sunnybrook Hospital Cancer Clinic on November 25 for initial treatment of a melanoma!

I made a plane reservation, and when I got back to Toronto, I was given bad news and good news. I did have a melanoma; the good news was that it could be removed. Apparently, this type of melanoma did not have the means to metastasize or re-appear once removed, but I would have to return about three more times. I felt the good news far outweighed the bad. On this first visit, the doctor attempted to get the length and breadth of the lesion so he opened it wide, and I had to return in one month for results.

In Mid-December, I returned and learned it was wider than he had first thought. So, he removed further tissue to where he thought the lesion ended. I had to return again about four weeks later in January, when it was determined the tumour was all gone. Now the doctor had to do some tissue-grafting to cover the opening, and again I had to return in three weeks. In February, I was assured that the plastic surgery had healed well, but I had to stay in Toronto for another week to ensure all was right. I was then allowed to return to Florida, with my follow-up visit booked for April when I returned to Canada. All was fine, and he would see me in one year. It was my good fortune that the doctor who saw me at Sunnybrook was Dr. V. Higgins, who was head of Head and Neck Melanoma Surgery as well as head of Head and Neck Melanoma Plastic Surgery. As a result, it is now almost impossible to recognize where the melanoma was. I was also told that I would not ever have to return to the clinic, as all was okay. He was right; this type of melanoma never metastasized.

During the treatments, I was seen on airplanes arriving with large white bandages on my face. I cancelled some of my sessions for Nova University, and the Century Village programs I was supposed to do that winter. When it was all over, it was great to get rid of those bandages and look forward to a relatively normal life ahead.

2013 had been an eventful year. I lost my eldest son—a tragic blow to our family. I also had to undergo a series of uncomfortable surgeries. The loss of my son James can never be forgotten by any of us, and each member of our family grieves in his or her own way. We began planning again for continuing our lives. At this point, I had heard nothing yet from Mariposa, but the investigation continued.

2014
Saying Good-bye to Pete Seeger
The year began as usual with another series of lectures for the many campuses of Nova University—about ten classes in total from January to March. Concurrent was a series of six classes for the Century Village Clubhouse, this time on Yiddish Music called "From Shtetl to Amerika". As Jews left Europe, they brought their songs and customs with them as they travelled to the New World. There was good response to this series, and it was fun to do and see the reactions on faces.

Early in the year, we learned of the death of my long-time friend, folk partner and mentor Pete Seeger, at age ninety-four. I learned so much about folk music and life from his books and recordings, and the personal meetings I'd had with him. He was an iconic figure in twentieth and twenty-first century folk music and had guided so many people. About a week after Pete died, I got a call from Rod McDonald, the person who had replaced me at FAU, asking that I appear with him on stage at FAU where he was supposed to do a class on Pete's life. We sang a couple of Pete's songs together at an emotional appearance again at FAU.

During the previous year, I had been asked to take part in a three-day Women's Conference of songs and lectures, held at Temple Torah in Boynton Beach on March 4, 5 and 6, 2014; so, I made my talks about the women of the turbulent 60s; Buffy Ste. Marie, Joan Baez, Mary Travers of Peter Paul and Mary, Ronnie Gilbert of the Weavers and others.

Just before leaving Florida, I learned about a memorial concert being planned for Pete Seeger in Toronto at Hugh's Room. The committee was headed by veteran folk singer Paul Mills, and the program would be a salute to Pete's life. I said I would love to be part of this event, which also included Sylvia Tyson, Sharon and Bram, and others from the Toronto folk community. Two concerts, one week apart, were planned for April.

As we discussed the order of the program, it was decided that, since I had the longest continuing history with Pete, I would close the first half of the show, and then return to head up the closing song. As I had when I said goodbye to James, I sang "Ramblin' Boy" to close this event. I thanked them all for the honour as I had only worked with a few of these people who, by my standards, were all "newbies" in the folk community. The event was a salute to a man who had been actually introduced to Toronto back in 1953 by The Travellers, long before any of the other performers had even been born. The first concert was a financial and artistic success. A second concert followed one week later and it was equally successful. I was happy to have been invited, and they were happy they had invited me.

August in Toronto that year marked the one-year anniversary of the death of son James. His brothers marked the occasion by inviting people and bands who had worked with James to perform again, to remember him, and to celebrate his life. Last year, right after James had passed, there was an event held at a club in the Ossington and Dundas Street area that he used to frequent. This year's memorial to James was held at the Horseshoe Tavern at Queen and Spadina, and was attended by the Blue Rodeo guys and several other bands. I also came, accompanied by Mike Daley.

I have very little family. My mother had an older sister who lived in Detroit, but that whole family was now living on the West Coast. One of my cousins had four tall and beautiful daughters who used to come into Toronto whenever we had a wedding or bar mitzvah. At the time of James' death last year, they did not have time to get to his funeral. They hadn't been to Toronto in years, but this year they came in for James' memorial for three days. It was one of the only times they had ever seen me perform live. When James had played on the West Coast with Blue Rodeo, they all came to see him perform with his band. *Now magazine*, a Toronto entertainment newspaper, sent a reviewer to the memorial, and he had this to say about the evening:

"James' family delivered the strongest performances. His three brothers swayed in unison during 'Sweet Brother James', a tender bluesy ballad written by Michael Gray the day after his brother died. Incredibly, the crowd began singing along to a song that they were hearing for the first time. James' father, the legendary Jerry Gray of Canadian folk heroes The Travellers, served up an extended version of 'This Land is Your Land' that damn near made everybody weepy. But seeing Gray Sr. perform with such gusto at eighty, and remembering his son with a smile on his face, reminded us all that this was a celebration of his life."

That sort of closed the year with a final salute to Sweet Brother James.

2015

I was going back to Florida as usual in early November—fit and ready for my usual busy January and February, that followed my early October birthday. Each birthday brought some worry about my mortality, but I returned to Florida in good health, confident in my ability to continue delivering the quality of performance I try to live up to. My theory is that it's best to stay away from calendars and mirrors to stay alive.

Usually, I drive to Florida and I stay one night in a motel. But my wife and children were saying this should be the last of the "one-night stands", so I agreed that on my return from Florida, I would include two nights on the road. I had driven minivans for the last ten years, but that year, I was down one size and just barely managed to get all my stuff in. With all the classes, shows and lectures I did in Florida, I had to bring all my necessary research notes and videotapes, and of course, my banjo and music gear.

As usual, Nova grabbed me to begin my winter program with two lectures in December. This gave me an opportunity to do classes about the seasonal songs of Christmas and Chanukah. Once we got into the New Year, here's a summary: I did ten venues for Nova and, for the sixth year in a row, I gave a six-week course at the Century Village clubhouse. This year in February, I did a special class at the main campus of Nova. This was basically an overview of folk music which I call "The Power of Song".

Again, as usual, the season ended in late March and I was ready for my trip home with a few upcoming events in Toronto. To keep my agreement to my wife and family, I planned for two nights on the road with the second night near Erie, Pennsylvania. Finding traffic to be light, I arrived there around 4:00 p.m.— a bit earlier than I expected and only three hours from Toronto. After some thought, I end up proceeding right to Toronto and staying the second night at my home. Maybe next year I'd take two nights.

Back in Toronto, I had two events waiting for me. In 2017, Canada would be celebrating its 150th anniversary. Early last year, I got a call from the CANADA 150 Committee asking me to be part of the celebrations, just as I had been in 1967. The Committee asked me to put together a program of appropriate songs to be used as part of the celebration, and present it to them. When I met with the committee and presented my program to them, they were quite happy with it; so, we planned on doing more as the celebrations drew closer.

At this meeting, I met a magazine author named Tom Douglas who I learned had also co-written some biographies. He and I begin chatting about his writing an article about me, but then he also talked about my writing an autobiography with his help. But first he wanted to write a magazine article for *Fifty-Five Plus,* a national magazine I just barely qualified for! So, we set that up for their fall edition, but it got delayed until the February edition. They said they would send a photographer later to get some shots of me for the cover.

Another commitment for May 2 was a second concert to remember Pete Seeger and his life, and the second year of celebrations of his life, again at Hugh's Room, but with a slightly different group of performers. It was the only event that year, but the cast and audience were all enthusiastic again. At the request of all the performers, I closed the night with an appropriate song, and thanked them all for letting me be a part of their celebration of Pete's life.

Theodore Bikel

I had appeared on many occasions with Theodore Bikel, a Jewish singer, actor and writer who was now approaching ninety. I had first appeared with Theo in Toronto at several of the concerts I had headed at the Hootenanny shows at the CNE in the 60s and 70s. I had appeared on stage with him at Jewish community events, and I began needling him by asking if he remembers when he "opened for me" at the CNE.

We met again in Florida on several occasions: One year, he played the Florida concert circuit, and the next winter he performed in two plays in South Florida. Greta and I, along with several friends, went to see him in a play in Coconut Grove. Before the play, Theo came over to our table where our friend Anna Burke was sitting with us. Theo, who is about six-foot two with a large girth, picked me up at my chair in a warm embrace. Friend Anna Burke still tells that story of my being embraced so energetically by Theo Bikel, impressed that he took the time to do it. That same year, I was doing a Yiddish history class at FAU and he was in the audience. The last song was "Zog Nit Kaynmol", a Holocaust song, and he came up on stage to do it with me.

Theodore Bikel and Jerry Gray

Theo later wrote me an email entitled "Shoyn Tsayt" (It's about time). He told me that he'd separated from his wife some thirty years ago. She remained in New York and he in Los Angeles. Now he had a new woman in his life so "it's about time" to sever the relationship with his wife, and remarry. He had just done that, and his new wife Tamara was an orchestral composer and choir leader, and now his constant companion.

Several years ago, he had invited me to KlezKanada, a Yiddish Folk Festival in the Laurentians, so I went as a co-senior performer with him. We sang together, and I showed him some Yiddish songs he had never heard. His wife Tamara was knowledgeable and protective of him, but sadly passed away prematurely several years later. I have followed Theo's career for the past several years as he completed a musical version of *Lies My Father Told Me* in Montreal, and a new musical play called *Me and Sholem Aleichim,* which he performed throughout North America. He also completed the latest version of his autobiography, updated from one he had written fifteen years earlier.

He invited me to the opening of *Lies My Father Told Me,* so Greta and I travelled to Montreal for that premiere. He was to come to the Jewish Film Festival in April 2018, but did an online interview instead as his doctors had advised him not to travel. He died in July 2015. His death prompted me to write an article for the *Canadian Jewish News* called "Where Have all my Mavens Gone?"—reflecting and asking questions about the deaths of many people in show/folk music business with whom I had worked and who were now gone. I mentioned people like Pete Seeger, Woody Guthrie, Alan Borovoy, some of the Weavers, and now Theo, and the many who had lived out their lives for the common good who were now missing from the performance stage.

Several days later, I was asked by a "Remembrance for Theo Group" to appear at a concert in Toronto in remembrance of his life. I was honoured to accept. The event was held at Temple Sinai on July 28 to a large number of people who had revered Bikel.

As the end of the year approached, on November 5, I was asked to return for the third time to speak and sing for a group of retired women teachers in York County. My subject was on the "Status of Women", bemoaning the fact that besides the men who had passed away, there were also women who were music mentors now gone: people like Ronnie Gilbert of The Weavers and Mary Travers of Peter Paul and Mary. It was an interesting musical lecture to a receptive group.

In early November, I got a call from the magazine, *Fifty-Five Plus* saying that they were now ready to do a photo shoot of me for the magazine cover, and for the story inside, written by Tom Douglas. Just before I left for Florida, a photographer came from Ottawa. I was honoured to have a photo shoot that resulted in some memorable pictures.

So, it was now time to head back to Florida. I'd still not heard from anyone at Mariposa, but I hoped that 2016 would be the year I would be able to reopen the Mariposa investigation. Perhaps.

2016

We travelled to Florida that year with two stops, arriving in Deerfield Beach at noon of the third day—not tired at all. I always wished I had relatives who lived along the way, so I could stay and visit for a while, but mine are all living in California.

My schedule started as usual with two places in December for Nova University, followed by the usual eight other places for them in January and February. I found the same friends waiting and taking part, with the loss of a few and some new people to take their places, and some new venues. On January 6, I appeared on *Michael Stock's Radio Folk Music Show* on WLRN in Miami. I was there to acquaint listeners with my upcoming folk music concert in the city of Coconut Creek, near Pompano Beach. That was a free concert at the city hall on the subject of "The Power of Song", for it dealt with the songs of the American civil rights movement of the 1960s. The course would include the song "We Shall Overcome", as well as all the many songs written by Pete Seeger and Guy Carawan intended to sway public opinion; to charge and change people's minds. That concert was well attended, and something new I hoped to repeat.

On January 21, Rod MacDonald invited me to assist him as he did a concert at FAU in memory of Pete Seeger, after Pete's passing the previous year. Rod is the person who replaced me at FAU, now some eight years ago. He is an accomplished musician, performer and song writer, and a year-round resident of the south Florida area. We both enjoyed the event. Since we remember different things about Pete and we're from different generations, we sang different songs about him. On January 5, I was supposed to do a series during January for Wynmoor, a community much like Century Village but in the city of Coconut Creek. The person in charge did not really do a great job in preparation, so I ended up doing only one class. When I arrived, there was no one there to clear the stage from the twenty chairs still there. There was also no one to help in the lighting and with the audio-visual equipment. There was also no one from the organizing committee present. This first lecture was well-attended, so I pushed the chairs to the side and did a live concert program without any audio equipment, and then walked away. Not what I expected with my long history of doing these classes for over twenty years! They did send me a cheque later when they woke up to their own inefficiencies. I considered doing next year, but only if they got their act together.

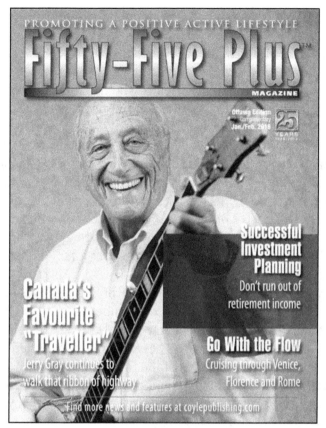

55-Plus Magazine, 2016

The national magazine, *Fifty-Five Plus*, came out in February in Canada. It was a wonderful six-page story about some of my life, and the cover photo was a collector's item; so, I collected quite a few copies as publicity tools. The lecture I gave at the main campus of Nova University was called "Where Have All My Mentors Gone?". On March 4, FAU asked me to return to the Boca campus to do a musical-lecture, also about the era of Dr. King. It was a nice crowd of older people who remembered the 1960s folk songs as well as new participants who wanted to learn more about folk music history. I received some interesting mail, but I'll finish here first and fill you in a little later about an email from Mariposa.

In April, we drove home to Toronto with two stops, just as we had done on the way to Florida. In August, I travelled to Ottawa to do a concert at the Jewish Community Centre after someone from Ottawa had seen a few of my Florida programs. A sell-out crowd enjoyed it as did I, and I met some long-ago friends who had moved to Ottawa. I'll tell you more about that gig a little later in this chapter.

I had just returned from Florida in April and, on April 17, Toronto singer Bill Heffernan was having a record launch at Lula Lounge. He and his back-up band played all the songs on his new CD, and at the end f the program, Bill, who was a huge Pete Seeger fan, invited me up on stage to talk about his love of Pete and my relationship with him. We ended by singing "This Land" with his back-up band and with the audience. It was a raucous evening in a club setting, but when Bill and I spoke about Pete and sang "This Land", everyone was listening and singing along.

Also waiting for me when I returned from Florida was a call from the Toronto Historical Board who were planning a tribute to Yorkville. It would take place in a few days at the Concert Hall, the old Masonic Temple at Yonge and Davenport. They were planning to dedicate three plaques to be placed on the sites of the former folk clubs in Yorkville.

Gordon Lightfoot had agreed to appear, and they hoped I would, too. Gordon was to sing, but decided not to without his back-up band, so they asked me to sing "This Land" while they projected the words on a screen behind me. Before that song, Gordon and I both spoke to the audience about the Yorkville scene. He spoke first, saying he knew The Travellers were the first people who performed folk music in Yorkville. I thanked him, and then said I really predated him as I was actually born in Yorkville at the original Mt. Sinai Hospital located at 100 Yorkville Avenue. The video they produced afterward shows Gordon singing "This Land" along with me. After the event, many people approached us: former Toronto mayor Barbara Hall, along with Klaus Van Graaf and Bruce Good and other original folkies from that era. You can see the plaques outside the original locations of The Riverboat and Purple Onion clubs. You can see the video on YouTube. It was nice to be asked, and be remembered as an original Toronto folkie.

Jerry Gray and Gordon Lightfoot, Toronto, 2017

Jerry Gray performs at The Toronto Historical Board, Yorkville, Toronto, 2017

On my return to Toronto in April, there was an email from Michael Hill the Mariposa stage director! This, after six years of receiving nothing from either him or Mariposa, and one extra year of waiting for him to answer his suggestion that we should get together to discuss what had happened six years ago back in 2010. His email said that I must be wondering about what had happened at Mariposa 50. "You bet your ass I was wondering," I wrote.

Mr. Hill explained. Apparently, Sid Dolgay had been a non-official helper at Mariposa and although he was never elected to a post, he attended an executive meeting. Although he had no vote, he announced that if Jerry Gray or The Travellers appeared or received any award from Mariposa in 2010, he would quit his non-elected position and not show up to help. When Mr. Hill asked him why, he said that Jerry Gray had "dissed him" at Mariposa 40 in 2001 by not allowing him to appear with us. I have a photo of Sid appearing on the stage with us at the new Orillia site in 2001! No one looked into his charges, nor did anyone take the time to corroborate them or check the validity of his claim. Mr. Hill was then a close friend of his, and simply accepted his charge as gospel without checking the validity of his claim against my history of appearing so many times at Mariposa, and being the featured act for the first four years of Mariposa and on and on.

But that's not the whole story. When Sid Dolgay attended the next board meeting and realized his position of banning The Travellers had been accepted, he then asked that no one be told what had happened, and apparently it was not to appear in the minutes. And they went along with this coverup. With this action, the board and Mr. Hill became complicit in the blacklisting by first agreeing to do this move, and then agreeing not to tell anyone, but most especially by agreeing to not include a significant decision like this in the minutes of Mariposa. He further explained that, since Mr. Dolgay had passed away just four months prior, he thought I "deserved" to know".

While I was certainly glad to know what had happened, this was by no means an apology for his role in a most arrogant betrayal of the principles of justice that had governed Mariposa for the forty-nine years up to that point. His opening line was that I seemed to be having some problems with Mr. Dolgay. In my response, I told him it seemed more like Dolgay had a problem with me.

I responded to Mr. Hill with an observation that he didn't seem to be apologizing at all, just reporting what had transpired, and never admitting that it was a wrong-doing. I also said that we needed to talk, and he agreed. He said he would be in Toronto soon, and would call me to set it up. After not hearing back from him again, I wrote back offering to drive up to Orillia to meet with him, or to any town in between. I wrote again reminding him that his promise to talk with me had not taken place. I also said I would be leaving for Florida in thirty days, and asked him to get back to me so we could set a time for this. In keeping with his head-in-the-sand attitude, he never responded at all, seeming to confirm that he felt no contrition in the collusion and the coverup he had participated in.

You've had an opportunity in this book to read about how I worked with people in show business, and with members of The Travellers, and I believe I always lived up to the principles of fairness in the running of my life and that of The Travellers. You may remember that, in 1965, when Sid was removed from the group in a legal vote, we discovered we were $7,000 in debt from our last trip to the British Isles. The Travellers had never publicized these facts, but we suspected there were problems. At the time, Sid was in personal bankruptcy and, after he was removed from the group, we found that his bankruptcy creditors had commandeered all the money from The Travellers' account—as the only two signers on the account were Sid Dolgay and his wife Ida. And he never told us. Consequently, our bank account was emptied by the bankruptcy folks, and we were left with a balance of exactly zero.

A year after Sid was removed from the group, I wrote a three-page letter to Sid about all the things we had discovered, but I received no reply. In that letter, I said we would honour the time he had spent in The Travellers' early years and I'd invite him to appear as The Travellers' guest at Mariposa events and anniversary concerts. In fact, I did this fifteen times over the years, yet his only comment to Mariposa was that he had been "dissed" by me. The other members of The Travellers were never happy with Dolgay's many appearances with us.

When I finally learned the real reason the group and I had been excluded from Mariposa, I wrote a letter to Ted Roberts, who'd been with the group for almost forty years, and asked him for his opinion. Ted had left the group after the death of Joe Hampson several years prior, but I always considered Ted as a sobering, sensible part of The Travellers. His comments in his return email are worth sharing. He wrote:

"For 38 years, you were a pillar of support for the rest of us in The Travellers, arranging accommodation and travel details with no compensation for yourself. The money earned was always split evenly between the members of the group; all we had to do was to show up. You were honest and hard-working at all times."

I remember that you would often book Sid with the group at times—not to our advantage, but to make him feel better. His instrumental work was bearable, but he would also insist on singing, if he could find an empty mike, and that was not bearable. Even though he ruined some of our arrangements, many of which I had written, I suffered in silence so as not to "hurt Sid's feelings." It occurs to me that Sid was a part of the group for about 10–12 years, while Joe, who replaced him, had been with us for 41 years, while I was there for 38 years, Don Vickery for 36 years and Aileen for 35 years.

In my long experience in the music business, when you are asked to leave a group, you don't hang around and pretend you have been done wrong, and keep on trying to get back in where you weren't needed or wanted. You could have started your own group or joined another one. Joining a group is not like getting married, but Sid seemed to think he had squatters' rights, because he had been a part of the first incarnation of the group and should be indentured.

Having said all this, I feel that you are in a no-win situation. Sid's input, whatever it was, has poisoned the well, and I doubt that Mariposa wants to go thru the trouble of understanding the situation. No one else was there with us for all those years when you kept The Travellers going, both in Canada and around the world. Sid sure as hell wasn't there and yet, he was given some credibility—by whom, I wonder?"

Ted Roberts

I had not asked Ted for his comments on all this as I wasn't seeking an endorsement, but I certainly appreciated his thoughts, from his having been with us for a remarkable thirty-eight years. His words, coming from an outside person, validate what I have said in this matter, that the stage manager of Mariposa was guilty of destroying its own credibility by doing what they did, then admitting it to me in writing, but neither apologizing nor even acknowledging the gross error in their decision and subsequent actions. And that is the shame of it. And now there was Mike Hill hiding behind his own lies, and not admitting that perhaps he had made a grave error. And there is more coming.

This has been a highly emotional betrayal for me to write about. Mariposa is a public trust corporation that I had had a large part in starting, and which I had helped out many times over the years. Through this action, it had abandoned its founding mandate for a misguided stage manager's whim. I am not seeking revenge. But I am looking for them to come forward and admit what they did and why they did it. Michael Hill, the director, knew very well that what he had done was wrong. *"J'Accuse"*.

#

For the past couple of years, I'd been doing concerts honouring our folk icons like Pete Seeger and Theodore Bikel who had passed away. In 2016, I read in the *New York Times* that guitarist Fred Hellerman, the last member of The Weavers, had passed at age eighty-nine. He was a well-respected member of the folk community from the mid-fifties, and had produced Arlo Guthrie's first record. The end of The Weavers was a mighty loss to me as they had actually started the folk music boom in the U.S. and led the way, despite incurring the wrath of Senator Joe McCarthy and the resulting blacklist.

In the winter of 2016, I did several concerts and courses in Florida as I often did. Then, someone from the Soloway JCC in Ottawa invited me to do a concert there in late August. Michael Regenstreif, editor of the *Ottawa Jewish Bulletin* and a folk fan since his childhood in Vancouver, wrote of an interview with me in advance of the concert discussing almost everything we had done. The August 22 concert was the first one I'd done in Ottawa in many years. There were many transplanted Torontonians present, and the sold-out concert was a cultural and financial success. Shelley Posen, one of my favourite songwriters, was also there. Shelley had a PhD in folk music from Newfoundland, and was in a group called The Finest Kind. He became the head of the Canadian Museum of History, and had recently retired. Some ten years earlier, when both his parents had died, he wrote and recorded two albums about his Jewish upbringing that were like a Holy Grail to me. It was nice to be able to speak to Shelley again in person, and I continue to sing his songs whenever Jewish holidays come around—which is often.

2017

As usual, I came to Florida around November 12, this year just after the Trump election, and did two dates for Nova University—in my tenth year of teaching for them. In January, I was supposed to teach a six-week course for Century Village, but a new person took over the scheduling, gave me a date to start, and then published a notice in the Century Village newspaper for two weeks later. I arrived on time, but only five people showed up. When I did not receive an apology from the "Staff Office" in charge of dates, I told them I would not continue. So, for the first time in about ten years, I did not do a course even for the people in my condo at Century Village East. For people who passed me on the street and inquired, I told them they had to ask the office what had happened. I must say it was nice to have more time to do other things, although I did have a total of nine more dates at Nova U. that lasted through to the end of March. I used the extra time that was now available to start writing this book.

Before I left, I was asked to do a four-week course the following winter at Wynmoor, plus my regular program at Nova. In addition, the Coconut Creek city hall had hired me to do another public concert in January 2018, so in December I appeared again on the folk music radio show with Michael Stock on WLRN to promote the upcoming concert. In October of 2018, I'd be turning eighty-five, and I was still able to be working into my sixty-fifth year of performance.

When I got back to Toronto, I found that son Michael and his band Hidden Stash, had made a recording and was getting a few dates to perform. He had a scheduled booking in early November at a folk club restaurant, and he wanted me to share the billing as I hadn't performed in concert in Toronto for a few years. So, that event was also on the books. I think Michael was always a musician, but had been overshadowed by his older brother James. When James passed away, Michael wrote twelve new songs and recorded them, and then planned a series of dates for his new band.

Hidden Stash (Michael Gray) first CD, Mixed Cassette Tape, 2016

In June, I got a call from the Canadian Museum of History in Ottawa asking if they could borrow some of my artifacts from my musical career for a new exhibit of Canadian music memorabilia during the years 1950–1970. They wanted things like the first copy of the sheet music for the new "This Land" and the first '45 recording, plus many other items. The exhibit would showcase items from people like Anne Murray and Gordon Lightfoot in a display that would open in December of 2018, and run for a year. I was the first person they called, suggested by Rob Bowman, and I looked forward to their featuring my items that had some bearing on the history of Canadian music. Unfortunately, the exhibit never came to fruition because of scheduling problems.

Early in 2017, I learned of the death of Bob White, the former and first president of the Canadian Auto Workers in 1984. I had a long relationship with Bob, beginning when he hired The Travellers to appear at CAW's first national convention. They held their conventions every three years, and after that, we sang at every single one, until they merged with the Paper Workers Union in 2016 to form UNIFOR. After leaving the CAW, Bob became president of the Canadian Labour Congress, and he arranged for The Travellers to appear at one national convention, and then again as Bob retired from that post. If you've read up to this point you know how many times, we sang for the UNIFOR partners CAW and CPE. Whenever we assembled to sing, Bob would be there to greet me and shake my hand. Ken Georgetti succeeded Bob at the CLC and, back in 2010, they had both written me a letter congratulating me on my investiture of the Joe Hill Award by AFL/CIO.

When I returned from Florida in the spring of 2017, I wrote a long letter to Michael Hill at Mariposa asking that he honour his promise to sit down with me to discuss his actions during the past seven years. After waiting a month with still no reply, I called someone I knew who was a lawyer for Mariposa, and it turned out he still was working in that capacity. (I thought that he was no longer with Mariposa, and that's why I hadn't reached out to him earlier.). I told this lawyer, Dave Warren, about Mr. Hill, his actions and emails. Within two days, I received Dave's response, saying a meeting would be arranged when

I returned from Florida in the spring of 2018, as Mike was leaving town for six months. I called, and we set the appointment for April 15, 2018. It has taken a long time to finally have a meeting with the new incoming president and vice president of the Mariposa Foundation. I guess truth takes a long time to be unearthed.

I have spent a lot of time getting this book together but it's been worth it to finally come close to the end. Hanging over the ending is what will be the outcome of our future meeting. I am glad that I am still around to write the ending for you and for me.

I did not do much that year on the performance level. On July 1, Greta and I celebrated our sixtieth wedding anniversary, and decided to go on a cruise later in the year. In early November, our cruise ship sailed from the port of Los Angeles—first to Mexico and Costa Rica, and then through the Panama Canal to the Caribbean. After several stops in Colombia and some islands along the way, it would dock in the port of Fort Lauderdale.

I planned this itinerary the way I had always planned travel arrangements for The Travellers. It might be interesting for you. On November 4, I had a gig in Toronto with my son Michael's band, Hidden Stash, and I finished my part of the show by 9:00 p.m. My car was already packed with what we'd need for the next five months and, after a few hours sleep, Greta and I planned to leave at 4:30 a.m., the next day for Florida. Keeping my promise to my family, we made two stops on the way there, and arrived at noon of the third day. We now had two days to unpack the car, and repack for our cruise. I had 20,000 Aeroplan points and used them to fly us both from Fort Lauderdale to Los Angeles for our cruise departure. That was a bargain but I still had to pay the tax, which worked out to be seven dollars and fifty cents each! I gladly paid it in advance, and once in Los Angeles, we met five of my cousins including one who had driven in from Phoenix. The cruise was a "Bucket List" event for me, because I had written to the cruise line that I'd be available to do a concert on board the ship. That worked out on the fifth day, and I performed for about forty-five minutes in front of 200 people, about the history of folk music. The cruise was fine, and we ended up back where our car was parked in the Fort Lauderdale port parking lot for cruise passengers. By the end of November, we were back in our rhythm of Florida life. I had two gigs in December for Nova University, and we hosted a Chanukah Hootenanny in mid-December. That trip took my mind off "L'Affaire de Mariposa," and I continued into the next year.

2018

That winter, I again had about ten dates for Nova University, including a concert for them at the Coconut Creek City Hall on March 1. Early in February, I received an email from the Canadian Museum of History in Ottawa updating me on the musical memorabilia display. I was now in the final stages of finishing the book, so I savoured the time to keep writing.

My final gig was on March 1 at the Coconut Creek City Hall, co-sponsored by the Radio Station WLRN's "Folk Music Show", and Nova University. Several weeks earlier, on February 14, the nearby community had had a shooting at the Stoneman Douglas High School in Parkland, not far from where we live. Seventeen people were killed and another seventeen were injured. The shooter was captured near the police station in Coconut Creek, so I dedicated my program to the Stoneman students. All the TV films of the kids showed them getting together and always giving each other hugs, while the shooter seemed to have had a life without hugs.

In our 1980 kids' record, Joe Hampson had written "The Hug Song" about people not getting enough hugs, so I sang it while being interviewed by Michael Stock of WLRN. I also did Joe's hit song from our 1970 record for kids called *Talk About Peace*. It was my most important event in South Florida that year, and encouraged a group of committed high school graduates to have an influence on coming elections in the U.S. Here are the lyrics of the "Hug Song":

Have you had a hug today? A warm and friendly hug today.
Everyone's entitled to a daily hug.
It's a scientific fact, if it's hugging that you lack, it can

change you from a lamb into a maniac.
But, if you've had a hug today, you know it feels good, and
it's free.
So, if you know of anybody, who might not have had a hug.
And you can tell by their expression, 'cause it gives your
heart a tug,
Don't put it off, do it now, one-two-everybody hug…
It'll make you feel so good, and you will see.
It'll make the world a better place to be."

Then I sang "Talk about Peace", also written by Joe Hampson, and the final words were really a message from me to the kids of Stoneman High.
"The people trying hardest to change the world have lived here the shortest time."

#

I returned to Toronto with the meeting scheduled for April 15 at the office of the new Mariposa president, Ken Rovinelli, and vice president, Pam Carter. Three days before the meeting, Mr. Hill informed us all by email that he would not be attending this meeting. I believe he did not have the guts to face me, as well as the new executives of Mariposa. The meeting proceeded with only the three of us. When I met them, I asked them how this was going to take place? They replied that they knew nothing about what had happened, and could find no evidence of it in the minutes of previous years.

I had brought along all the emails exchanged between Mr. Hill and me. These included a letter from him threatening me with a lawsuit if I exposed his emails to any member of the press, but mainly having to do with his admission of why I had been blocked from appearing, and Mr. Dolgay's involvement. I also had an email from Mr. Hill telling me exactly why he disallowed me from attending. You just can't get better self-incriminating evidence than that. In a later book, that Mr. Hill wrote, *"The Mariposa Folk Festival: A History"*, published in 2017, he wrote about having two choices: one to listen to Sid's plea that he had been wronged and not allowed to appear with The

Travellers at Mariposa 40 in 2001, even though I have a photo taken of The Travellers singing at that Mariposa with Sid Dolgay being on stage with us. The second choice that Mike Hill had was not to believe Sid and stay true to the rules of his hiring by the Mariposa Festival. Michael admitted making the first choice. I explained the background of this situation to at our meeting on April 15, 2008.

They were shocked with the evidence I had brought, and assured me it would be taken care of at the next executive meeting of Mariposa in early June. I told them there were only two things I wanted: Firstly, I deserved an official apology from Mariposa, and not from Mr. Hill as he was speaking and acting in the name of Mariposa. Secondly, this matter should be exposed in some way to show that I was a victim of a rogue director. I also said it was up to Mariposa as to whether they still wanted me to receive their Lifetime Award, and if they wanted me to appear again at Mariposa as had been promised eight years ago.

Two days after their executive meeting, Mr. Rovinelli called to inform me that the executive was shocked, and immediately invited me to receive the Mariposa Award, not because of what had happened, but because I really should have had it eight years ago. He said that more information would come later, as well as an official invitation for me to appear. The last edition of The Travellers would be invited to perform at the investiture at Mariposa 2019. They gave me the choice of receiving the award right away, or wait another year for Mariposa 60 in 2020. I told them that, despite being in good health, I still did not buy green bananas, and I would rather accept the award at the next Mariposa Festival in 2019 and not wait another year.

Looking at the final chapter of the book but not of my life, I planned to drive to Florida in early November and make two overnight stops, of course. I already had ten dates for Nova University up to the end of January, including an invitation from a synagogue in Hallandale. The theme for all my classes would be another look at the American civil rights stories from the 1960s. I chose this theme because of the Spike Lee movie *Black KkKlansman* screening then, a new book about the lynching of Emmett Till, as well as the political situation under Trump. It seemed like a good time to show a film, tell stories, and sing songs like "We Shall Overcome" once again. I would probably be on radio in Florida to publicize these appearances.

Before I left for Florida, we hosted an 85th birthday party for me in our party room with 85 people, many of whom had been my personal friends for 85 years

In the fall of 2018, Greta and I drove to Florida, making the two stops now designated by her and my family. Before leaving for Florida, in October we drove to Connecticut for a lavish family bat mitzvah, for the granddaughter of one of my cousins, Rabbi Paul Schneider of Baltimore. I met some relatives of my Aunt Goldie, whose family grew up in Detroit before dispersing to various cities in the U.S. (This is the only family I have from my parents, so we make the effort to attend whatever family events we can.).

Late in 2018, we arrived in Florida, and I had three performance/lectures in November and December lined up for Nova University. All the lectures were on the subject of Dr. King's story, and my talk on the American civil rights movement. The wave of re-interest in the Dr. King era had been prompted by the recent release of three films: *Selma, KkKlansman*, and *The Green Room*. There seemed to be a need to review the results of the "King era", and to revisit and evaluate whether we had, in fact, "overcome". In January, I delivered six more classes on the same topic for Nova at their satellite campus locations.

On December 6, Greta and I had to fly back to Toronto for the bat mitzvah of son Rob's daughter, Jadyn. This event was followed the next day by a big Chanukah party held at the somewhat palatial home of a friend and distant relative of the family. They had been holding this Chanukah party for some ten years, but we'd never been able to attend because we were already in Florida. But this year, we were finally able to make it as we were back home in Toronto with our family, who all came to this great party. We usually host a Chanukah Hootenanny at our place in Florida, so when we returned, we instead held a regular Hootenanny just after Christmas. At this event, I was accompanied on guitar by friend Len Caplan, and a new Florida resident from Montreal who also plays a five-string banjo. We sang for ninety minutes straight, and, as no one was used to doing that, everyone had a sore throat afterward! At that event, we served everything but *latkes*.

2019

This is the final chapter I will write for this story of my life. Not that I'm in any immediate danger of passing away, but I have selected someone to edit my writings, and transfer it all from a self-gratifying story into one that tells the actual story of what I've done in a lifetime of events for the public good—events that deserve to be made known. There are some events waiting to take place this year; so, as in previous years, I will list now the events where I've appeared, and what future events I know about that will follow as the book goes through the next stages of publishing and distribution.

I had six more classes to do for Nova, and finished up in late January. On February 13, I did a concert in a nearby gated community in Delray Beach on "The History of Folk Music". The next day, Valentine's Day, I gave a one-hour concert for the Canadian Club at Century Village on the story of my life in Canadian folk music. It turned out that my cousin, Rabbi Paul Schneider, whom we had recently seen in Connecticut, was visiting in nearby Boca Raton. Also in Florida were close friends from Toronto, Irv and Marsha Feldman, whose daughter and son-in-law, Avi and Fonda Roth, had hosted the elaborate extended family Chanukah party in early December. My sister-in-law, Fay Goldfarb, was also staying nearby, so they all came to my Canadian Club concert in the Century Village Theatre!

That day, I did what would probably be my last ninety-minute concert in Florida, and the event was special because close friends and relatives were there who had not seen me on stage in many years. It was probably my best performance for some time, and for an audience of mainly Canadians. I closed my concert by showing a video of my conducting the Mormon Choir, a video I show at all my gigs where I can. At the end of this concert, I received a long, standing ovation to close off my season in Florida.

Now with five more weeks in Florida, I had no singing commitments, and I was on vacation. Greta and I would leave on April

5 and drive home with two nights on the road. As I finish this writing, here is what I have before me for the rest of this year:

My first stop in Toronto is to undergo two cataract operations on April 9 and 11, at the well-known Bochner Clinic, and I do not anticipate any problems. I have several people to see regarding the publication of this book. On June 4, I'll be appearing at The Yiddish Vinkl at the Free Times Café, for Sol Hermolin. There, I'll be telling of my life story through song, and singing of the important life events that you've read about so far. My son Michael has invited me to do a gig with his band in October, and I've been asked to teach an autumn course back at Ryerson University where I began teaching twenty years ago. I hope it comes through, as it's been many years since I taught a course in Toronto.

You may be wondering about the final disposition regarding the drama surrounding my relationship with the Mariposa Folk Festival, a dispute which had taken up almost ten years of my life. In November of this year, I received the formal invitation from Pam Carter, now president of Mariposa, to appear at Mariposa 59 in July of 2019. I include it for you here now:

P.O. Box 383, 10 Peter St. S.
Orillia, ON L3V 6J8
P 705.326.3655
www.mariposafolk.com

November 8, 2018

Gerald Gray

Mariposa Folk Foundation Hall of Fame

Dear Gerald

I am extremely pleased to inform you that the Mariposa Folk Foundation Board of Directors has elected the Travellers for induction into the Mariposa Folk Foundation Hall of Fame.

The mandate of the Foundation is the preservation of folk art in Canada through song, story, dance and craft. Induction into the Hall of Fame is reserved for those individuals or artistic groups who have demonstrated long-term dedication and commitment to the betterment of the Mariposa Folk Foundation and the preservation of folk in Canada. The Travellers' musical body of work reflects the social responsibility and inclusion inherent in Canadian values, and in the stated values of the Mariposa Folk Foundation

The Travellers have had a long and storied history. Perhaps one of the Travellers' greatest contributions to the Canadian folk music scene was to rewrite one of Woody Guthrie's most famous songs, This Land is Your Land, in a Canadian context. It remains an unofficial national anthem. A recording of the song appears on the Mariposa 2000 compact disc.

The induction ceremony will take place at the Mariposa Folk Festival July 5 – 7, 2019. The exact day and time of the ceremony is yet to be established. We may request you to do a video interview which will be displayed on the Main Stage monitor at the time of the induction ceremony. We are looking forward to your performance at the 2019 festival and to your induction into the Hall of Fame. We are proud of our relationship with the Travellers and for all the great music the Travellers have brought to Mariposa and the folk community across Canada and beyond.

If you could let me know that you have received the email and plan to attend it would be appreciated. I will get back to you with further details as they become available.

I expect that the success of this year's festival will surpass previous festivals and look forward to your participation and well-deserved recognition. Congratulations!

Sincerely
Pam Carter
Mariposa Folk Foundation President

The date of the ceremony was later confirmed as July 6, 2019, and I was happy to accept the award at last. So, I have lived long enough to solve the final unbelievable mystery "whodunnit" of my story and let you in on the final outcome.

I should tell you about the induction ceremony at Mariposa on July 6 and 7. Pam Carter, Mariposa president, did all that she had promised in her letter to me. I was given a special spot at the invocation ceremony, along with Owen McBride, Sharon, Lois and Bram, and The Travellers. I had suggested that, since Joe Hampson of The Travellers had passed away, his family, who were present at the invocation, should receive one of the awards to The Travellers.

Joe was with me for forty-one years and his daughter, Randi, received the award in his place.

The next day, the three inductees did a one-hour stage workshop singing songs of our many years as part of Mariposa, in front of a large appreciative audience. It is quite fortunate that I decided to accept the nomination at Mariposa 59 in 2019 as had I waited for Mariposa 60 in 2020 or in 2021, because of the Covid Virus cancellations, I would still be waiting.

Mariposa Lifetime Award presentations: Jerry Gray, Randi
Hampson, Sharon Hampson, Bram Morrison, Owen McBride,
Orillia, 2019

THE MARIPOSA INDUCTION CEREMONY

Was videotaped by the archives department at Mariposa and you
can catch the Jerry Gray section by plugging in at:

https://youtu.be/-DRHac2GJX8

ACKNOWLEDGEMENTS

There are always people after a project like this that one must thank and honour, and this is a great opportunity to do it. First, I want to thank everyone who has taken the time to read these pages about what I was trying to do—to entertain inform and to teach. Thank you for reading this book, and for travelling with me across Canada and around the world. I enjoyed all the trips and hope you did, too.

At the personal level, I give thanks to Fagel Gartner, my "musical muse. " Fagel was the pianist for the Toronto Jewish Folk Choir and wife of its conductor, Emil Gartner. Early on at Camp Naivelt, Fagel recognized my musical talent and ease with Yiddish, and often chose me to sing solos in the Saturday night concerts. She then selected me to join her on a cross-country tour with "The Fagel Gartner Singers", an experience which, at age eighteen, had a significant impact on my life and introduced me to a life as a musical "Traveller". Fagel, I am forever grateful for your appraisal of my potential, pointing the way to my future.

I must salute and thank every person who ever sang on the stage with me as a member of The Travellers. The original group that formed in 1953 was comprised of five members: Jerry Goodis, Oscar Ross, Sid Dolgay, my sister Helen, and me as the youngest. By 1965, I was the only original member left of this group, who had auditioned their way up the ladder by appearing often on the new CBC-TV network, and rewriting Woody Guthrie's "This Land is Your Land"— all before there were any other folk groups in Canada.

The second edition of the group consisted of Ray Woodley, who replaced Goodis, Simone Johnston who replaced my sister Helen, Joe Hampson who replaced Dolgay, and me. From 1964–1969, this group made headlines by appearing for the Queen, doing 186 concert appearances all across Canada during our 1967 centennial year, and recording some nine LP's, including the first children's LP in 1969. This group toured the country from sea to sea to sea, setting up their own equipment each day and establishing the quality of performance which set the standard for the rest of our years.

In 1970, Simone left and was replaced by Pam Fernie; we added Ted Roberts as a guitarist and arranger, and Don Vickery as a drummer. After five successful years, both Pam and Ray Woodley left. Ted Roberts then moved to the front line and singing, and Aileen Ahern replaced Pam Fernie. This was the group that stayed together for some forty years until Joe Hampson's death in 2006, setting a record for the group staying together without a break, for so many years. Ted Roberts' unsolicited letter to me in 2016 spoke about our ongoing relationship and our success together.

All told, there were about four editions of the group, all successful, as we changed the repertoire as "the times they were a'changin". I salute them all individually and collectively for sustaining the original principles from the time when we first founded the group, although some put their personal interests ahead of the historical principles of the group.

I must also mention and give thanks to Professor Rob Bowman, head of music at York University. In 1993, I sent thirty years of archives to what was then called The National Museum. The articles were assessed by Rob, his first introduction to me. He was then assigned the task by Sony, to write the liner notes for their new CD of the best of our seven Columbia LPs. To do this, Rob interviewed me some six times, during which time, I showed him the history of the group. This resulted in Sony publishing a twenty-page story of the songs of the 60s, as the award-winning liner notes for the recording.

In 2012, Rob also took twenty minutes to introduce me to a meeting of American authors in Edmonton, who had written about Woody Guthrie, really acknowledging me for all I had done to keep Woody's spirit alive in Canada. Rob continues to follow my career, and I thank him for his interest in keeping Woody's song and story alive in Canada. With the death of *Toronto Star* reporter Sid Adilman in 2006, Rob was now the main "grey eminence" of knowledge and support for me and The Travellers. I thank him often, and love being one of his dedicated fans.

Thanks are due also to Heather Reisman, president of Indigo Books, who helped in the release of the Sony album, as well as the re-release of *The Travellers Sing for Kids*. Heather wrote in her monthly column that "anything that The Travellers had done for Canada was appreciated by Indigo, and would provide help in the future". I have always appreciated her support and hope that Indigo can help in the release of this history, that agrees with her store policy, in her letter to me, "to support The Travellers' initiative to bring songs and stories to Canadians. As a dedicated wall in each of our stores says, "The World Needs More Canada" and what better place to start but at home".

Tom Douglas, author, Canadian biographer and magazine writer who, after meeting me in 2015, wanted to do a story about me and my career for the Canadian magazine, *Fifty-Five Plus*. When he published the interview in early 2016, he said my story required a full book on the history of myself and The Travellers, and he volunteered to help. Inspired and motivated by his words, I started. It took me about two years to write this story, but by that time, Tom was unavailable to help, so I did it anyway. Tom's professional suggestions gave me the inspiration and the impetus to write the story, and I thank him deeply for giving me the idea, and for the courage he instilled in me to live up to his suggestions.

As I completed the manuscript in 2019, I received suggestions from various editors to edit this story to make it easier to be read. In October, I hired Torontonian, Anne Dublin, a many-published author to edit the manuscript with infinite care, and this readable story shows her dedicated work.

To my family, who were all aware of my writing, but not privy to the contents, but my thanks go mostly to youngest son, Michael, who has often been my "scribe" by helping with the technicalities of building and sustaining the manuscript and helping with the sending it on for publication. It would not have been possible without Michael's help.

And last but certainly not least, to my loving wife Greta. I can never thank you enough. You have supported me through all my musical and creative endeavours, and misadventures, and through sixty-two years of marriage and life adventures, and this book is no different as the story continues.

FOLKFULLY
JERRY GRAY

AIN'T NOBODY LIVIN', CAN EVER STOP ME, AS I GO WALKIN' THAT FREEDOM HIGHWAY. AIN'T NOBODY LIVIN', CAN MAKE ME TURN BACK, BECAUSE THIS LAND WAS MADE FOR YOU AND ME.

WOODY GUTHRIE 1950

NEWSPAPER REFERENCES

There are many references in this book that refer to stories and interviews by the press. If you are interested in following up for the full texts and stories, please consult the following on line about The Travellers and Jerry Gray

1. The Canadian Encyclopedia of Music
2. Wikepedia
3. Heritage Toronto re Yorkville plaques
4. Mariposa award to The Travellers in 2019
5. Newspaper articles and interviews with Jerry Gray
6. Ottawa Jewish Bulletin
7. Canadian Jewish news
8. The many Toronto Star interviews and stories by Sid Adilman